Visible Learning into Action

Recently at the Visible Learning Conference, Professor John Hattie stood up in his opening address and said, "I'm looking at you all and thinking 'What if I got this wrong?'" I feel the same way when educators ask to visit and I always end up in the same place – that Keilor Views is a living, breathing example that he didn't.

Charles Branciforte, Principal of Keilor Views
Primary School, Melbourne, Australia

Visible Learning into Action takes the next step in the evolving Visible Learning story. It translates one of the biggest and most critically acclaimed education research projects ever undertaken into case studies of actual success stories, implementing John Hattie's research in the classrooms of schools all around the world.

The evidenced case studies presented in this book describe the Visible Learning journeys of 15 schools from Australia, USA, Hong Kong, UK, Sweden, New Zealand, and Norway and are representative of the Visible Learning international community of schools in their quest to ensure all of their students exceed their potential for academic success. Each school's story will inform and inspire, bringing to life the discussions, actions, and reflections from leaders, teachers, students, and families.

This book features interactive appendices containing study guide questions to encourage critical thinking, annotated endnotes with recommendations for further reading, and links to YouTube and other online resources. Drawing on the latest research into the major principles and strategies of learning, this essential resource is structured into five parts:

- Know Thy Impact
- Effective Feedback
- Visible Learners
- Inspired and Passionate Teachers
- The Visible Learning School

Visible Learning into Action is aimed at any student, teacher, or parent requiring an up-to-date commentary on how research into human learning processes can inform our teaching and what goes on in our schools.

John Hattie is Professor and Director of the Melbourne Education Research Institute at the University of Melbourne, Australia and chair of the Australian Institute for Teaching and School Leadership. He is the author of *Visible Learning*, *Visible Learning for Teachers*, and *Visible Learning and the Science of How We Learn*, and co-editor of the *International Guide to Student Achievement*.

Deb Masters is a principal consultant at Cognition Education and the Global Director of Visible Learning[plus]. She has established the internationally-acclaimed Visible Learning[plus] school change model.

Kate Birch is an education consultant in the Visible Learning[plus] team at Cognition Education. She also works as an independent literacy consultant in schools.

Visible Learning into Action
International Case Studies of Impact

John Hattie, Deb Masters,
and Kate Birch

Routledge
Taylor & Francis Group

LONDON AND NEW YORK

First published 2016
by Routledge
2 Park Square, Milton Park, Abingdon, Oxon OX14 4RN

and by Routledge
711 Third Avenue, New York, NY 10017

Routledge is an imprint of the Taylor & Francis Group, an informa business

British Library Cataloguing in Publication Data
A catalogue record for this book is available from the British Library

Library of Congress Cataloging-in-Publication Data
A catalog record for this book has been requested

ISBN: 978-1-138-85373-7 (hbk)
ISBN: 978-1-138-64229-4 (pbk)
ISBN: 978-1-315-72260-3 (ebk)

Typeset in Bembo and Helvetica Neue
by Saxon Graphics Ltd, Derby
Printed by Bell and Bain Ltd, Glasgow

Contents

Illustrations

Figures

Tables

Acknowledgments

The completion of this book is one of many milestones in the Visible Learning journey. The publication of John Hattie's research, *Visible Learning: A synthesis of over 800 meta-analyses relating to achievement* in 2009 has inspired and challenged educators around the world to undergo a rigorous self-review to evaluate impact in their own contexts. We acknowledge John Hattie for being the inspiration for this collection of stories. We would like to thank him for personally reviewing each and every story, providing feedback and challenging us to ensure the stories were indeed true to the story of impact. We also acknowledge Deb Masters who, as the Director of Visible Learning[plus] for Cognition Education Ltd, New Zealand, has masterminded the translation of the research into a professional learning framework that has enabled educators to take the theory into practice. She has worked with the Cognition team in New Zealand as well as partnering with other consultancy teams in Australia, North America, the United Kingdom, Scandinavia, and the Netherlands to take Visible Learning[plus] across the globe. Deb has worked with John Hattie and Kate Birch to write the introductory chapter, which provides both an overview and the rationale for this book. She has overseen the development of this project and has always been willing to advise, encourage, and follow up in a myriad of ways. Thank you, Deb – your impact has been profound.

However, there are many others who deserve acknowledgment: the principals, the teachers, and the students in these stories who have willingly shared their stories for us all to learn from. Thank you to the senior leadership teams who have spent many hours collating their stories, checking and double-checking, and communicating with the Cognition team to ensure the information is accurate. They are the first to admit that they have not got the educational silver bullet, but they are well on the way to ensuring optimal educational outcomes for every student in their care.

Thanks and appreciation are also due to the Visible Learning[plus] consultants who have nominated and worked with these schools to capture their work on paper: Ainsley Rose (Corwin USA), Marianne Skogvoll (Challenging Learning), Bitte

Sundin (Challenging Learning), Jayne-Ann Young (Cognition Education), Helen Butler (Corwin Australia), and Craig Parkinson (Osiris). Their many hours of editing and emailing will bear fruit when other schools can see, hear, and feel what it is like to develop Visible Learning communities and be similarly inspired and motivated. We are lucky to have an international team of inspired and passionate consultants to work with schools to bring Visible Learning to life.

Most especially, we need to acknowledge and thank the engine room. Behind the scenes has been a writing team that has taken the raw material from 15 schools and crafted it into the stories within each chapter. Kate Birch (Cognition Education) has led the writing of this book, working with consultants and educators around the world. Her attention to detail, her gentle pressure, relentlessly pursued, and her passion for Visible Learning is evident from the many hours of work and the stunning result represented by these case studies. Kate Dreaver, from Wellington, New Zealand, writes with style and sincerity to tell stories that will not only captivate but also provide rich details that add context. She has put endless hours into researching each and every school to paint as full and accurate a picture of their journey as possible. She has been ably assisted by Peter deWitt, an author of educational renown in his own right, who has collaborated with Kate to craft some of the northern hemisphere stories. Thank you all for your enthusiasm, your senses of humor at all hours of night and day, and your willingness to be perfectionists, naggers and champions! We couldn't have asked for a more able team to bring this book together.

Lastly, we would like to acknowledge Bruce Roberts from Routledge, who has given so much encouragement and mentoring to ensure the successful completion of the book.

Terry Bates, CEO Cognition Education NZ Ltd

Overview and introduction

This book brings together stories of schools from around the world that have been part of the Visible Learning^plus professional development program. The program is founded on the research of John Hattie and was developed by him in partnership with Cognition Education's team of professional facilitators. It supports schools and individuals to examine their evidence and make adjustments to their professional practice in relation to its impact on the outcomes they seek for their students. The stories are far from over, either for the schools or for the program as a whole. What you see here are moments in time, but moments that we hope richly exemplify what happens when we seek to truly understand and take responsibility for our impact on the young people we are here to serve.

The research perspective, *by John Hattie*

One of the first things that struck me as a young teacher, and later as a teacher educator and an academic, was the pervasiveness of the pursuit for what truly makes a difference to student learning. It seemed that everyone was seeking that knowledge, but seeking it in different places. The proffered solutions were so varied – how could they all be correct? And if we do know the "truth about what works," then why are we not all doing it? And do they all work equally well? Surely some solutions must be more important than others? It was the search for the answer to these questions that led to my synthesizing the many meta-analyses that now underpin Visible Learning.

What I discovered was that if we just ask the question "What enhances learning?" the answer is "almost everything." Over 95% of all average effects from the (now) 1137 meta-analyses are positive. But just asking "What works?" is pretty meaningless. Evidence can be found to support almost anything under the educational sun. We need to move from a focus on "What works?" to "What works best?" Fortunately, the work of thousands of researchers, practitioners, and students who have allowed their teaching and learning to be the subject of scrutiny means that we have the information we need to address this critical question.

Figure 0.1 makes the point. It plots the number of influences described in the research literature in relation to the magnitude of their effect on the desired student outcome. It demonstrates that there are very few influences that decrease student achievement (that is, that have an effect size below 0.00). There is a fairly normal curve of effects, with about half above 0.40 (the green zone) and half below (the red zone). The key to improvement in education is for us to explain the influences above and below this average. This was the major purpose of the previous Visible Learning books.

As Figure 0.1 shows, many teachers and schools are already in the green zone, selecting strategies that have an above-average impact on student outcomes. Our purpose is to understand this above-average effect and to invite all educators into this zone. For teachers and schools already in the green zone, then all we need to do is give them the permission to keep doing what they are doing, understand how they think and what they do, and value and privilege them as part of the coalition of success in education.

Importantly, the Visible Learning research shows that we are surrounded by success. We do not need to go to Finland, or Shanghai, or a rich school in a neighboring suburb to see success: it is all around us. Do we have the courage to reliably identify where we can locate success, to understand it, to value it, and to

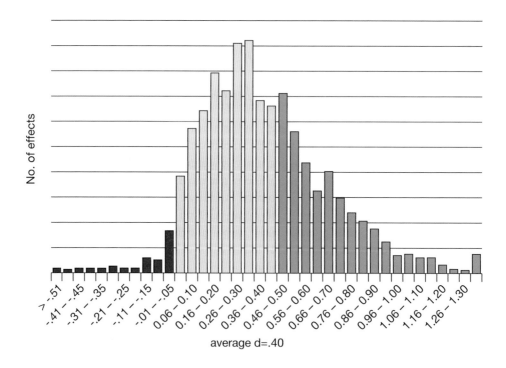

Figure 0.1 Average effect sizes

use success as the basis for building a coalition to transform schools and systems? Do we have the good sense not to denigrate those who are not yet in the high-impact zone, but to find ways to support them as they work towards it? The schools whose stories are told in this book exemplify this courage and this thoughtful, intelligent approach to improvement. Each began in a different place in terms of their improvement trajectories, but with a thoughtful evaluation of their aspirations for their students, the resources they had to support improvement, and the things they needed to do to get better.

A fundamental belief of many teachers is the importance of allowing for individual differences. Indeed, the claim is that each class is unique and teachers need to adapt whatever teaching method and resources to their particular students. This is true and can be intimidating: it suggests the need for teachers to understand and apply every one of the influences on student learning. What we now know is that the "adaptive practitioner" (see Timperley, 2011) is not a superhuman but a learner – someone who is able to engage with evidence from research and from their own context and use it to break new ground and meet new challenges.

The previous Visible Learning books combine to tell a story about what underpinned the influences that had the greatest effects on student learning compared to the influences that had the least effects. This creative process of seeking to provide a more convincing story in light of the evidence is at the heart of the science of teaching. Yes, there are lots of data-points, many millions of students (about 250 million), and we could dispute some aspects of these numbers. But this misses the major point – is the overall story a convincing explanation?

This story began over 20 years ago and has been told in various articles and books over the past 15 years. Its themes are articulated in the strands and mindframes of the Visible Learning^plus program. So far, few have contested the Visible Learning story, and there have been no alternative explanations that we can locate. The stories in this book contribute to this legacy by demonstrating what happens when teachers and school leaders engage with the big ideas of Visible Learning and use them as a framework for considering research-informed strategies in light of the specific needs, strengths, and aspirations of their learners in their context.

Know Thy Impact

The story starts with the notion "Know Thy Impact." What is the current impact of a particular teacher, school, or system leader on the outcomes that are sought for the learners for whom they are responsible? If this impact is above what is acceptable, then the aim is to continue this practice. If the impact is not yet where it should be, then the aim is to refine, adapt, and change. Validating the practice of those who systemically get higher-than-agreed effects is a major part of the Visible Learning story, and in many cases all Visible Learning does, as noted above, is give permission to continue as before. But there are some critical parts to Know Thy Impact: the nature of the impact, its magnitude, and its pervasiveness.

First, what is impact? As Chapter 1 of this book illustrates, this is a key question with no easy answers. The answer is not as simple as "effect sizes." One of the key starting points is school leaders having a robust discussion about what impact means in their school – across subject domains, and across surface and deeper learning. Of course, the curriculum should assist to the degree that it provides expectations, progressions, and steps towards outcomes. It is unfortunate that many curriculum documents are adult "group think," setting out what we adults believe is the right stuff to be taught, apportioning this into domains and topics, and often dominated by surface knowledge. Instead, schools need to understand how students progress through a curriculum and that it is likely that different students will progress in different orders and at different times. Knowing what impact means involves an understanding of progressions, where students are in this progression, allowing for multiple ways up these progressions, and not prescribing one progression for all. This knowledge must be shared; otherwise, if a student meets a new teacher who has a different conception of challenge and progression, their learning may be disrupted. It must also be apt: teachers with low expectations can be very successful in realizing low progress, whereas teachers with high expectations are as successful in realizing high progress (Rubie-Davies, 2014).

The power of teachers and school leaders having shared understandings of impact is increased when students share these as well. This is why there is so much attention to success criteria (as seen particularly in Chapter 3). The Visible Learning research indicates that if learners understand the nature of success as part of their initial learning of a concept or series of lessons, then they are more likely to efficiently move towards this success. What is more, a deep understanding of success criteria seems to be critical to changing the relationship between teacher and learner so that the power of learning is shared. At Hodge Hill Primary School, for example, teachers introduced a color-coding strategy that students could use to monitor their progress towards achieving success criteria for their written work. This became the basis for deep learning conversations that went beyond student learning to how teachers could adjust their practice to better support that learning.

Second, knowing thy impact requires discussion about the desired magnitude of this impact. As noted above, merely enhancing a student's learning is hardly ever enough. What matters are the teachers' understandings of this magnitude. When there is good assessment, growth effect sizes can be a valuable tool for informing these understandings. Fundamentally, though, it is not the effect size or the test score that matters. On every school day and in every lesson, teachers and students are making judgments, and it is these that are critical, rather than the data, the test scores, or the effect sizes. How to interpret measures to best inform teacher judgments is the core of the Visible Learning story. Does the impact match what we desired (which means having an upfront sense of the desired impact)? Is the impact appropriately evaluated by whatever measures we are using? Is the impact related to the right proportion of surface and deep learning? Is the impact of sufficient magnitude? Which aspects of the impact were realized, and which were not?

The third consideration is the pervasiveness of the impact. In every lesson, sometimes despite our efforts, at least some of our students learn at least some of what we want them to learn! Yes, we can claim these students as part of the success story, but the key is the number of students who have had the desired outcome. Have some been left out because they were left behind? Have some missed out because they had already achieved the intended outcome and had not been given an opportunity to extend themselves? Wodonga Primary School and Discovery College are examples of schools that were perplexed to find that some of their students were achieving well with regard to the intended outcomes but whose rates of progress were poor in contrast to their peers.

Only after these three issues of nature, magnitude, and pervasiveness are addressed should we ask about causes and explanations. Too often in schooling we rush to an explanation before we have understood our impact. In Visible Learning schools such as those featured in Chapter 5, leaders prioritize the time and learning needed to address these questions with staff. School leaders engage with their teachers to discuss these issues in light of lessons learnt; this is reflection based on evidence. The data cannot provide the reflection or judgment: that is the role of the professional. But the data are the basis for making judgments about success, where to go next, what to delete, and where to focus.

Note that the mantra is "Know *Thy* Impact": "Thy" refers to the plural and thus the emphasis is on working in teams. Collaborative action across teachers (and students) is a critical part of the Visible Learning message. This means that the role of school leaders is critical to the success of the model in schools. Tools such as the Visible Learning[plus] Matrix support school leaders to engage teachers in the process of gathering, analyzing, and interpreting data from a wide range of sources. In the case of Monmia Primary School, this process engaged all staff in focusing on the nature of effective feedback, and on how they might make better use of student achievement data and the student voice to plan for lessons and support students to become assessment-capable visible learners.

The system

One of our pet dislikes is when educators claim that a school or system is only as good as the teacher. This places too much reliance on the individual teacher, when the messages from Visible Learning clearly show that educational outcomes rest upon the teachers (plural), led by school leaders (plural), supported and nourished by the system as a whole. In other words, it is the combined expertise of teachers and school leaders that makes the difference. Developing such expertise, nurturing it, and building a coalition of expertise is among the most expensive but worthwhile investments a system can make to enhance learning.

There are many distractions in the education enterprise and too many of us are enamoured by these distractions. Such distractions include the size and shape of buildings and classes, the ways we sort students into classes, the curricula and assessment regimes, and the employment of untrained adults (such as teacher aides). We are not saying these are unimportant, but if they become too important they can distort the success of teaching and learning.

The conditions in which schools operate are important. We use a tremendous amount of resources establishing these conditions and there is no excuse for not having optimal conditions. But it seems clear that there is a tipping point above which spending more on external conditions has limited return. Most Western democracies are well past this tipping point, so our concern should be how to best utilize the resources we have rather than asking for more.

Given that we know that the greatest lever for system improvement is developing the capabilities of the adults in the school, this is where resources should now be focused. The system can support the growth of these capabilities by:

- investing in evidence-based teacher education (see the new Council for the Accreditation of Educator Preparation standards[1] for a model for supporting such evidence-based programs);
- providing resources for teachers and leaders to readily evaluate their progress (such as clear curriculum progressions based on evidence of student learning and not adult group-think); and
- devising assessment systems that support teachers and leaders to share common judgments about progression. (For example e-asTTle,[2] which my team developed, is a system tool that provides detailed teaching and learning information and can also be used to aggregate and report on that data.)

Translating research into practice

We know that the one-off professional learning opportunities are unlikely to have a big impact (Timperley et al., 2007). In the early days of my own work, I often presented at schools and conferences. The immediate response was often personally reinforcing for me, but I knew that the long-term impact, if any, was slight. After the first Visible Learning book was published, the number of requests for presentations increased exponentially, but my awareness of this slight impact was worrying. For this reason, I formed a team of professional development experts who converted the major ideas into various programs for use in schools. This is the basis of Visible Learning[Plus], the program that is exemplified in the various stories in this book. The program is successful if – and only if – the coaches can demonstrate that their professional learning offerings have had a demonstrable and sufficiently large impact on the majority of the students of the principals and teachers who have participated. The measure is not whether the teachers were satisfied, enjoyed the sessions, learnt lots, liked the presenters, and found the seats comfortable (although there is no reason why this should not be so). The measure is the impact on students. The model the Visible Learning[Plus] team has developed is premised on showing this impact, and the stories in this book are part of that evidence.

As Visible Learning shows, there is a "practice of education": we do know things that work best and things that work least. However, when I review the professional development offerings in many schools, you might not think this. Too often, teachers approach professional development like magpies: they pick and choose the bits that fit with their theories. Simultaneously, many providers bypass teachers' theories and fail to take into account the contexts in which they operate and the priorities with which they are concerned. The Visible Learning[plus] program outlined below seeks to treat theory and practice with equal respect. When evidence of impact is prioritized, conversations, practices, and routines are initiated that continue long after the providers of professional learning have left the school.

The professional development model, *by Deb Masters*

In 2010, the Visible Learning[plus] team at Cognition Education[3] began the task of translating the Visible Learning story into a new professional learning program. The Visible Learning[plus] program consists of a series of workshops that provide school leaders and teachers with the knowledge and tools to engage with the research and consider what works best for their students. Its rigor is assured by the close and ongoing collaboration between Program Director Deb Masters and John Hattie.

The program's purpose is to set up a professional learning process that will continue after the providers have disengaged from a particular school, cluster, or system. This involves setting up systems, routines, and ways of talking that keep educators moving around the impact cycle described on pages 10–11. It is a process that grows adaptive practice in individuals and organizations, and it demands adaptive practice from the program's impact coaches as they respond to the specific aspirations, capabilities, and needs of different people in different places.

Most often, participants attend a Foundation Day (or, in our internal language, the Big Day Out). This is where the research is outlined and the story is reinforced. It includes an overview of the notion of impact and how it can be evaluated, and an introduction to the key messages relating to feedback, assessment-capable learners, and the major mindframes that underpin the whole professional development model. Then schools can move through the Foundation Series, where they are supported through an initial process of self-review, and on to the Inside Series, which includes the development of a targeted action plan for improvement.

The Foundation Series focuses on the concept of instructional leadership and on how school leadership teams can work collaboratively with their colleagues so that the whole school is included in the journey. It provides leaders with the tools and support they need to consider what is and is not currently working in the school. After this evidence has been gathered and analyzed, schools develop an action plan based on their findings.

Schools are busy places and while the planning for the new directions may happen quite quickly, the task of driving those changes can often be more difficult. The action plan process is based on the work of Michael Barber (Barber et al., 2011a; Barber et al., 2011b). It is led by a school-guiding coalition and implemented

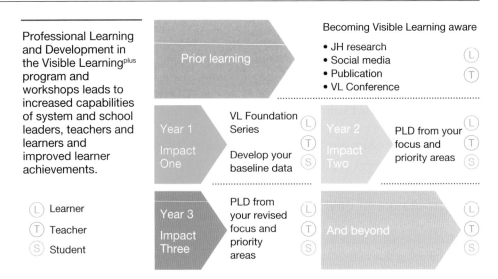

Figure 0.2 Building a sustainable and measurable capacity in your school

by a delivery team. Together, the guiding coalition and delivery team plan actions, set targets, and develop a timeline that includes monitoring activities. The goal is for the new activities to become part of the school's normal operating routines rather than "add-ons."

The Inside Series workshops can be a next step in that plan. These workshops allow teachers to learn more about the five strands that synthesize the essential Visible Learning elements. Those strands form the basic structure of this book and are exemplified within each chapter.

The Visible Learning^plus materials provide a framework for the multiple, varied, and "one-size-fits-one" discussions that schools, school districts, and whole states and territories might have as they interrogate practice and evidence. There are many entry and exit points for schools as they work through the materials and discussions. In some cases, a school might provide Foundation Day training for all teachers; in others, the school leadership team may choose to introduce these key messages themselves and plan their own ways to introduce the new learning and evidence-gathering tools. Sometimes an individual teacher may choose to attend a Visible Learning into Action for Teachers workshop while the rest of their school may not be widely involved.

Some of the schools featured in the case studies are part of the Collaborative Impact Program that is designed to facilitate system-wide change. A system can range from a cluster of schools to a whole state or even a country. Deep system-wide change will happen most effectively when schools collaborate and policy leaders work alongside the schools to align systems and processes (Levin, 2012). For this reason, the Visible Learning^plus team has worked with colleagues and system leaders around the world to develop processes and tools for identifying the strengths and problems in an education system. Once the evidence is gathered, the team works with the system's guiding coalition to clarify the knowledge and skills that teachers and leaders need to develop in order to achieve the outcomes sought for students. This information is used to co-design a professional learning program that uses many of the components of the Visible Learning[plus] program. As with schools in the Visible Learning[plus] program, however, the journey each group takes through the Collaborative Impact Program varies according to their aspirations, contexts, and needs.

The Collaborative Impact Program has been explicitly designed to build capacity and capability within the system. Evidence shows that effective professional learning can take three to five years and involves external expertise (Timperley et al., 2007). For this reason, the program has been designed as a series of impact cycles. At a system level, these cycles typically take place over a school year, while at a teacher level they generally take place over three months. By gathering the evidence, planning the change based on that evidence, implementing the change, and then monitoring and tracking the impact of that change, schools can be sure that their Visible Learning journey is meeting the aspirations of the group. To build capacity and sustainability into the program, a team of impact coaches is supported to be the champions of the work in schools. Through collaboration and new learning, members of this group become the flag bearers of Visible Learning, alongside the school and system leaders. The Collaborative Impact Program's integrated approach to Visible Learning creates a common language with shared and explicit goals visible across the system.

In order to meet the international demand for the learning from the Visible Learning research, Cognition Education Ltd has established partnerships with Corwin Press in Australia and the United States, Osiris Educational in the United Kingdom, Challenging Learning in Scandinavia, and Bazalt Group in the Netherlands. Partners use the materials developed from Visible Learning[plus] by Cognition Education. Consultant teams are trained by Cognition to enable the implementation of Visible Learning[plus] programs within each country's unique context and curriculum. Cognition Education has put in place quality control processes to ensure that all workshops around the world are equally faithful to the Visible Learning research. These include processes for monitoring the impact of every workshop on participants, their schools, and − most importantly − the students in these schools.

Stories from practice, *by Kate Birch*

The major messages

The stories presented in this book describe the Visible Learning journeys of 15 elementary and high schools from across the globe. Each represents a unique context but is selected as being representative of the Visible Learning international community of schools. These are schools that have been deliberate and determined in their quest to ensure that all of their students exceed their potential for academic success.

Although there are many entry points to Visible Learning implementation, each school's story follows a similar structure, bringing to life the discussions, actions, and reflections from leaders, teachers, students, and families. In Visible Learning this is described as an "impact cycle": an evidence-based cycle of inquiry and knowledge-building. The cycle is founded on a resolute desire to improve the outcomes a community wishes its young people to achieve and takes place within an ongoing exploration of how John Hattie's research findings can facilitate that improvement. The cycle (Figure 0.3) has five distinct stages:

1 Determining student outcomes: What are my students' learning needs? What does "impact" mean in this school?
2 Educator knowledge and skills: What are my learning needs in relation to student needs?
3 Changed actions: Identifying the required actions and behaviors in planning and implementation.
4 Evaluating impact: Gathering evidence to monitor and evaluate the impact of the teaching on the learning.
5 Renewing the cycle: Planning for "where to next." Using a range of tools, leaders and teachers gather evidence of their current situation under the five strands of Visible Learning:

Know Thy Impact
The Visible Learner
Inspired and Passionate Teachers
Effective Feedback
The Visible Learning School (systems, processes, and structures).

The learning from research provides a theoretical lens through which the school, led by the guiding coalition, looks at its own data and the messages from the Visible Learning research to ask the three major feedback questions:

Where am I going?
How am I doing?
Where to next?

These questions ground and drive decision-making and are employed at each stage of the cycle. From this baseline evidence, schools determine their starting place. With aspirations, focus areas, and targets clearly established, a school then enters the next phase of the impact cycle. Implementation of the plan is around building knowledge and changing the actions and behaviors of teachers, students, and all other stakeholders. Often, this is supported by resources such as workshops, and consultation with and mentoring by Visible Learning[plus] consultants.

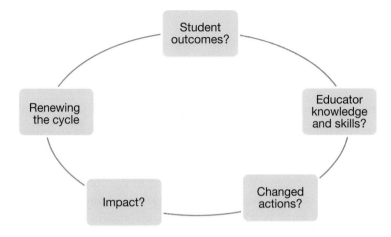

Figure 0.3 The Visible Learning impact cycle

The paramount concern is the impact of these changes. Quick wins have empowered schools to persist, to challenge, and to be confident to continue, fortified by the evidence that they are indeed making a worthwhile difference. Knowing their impact has enabled them to review and refocus, grounding and informing their decision-making process for the next cycle of impact. Just as importantly, this impact information has allowed the schools to celebrate their success at various stages.

This is how one school has described their process:

> What's worth keeping? How much of what we do and how we do it positively impacts on the learning of our students … not "what they do" but "what they learn?" … Our action research into Hattie's work was the stimulus that prompted many significant changes, and through the perspective of a different lens we began to declutter, debug, and disrupt tradition; there were "sacred cows" dying all around us!
>
> (Guiding coalition, Keilor Views Primary School, Australia)

This book is structured into five parts. Each of these parts reflects the strand that best reflects the focus for the school. Of course there is always an overlap, as the five strands of Visible Learning knit together to make a strong fabric that becomes the way of working for a school and its community. Within each part are chapters, which are the individual school stories. In total there are 15 chapters.

Part I: Know Thy Impact

Part I is focused on the strand of "Know Thy Impact." It illustrates how three schools – Keilor Views Primary School, Discovery College, and Sadadeen Primary School – have implemented the use of data.

> For me, the two questions that drive things from the leadership point of view are: "What evidence do you have that you are making an impact?" and "How do you evaluate that evidence?" So the principal needs to involve the teachers by saying, "Is this good enough?" and "Is there evidence that this is good enough?" and then "What are we doing in light of that evidence?"
>
> …Now this notion about impact requires opening up classrooms. It has to do with looking at what the impacts on student learning are, looking for evidence in the artefacts of students' work, and then leading those dialogues and discussions. For example, "What does progress look like in your area?" or "What does challenge look like to you?" And then, particularly in a high-school setting, "How do you know that each student is making progress across all the subjects?"
>
> (Hattie, interview, 2013, p. 15)

Chapter 1: Keilor Views Primary School, Australia

At Keilor Views Primary School, continual inquiry into impact drives improvement at all levels. Teachers and leaders at Keilor Views Primary School are learning to look for evidence of their impact on students, considering this evidence through their students' eyes, and taking on board the lessons for their own learning and practice. The school decided that their central purpose was to support each student to achieve at least "one year's growth for one year's work." Its strategic outcome for students – the outcome through which this purpose would be achieved – was to grow students as visible learners.

> This is our aspiration for Visible Learning in our school: All students at Keilor Views Primary School will show a greater than 0.4 effect size in all learning disciplines and they will exhibit qualities of assessment-capable visible learners. The language of learning, assessment, and feedback will be embedded across the school.
>
> (Keilor Views Primary School, Visible Learning Plan, 2013)

Chapter 2: Discovery College, Hong Kong

Discovery College is a private, independent school situated on Lantau Island in Hong Kong. The school is run by the English Schools Foundation (ESF) and it combines a primary and secondary school. At Discovery College, knowing thy impact has become the key to a staff development process that has driven improved student outcomes across a large, multi-levelled student population that had already been doing well by international standards prior to any work with Visible Learning. However, the leaders did not want to lead a school that was just doing well. They wanted to lead an improving school where all students were extended, including those who were already achieving two or three years ahead of expected levels.

In this story, we look at how the leaders of a large and successful school reoriented staff to the use of evidence-based inquiry as a means to improve their practice and thus their impact on students. It includes six brief vignettes describing inquiries undertaken by teachers at different levels of the school, each with evidence of impact on student achievement.

Chapter 3: Sadadeen Primary School, Australia

In 2012, John Hattie visited Alice Springs and spoke about his research. At Sadadeen, the leadership team was excited and keen to engage with the program, seeing it as a powerful way to tackle the problem of long-term poor results for their Indigenous Australian students. The data from their initial survey highlighted what they already knew: they had a long road to travel. Throughout 2013, the leadership team built a focus for professional development based on John Hattie's nine mindframes. This resulted in the development of a stronger belief that teachers have the power to change their thinking around the students, realizing that "we can't change their situation but we *can* change our thinking around them." And they have the data to show their impact.

Part II: Effective Feedback

There is a lot known about feedback, but there is much more to be discovered about how to optimize its power in the classroom. On the one hand, feedback is among the most powerful influences on achievement; on the other hand, it is among the most variable of influences. For feedback to be received and have a positive effect, we need transparent and challenging goals (learning intentions), an understanding of current status relative to these goals (knowledge of prior achievement), transparent and understood criteria of success, and commitment and skills by both teachers and students in investing and implementing strategies and understandings relative to the goals and success criteria.

(Hattie, 2012, p. 134)

Part II describes the implementation of effective feedback strategies in two schools, Monmia Primary School and Presbyterian Ladies' College. It includes a focus on the giving and receiving of feedback, and how teachers know that students can understand and act upon the feedback that they receive.

Chapter 4: Monmia Primary School, Australia

The school is characterized by diversity, with students from over 30 different cultures. Two thirds of students are from low socio-economic backgrounds. This story is primarily focused on the school's implementation of the Visible Learning feedback model. Principal Lorraine Bell comments:

> Visible Learning has influenced a change in my leadership style, my mind frame, and my understandings about the power of effective feedback. This is not just another initiative – it is a process based on solid research and with demonstrable evidence that empowers students to understand their learning and articulate what they need to know and where they are going next.

Chapter 5: Presbyterian Ladies' College, Australia

When the senior leadership team at Presbyterian Ladies' College attended some Visible Learning[plus] introductory workshops early in 2012, they responded to the strength of the messages from research. They were especially taken by the insights into feedback and its role in cultivating assessment-capable learners who are able to regulate their own learning.

These insights were the catalyst for a critical review of the quality of the feedback provided to students and parents in the written reports made at the end of the first semester. The school leaders decided on the following student outcome as its first priority: "Develop assessment-capable learners, who can act on the feedback provided, and who can identify where they were, where they want to go, and how they are going to get there." This story describes how they have worked to achieve this.

Part III: Visible Learners

Part III focuses on the strand of Visible Learners. Visible learners know about and are active in their learning. They understand where they are at, how they are doing, and where they are going to next. Four schools feature in this chapter: Stonefields School, Hodge Hill Primary School, Åsgård Skole, and Gustav Vasaskolan. Each is on its own path to fostering in its students the characteristics of visible learners who take responsibility for their own learning and see themselves as their own teachers. The processes the schools have used to achieve that are described from the perspectives of the various stakeholders.

Chapter 6: Stonefields School, New Zealand

In this story, you will read about the processes Stonefields School has undertaken to develop in students the confidence and ability to take control of their own learning processes and progress. It describes some of what the school has done to create a community of visible learners, and profiles Katherine Jackson, a teacher of students in years 0–2. Katherine is an experienced early childhood and new entrant teacher who has taught in both the United Kingdom and New Zealand. She has a passion for developing assessment-capable learners and this begins when students enter her classroom at five years of age.

Chapter 7: Gustav Vasaskolan, Sweden

In 2011, the Swedish government brought in sweeping reforms which included the introduction of a new national curriculum that allows greater flexibility for school planning. At the same time, it set up a much stricter system of accountability, with the expectation that schools must be much more focused on student outcomes. The leaders at Gustav Vasaskolan embraced the changes. They valued the opportunities offered by the new curriculum and the new focus on student outcomes. Visible Learning has been a springboard for Gustav Vasaskolan School to embark on a very new concept in Swedish schools: they have been working hard to find out how to work with students, challenging them to know where they are in their learning, where they are going, and what they must achieve and learn to get there. They have introduced learning intentions and success criteria and have focused feedback around these. At the time of writing, Gustav Vasaskolan is early in its journey, but this story shows that given a context where teachers and leaders are already open to learning and can see its purpose, quick gains are possible. Interactions within classrooms and between colleagues are now far more learning-focused, and systems and routines are being set up to allow progress to be understood and monitored. Students at Gustav Vasaskolan are already beginning to exhibit some of the important characteristics of visible learners.

Chapter 8: Hodge Hill, UK

In this story, you will learn how teachers and school leaders at Hodge Hill Primary School transformed the way their students thought and talked about their learning. Hodge Hill Primary School is a large primary school in the city of Birmingham and over 90% of the school's students are Asian, predominantly Pakistani. A significant percentage of the students are English language learners, and many are from low-income homes. The school needed a robust vehicle that could stand up to the disruption caused by the burgeoning student numbers and the ever-expanding teaching staff that this necessitated. Visible Learning has proven to be that vehicle. In only one year of implementation, there has been a remarkable shift in the relationships between teachers and students, leading to a situation where students have significantly more control over their learning and are rapidly acquiring the characteristics of a visible learner. Recent data analysis indicates that this has contributed to an impressive rise in student achievement.

Chapter 9: Asgard, Ås, Norway

Åsgård Skole is a primary school serving 330 students aged from six to 12 years old. The school is set in the small municipality of Ås, which is outside Oslo, Norway. It is situated in a high socio-economic area with one of the highest average levels of education in Norway. Åsgård Skole was regarded as a high-achieving school for many years, but when the school's leaders began to dig deeper into their student achievement data, they found that they were not maximizing student growth. This story of impact describes the first year of the school's Visible Learning journey. In that time, the guiding coalition focused on the use of learning intentions, success criteria, effective feedback, and effect sizes as a means to improve students' achievement outcomes and assist them to become assessment-capable visible learners.

Part IV: Inspired and Passionate Teachers

Part IV is about "Inspired and Passionate Teachers." It profiles two schools and one district that have established processes for teachers who strive to achieve excellence in their daily work. The inspired and passionate teachers at Clevedon School, Wolford Elementary School, and Moberly School District seek to impact positively on all students in their class. This is no accident. Their school or district leaders have established processes and systems to support the teachers to plan collaboratively, develop positive relationships, and track the effectiveness of their teaching.

Chapter 10: Clevedon School, New Zealand

This is the story of a school that has emerged from a time of trouble to recreate itself as a learning community that shares a passion for ensuring success for all. The school leadership team aspired to have teachers who:

- are inspirational and know the impact they are having on student progress and achievement;
- are collaborative and supportive, who work together to maximize impact on student learning; and
- have a culture of feedback which improves systems and processes in the school.

This story provides an insight into the school's journey, finishing with the impact it had on the professional growth of novice teacher Rachael Baker. Rachael is a year 5–6 class teacher who is passionate about writing, e-learning, and the use of digital tools to enhance learning. She is focused on knowing her impact on students' learning and on students knowing themselves as learners. She has established positive relationships with her students and works to ensure all students in her class are assessment-capable and able to discuss their learning. She tracks student achievement closely and plans to meet individual needs. Rachael has a "growth mindframe" – she is willing to try new initiatives and ways of doing things.

Chapter 11: Moberly School District, USA

Tara Link serves several roles, but primarily she is the professional development facilitator for her school district. More importantly for this story, she created a

New Teacher Induction Program (SHINE), focusing on Visible Learning, which serves the Pre-K–12 teachers. This story describes how she has worked to develop these new teachers into "Inspired and Passionate Teachers" who demonstrate the essence of this Visible Learning strand. Her goal is to bridge the gap for teachers between educational research and practical classroom application. She began with a focus on learning targets and feedback. This has emerged into student self-reflection as a form of feedback and the use of assessments for students and teachers. Student language has shifted away from "what I am doing" to "what I am learning." As formative assessments and student self-reflection have become a part of daily practice, student engagement has increased. In addition, district data continues to show increase in performance on state tests.

Chapter 12: Wolford Elementary, USA

Wolford School's goal is always 100% success in student learning. Its leaders believe that when one child fails to learn, it may have a small impact on the school, but it represents 100% failure to the child and their family. In August 2012, the Wolford School campus engaged in a professional development initiative that focused on the effects teachers have on their students. They examined their practices in comparison to John Hattie's effect sizes and questioned their own practices. They focused on developing highly collaborative grade level teams where teachers designed challenging and engaging lessons, utilized high-yield practices in instruction, and focused on student learning.

> We have to work within the constraints of the State of Texas and Federal government. We have curricular requirements and state-mandated assessments. Teachers don't have a lot of autonomy in what to teach or daily time requirements. They can, and do, control their level of collaboration; the "how" of their instruction, the effects they have on their students, and the focus on student learning.
>
> (Carol Turquette, principal)

Part V: The Visible Learning School

Part V describes the strand that focuses on the systems, processes, and structures that feature in a Visible Learning School. The schools featured in this chapter accept that it is their moral purpose to help students exceed their potential and do more than they thought they could. Each has used the Visible Learning Matrix as the basis for inquiring into systems and practices that support effective teaching and learning. They make time for collaboration, have regular classroom walkthroughs and observations, and engage in evidence-based discussions with teachers about their practice. The three schools featured are Oxley College, Tobermory High School, and Wodonga Primary School.

Chapter 13: Oxley College, Australia

Oxley College has always espoused a commitment to excellence in student learning. Prior to its involvement in Visible Learning, it had engaged in a range of staff professional learning and other initiatives intended to achieve that vision. However, there was little hard evidence to suggest that they had been successful. Increasingly, both students and families wanted that evidence. The school's leaders realized that to provide students with a continuum of effective teaching throughout their schooling, they needed to move away from a narrow approach to one where teachers took collective responsibility for all students' learning. When deputy head Kate Cunich attended a presentation on Visible Learning in September 2012, she recognized an opportunity to engage in whole-school improvement. Kate explains that they set out to become a school respected for excellence in student learning. The change has come over time. As the school implemented the Visible Learning framework, refocusing from curriculum to learning and from assumptions to evidence, the characteristics of visible learners have become manifest, not just in students but also in teachers and school leaders.

The change has not been an easy one and the journey has not been the same for everyone. This story gives you a glimpse into the successes and challenges that have been part of Oxley College's ongoing transformation into a Visible Learning school.

Chapter 14: Wodonga Primary School, Australia

The process of change described in this story was prompted by the leadership team's recognition that while student outcomes were "adequate," as indicated by the school's five-year standardized external trend data, they were not what they could be. The school's achievement outcomes had plateaued – the leadership team wanted to see an upwards trajectory and believed that the solution lay in professional learning for staff.

This story describes how Wodonga Primary School implemented a change process that integrated inquiry, action, and reflection. Through this process, the school has transformed itself into a Visible Learning school. In that environment, school leaders are "instructional leaders" who make time for collaboration, have regular walkthroughs, and engage in evidence-based discussions with teachers about the relationship between practice and its impact on student outcomes. Leaders, teachers, and students open their learning to themselves and to each other, taking control of their own destiny and driving towards a shared vision of a school where the focus is always on learning.

Chapter 15: Tobermory High School, UK

Tobermory High School, a rural school located in Scotland on the Isle of Mull, has a mission: "To work together to create a community with a culture where our young people are included, successful, ambitious, and creative and where they can aspire to be the best they can be." Craig Biddick, appointed to the position of principal in 2012, is the first person to admit that the school's Visible Learning journey has only just begun, yet he and his staff have been rigorous in their self-review, using evidence collection tools to give them valuable information about learning across the school in a more targeted way. Subsequently, they have developed a coherent plan from the initial evidence into action phase.

His comment to other educators at a recent Visible Learning conference was that with Visible Learning you are not buying into a box that you fit into; rather you are given the tools to investigate, design, and build your own box. Craig knew it would take some work to get teachers on board and that a commitment to become a Visible Learning school is a matter of years, not months. Nevertheless, thanks to his commitment and that of his staff, Tobermory has seen big changes in less than a year.

Active reading guides/Theory to practice activities

As you will see, the Visible Learning[plus] program is not about schools working through a lockstep process of implementation, but about working through the evidence from the Visible Learning research and the evidence from their own context to design and evaluate solutions and approaches that will achieve the best possible outcomes for their students. It is a messy, complex, and above all active process.

While the schools all demonstrate early success in their application of the Visible Learning principles, they are not intended as exemplars of Visible Learning; rather, they exemplify certain key messages from the research. To get the best out of your reading, we encourage you to read, consider, and act with the same curiosity and deliberate intent as the educators in these stories. For this reason, each part concludes with a suggested activity intended to help you read each chapter deeply and more fully understand the learning from the story. Reading guides have also been designed for you to read at the conclusion of a chapter; they are intended to help you to look forward and consider how that learning might be relevant to your school and are located in the appendices at the end of each part.

Notes

1 http://caepnet.org/
2 http://e-asttle.tki.org.nz/
3 Cognition Education is a global education consultancy and training provider based in New Zealand and owned by the Cognition Trust (which returns education grants to local schools). See http://cognitioneducation.com/

Know Thy Impact

1

Keilor Views Primary School

Australia

For me, the two questions that drive things from the leadership point of view are "What evidence do you have that you are making an impact?" and "How do you evaluate that evidence?" So the principal needs to involve the teachers by saying, "Is this good enough?" and "Is there evidence that this is good enough?" and then "What are we doing in light of that evidence?"

… Now this notion about impact requires opening up classrooms. It has to do with looking at what the impacts on student learning are, looking for evidence in the artefacts of students' work, and then leading those dialogues and discussions. For example, "What does progress look like in your area?", or "What does challenge look like to you?" And then, particularly in a high school setting, "How do you know that each student is making progress across all the subjects?"

Interview with Hattie (2013, p. 15)

Essentially, knowing thy impact means connecting what we do as educators with what happens to learners. At Keilor Views Primary School, this continual inquiry into impact drives improvement at all levels.

Context

Keilor Views Primary School was formed in January 2010 from the merger between Keilor Downs Primary School and Calder Rise Primary School. It is located in Australia, 25 kilometers north west of Melbourne in the suburb of Keilor Downs, and on the former site of Keilor Downs Primary School. Since the merger, this "new-old" school has gone through a process of regeneration, including a major building program. This has seen the refurbishment of 10 classrooms and the construction of six additional classrooms, a library, and an outdoor sports facility.

Figure 1.1 Welcome to Keilor Views Primary School[1]

Keilor Views has 420 students, ranging from the preparatory level (five years old) to year 6 (11–12 years old). The students are ethnically diverse, with many speaking a language other than English. Many are from homes where the income is below the national average.

The 24-member teaching staff is drawn largely from the two former schools. It is led by principal Charles Branciforte. His senior leadership team consists of assistant principal Matt Borg and leading teachers Gloria Puopolo and Rita Scuteri. Rita is also the school's teaching and learning coach.

The school's motto is "Vision, Integrity, Pride."

Overview

Professional learning has always been prioritized at Keilor Views Primary School, but the journey has not always been straightforward. Prior to the schools' merger, Charles was principal at Keilor Downs Primary School. He had a strategic plan for improvement that included professional development for himself as a leader of teaching and learning. The curriculum focus was on literacy, with educational consultant Sally Slattery employed to mentor and coach selected teachers. Sally also took on the role of critical friend to the leadership team. This approach bore fruit but could not be sustained due to the expense of the merger process. Instead, building on what they had learnt, Matt and Rita implemented an internal coaching model supported by a new reading assessment system. In the meantime, Charles worked with the regional education authority to establish a professional development conference center. This initiative has provided a revenue source that has helped fund new professional learning initiatives. One of these was the employment of consultant Sue Costello, who supported staff in the use of exemplars as an approach to literacy assessment. This led on to an interest in Visible Learning and the school's inclusion in a 2012 study tour to New Zealand organized by Cognition Education and the Keilor/St Albans Network. Alongside other schools in the network (including Monmia School, whose story is also told in this book), the school was convinced by what they saw in the Visible Learning schools they visited. They consequently embarked on a Visible Learning journey of their own that has seen impressive improvements in student outcomes.

This story is primarily focused on the concept of "Know Thy Impact." It looks at how teachers and leaders at Keilor Views Primary School are learning to look for evidence of their impact on students, considering this evidence through their students' eyes and taking on board the lessons for their own learning and practice.

Featured leaders

This story is based primarily on the reflections of the guiding coalition as a whole, but three leaders are quoted directly:

In 2013, the state government acknowledged principal **Charles Branciforte's** success as an inspirational leader of learning by making him the Victorian Primary Principal of the Year. Charles explains, "Our learning community is what motivates me; it motivates me to provide excellent learning opportunities and to provide the best possible resources for our kids, our staff, and our learning environment. What drives and inspires me is providing opportunities for kids from diverse backgrounds to succeed."

Matthew Borg has been the assistant principal at Keilor Views Primary School since January 2012. He has been a specialist teacher, classroom teacher, and leading teacher. Matt says, "My passion in teaching and learning is to amplify every opportunity for the students we teach; together, we work out what's worth keeping."

Rita Scuteri began her teaching career at Keilor Downs in 2005 and was given the role of literacy coordinator in 2009. At the same time, she was given the opportunity to receive coaching from Sally Slattery and to work with Matt on the new reading assessment system. Rita says, "This was the beginning of the journey for me. It suddenly all became clear! I understood how simple pedagogy and explicit practices could transform the learning that occurred in the classroom." Today, she is helping to drive changes to the school's curriculum and pedagogical practices through coaching and the Visible Learning whole-school improvement strategies.

Keilor Views Primary School's Visible Learning story

What were the desired student outcomes?

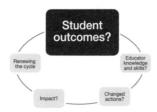

While the merger of the two schools provided a significant challenge, it also gave the school community the opportunity to redefine its aspirations for students and to revisit its basic beliefs and practices, evaluating them in light of their contribution to the intended student outcomes:

> This was a unique position to be in. We seized the opportunity to have a deeper look at "what was worth keeping." We reviewed everything from our uniform and logo to what would stand as our school's core values and our core purpose. In order to ensure enduring success for our students, our values and purpose would remain fixed at the same time as we ventured into the process of exploring, trialing, and developing strategies and practices that enable adaptation to a changing world.
>
> (Charles Branciforte)

By 2011, Charles and his team knew that student achievement was not where they wanted it to be. While their data told them that previous initiatives had led to improvements, the situation remained that students were not progressing at the national average. There were pockets of success, especially in literacy, but there was also considerable variation in student achievement across the school. This is exemplified in Figure 1.2, which shows reading progress in one class, over one year.

Figure 1.2 reflects the situation at an early stage of implementation and demonstrates that the use of a new tracking sheet and newly-devised benchmarking system was already having an impact. It made the growth patterns clearly visible so they could be interpreted, analyzed, compared, and discussed. This sort of clarity is essential if teachers are to understand their impact.

As a consequence of the classroom observations and walkthroughs that had become a normal part of the school's routines, the leadership team had a good idea of what was going on inside classrooms. This was affirmed through implementation of the Visible Learning[plus] tools and processes, such as student interviews and focus groups. It was clear to the team that students were often not at the center of teaching and learning and certainly did not have the understandings and strategies they needed to "see themselves as their own teachers." When the student focus

KEILOR VIEWS PRIMARY SCHOOL - READING BENCHMARKING TRACKING SHEET 2012

FIRST AND LAST NAME   GRADE: 3   TEACHER: *****

Fountas & Pinell	A	B	C	D	E	F	G	H	I	J	K	L	M	N	O	P	Q	R	S	T	U	V	W	X	Y	Z
Rigby	1	2	3/4	5/6	7/8	9/10	11/12	13/14	15/16	17/18	19/20	21	22	23	24	25	26	27	28	29	30	30+				
VELS Standard	0.5	0.5	1	1	1.25	1.25	1.25	1.25	1.5	1.75	2	2.25	2.25	2.25	2.5	2.75	2.75	2.75	3	3.25	3.5	3.75	3.75	4.25	4.35	4.5
Grade Level	P	P	P	EOP	1	1	1	1	EO1	2	EO2	3	3	3	EO3	4	4	4	EO4	5	EO5	6	6	EO6	7	7
Student name											98%	97%	97%	98%	98%											
Student name												96%		96%	96%	96%										
Student name												99%			96%	98%			98%							
Student name											98%	99%		99%	98%	97%										
Student name									99%		97%	98%		98%		97%	98%									
Student name										99%	99%	97%	98%		97%	99%	98%									
Student name												98%				98%										
Student name												97%			99%	98%	98%		100%	100%						
Student name												97%			98%	98%			98%							
Student name														100%	97%				99%	100%	99%					
Student name									98%		96%	97%						96%								
Student name												97%			100%	98%	97%									
Student name										98%	97%	99%	96%		96%	97%										
Student name									97%			96%		95%	96%											
Student name							96%					99%														
Student name									98%		99%	98%	96%		98%	98%			97%	100%	98%					
Student name										96%	96%															
Student name									98%		96%	99%	96%		99%	99%										
Student name												98%	97%		97%	97%			97%	100%	98%					
Student name											98%	98%	97%	100%	97%	97%			97%							
Student name				98%																						

Beginning Term 1   End Term 1   End Term 2   End Term 3   End Term 4

☐ is end of year 2 PP

Figure 1.2 Reading benchmarking data

group were asked about what they thought a "good learner" looked like or did, they made the following responses, most of which indicated a passive approach to learning:

"Listen to the teacher."
"Doing their work."
"Well-behaved."
"Listens."
"Not distracted by others."
"Always listens to the teacher / attentive to the teacher."
"Tries their hardest."
"Tries their best."
"Starting their work straight away."
"Very little talking / don't talk very much."
"Head down."
"Does neat work."
"Focused."
"Asks questions."

The opportunity to visit successful Visible Learning schools in New Zealand demonstrated what could be: that students with the skills and capabilities of visible learners are able to achieve the kinds of learning outcomes that make for success and fulfilment in later life.

As a consequence of this inquiry, the school decided that its central purpose was to support each student to achieve "at least one year's growth for one year's work." Its strategic outcome for students – the outcome through which this purpose would be achieved – was to grow students as visible learners.

This is our aspiration for Visible Learning in our school: All students at Keilor Views Primary School will show a greater than year's growth for one year's input in all learning disciplines and they will exhibit qualities of assessment-capable visible learners. The language of learning, assessment, and feedback will be embedded across the school.

(Keilor Views Primary School, Visible Learning Plan, 2013)

What knowledge and skills did the teachers and school leaders need to support these outcomes?

Following the trip to New Zealand, Keilor Views Primary School joined with 21 other schools in the region to enrol in the Network Visible Learning[plus] three-day series. Visible Learning[plus] consultant Helen Butler took on the role of critical friend and external coach, guiding the school in its review of learning needs for students, teachers, and leaders. The school formed a guiding coalition, with the leadership team of Charles, Matt, and Rita taking responsibility for planning the whole-school journey and selected teachers invited to focus on classroom practices.

Charles explains the strategic decision-making that went into his selection of the guiding coalition:

> Initially, the mindframes and beliefs have to be shared by leadership with a guiding coalition. I appointed a team that shared the vision. This is not easy, as it requires hard conversations with incumbents, potentially not renewing contracts, outside appointments, or a disruption to the "hidden promotion agenda" within a school.

The review affirmed the leadership team's impression that the variability in student outcomes was the consequence of the variability in teacher effectiveness. However, the same connection between student achievement and teacher practice was not being made by many teachers. They were not paying enough attention to what students were saying or doing and they were not using their learning from that kind of inquiry to determine what to do next. A particular area of concern was that many teachers did not understand the importance and function of learning intentions and success criteria as a means of ensuring they and their students truly understood the purpose of learning and could monitor its progress.

> We did a lot of work expelling the "but" culture, for example, "but our kids are poor," "but our kids don't read at home." Teachers who looked more deeply into this notion began the wave of improvement at a classroom level.
> (Guiding coalition)

The two statements below reflect the team's understanding that the school's intended outcomes for students needed to be intimately connected to the intended outcomes for teachers and school leaders. The first statement indicates the importance of developing the characteristics of visible learners in educators as well as in students:

> We are an inclusive educational setting that prides ourselves on the delivery of a quality curriculum based on the principles of Visible Learning where we are building assessment-capable learners. When teachers see learning through the eyes of their students and students see themselves as their own teachers, we become highly visible learners together.
> (Keilor Views Primary School, 2013 Annual Report to the School Community)

This second statement reflects the school's commitment to the use of data to "Know Thy Impact."

Our refined data collection and analyses enable strategic intent for individual students and cohorts of students.

(Ibid.)

These concepts about Visible Learning, assessment capability, and knowing thy impact informed an analysis of how teachers were doing and the kind and degree of support they would need to improve. Using the analogy of the lifecycle of a butterfly, the school leaders mapped teachers' readiness for the journey ahead (Figure 1.3). Caterpillars were those who were happy with the status quo and resistant to change, while the butterflies were effective practitioners with a deep and abiding interest in improving their own professional knowledge and skills in the interests of student learning.

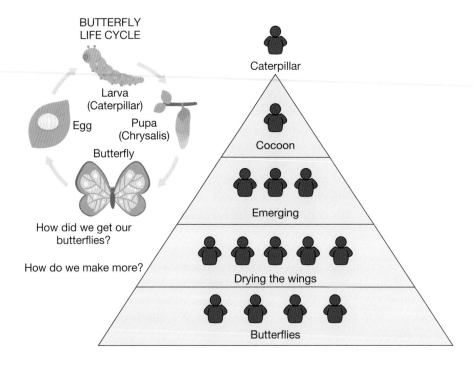

Figure 1.3 The butterfly diagram

What new actions did the teachers and school leaders try?

The leaders were careful to share the learning journey with the whole staff, bearing in mind the differences in teachers' readiness for what they had to learn and change. Whole staff sessions included opportunities to engage with the research – both Hattie's Visible Learning research and that of colleagues such as Shirley Clarke and Helen Timperley. All these researchers share a fundamental commitment to the concept that assessment must primarily be a tool for understanding progress in relation to valued student outcomes, and for using that understanding to make decisions on next steps in classrooms and across the school.

The learning from research provided a theoretical lens through which the school, led by the guiding coalition, looked at their own data and the messages from the Visible Learning research to ask:

> What's worth keeping? How much of what we do and how we do it positively impacts on the learning of our students … not "what they do" but "what they learn?" … Our action research into Hattie's work was the stimulus that prompted many significant changes, and through the perspective of a different lens we began to declutter, debug, and disrupt tradition; there were "sacred cows" dying all around us!
>
> (Guiding coalition)

A commercial spelling program provides an example of a "sacred cow" that had to go. Regardless of the relevance to purpose or content, the student's spelling level, or the student's ability to comprehend individual words without context, teachers kept asking students at the same time each day to "work from their Smart Words" booklet. For many students, this was a waste of time.

Of course, ending one approach that is comfortable and known leads to the question, "What do we replace it with?" The school needed to identify what might be "better" and more effective. The Visible Learning research provided the principles and framework necessary to construct a new shared pedagogy based on the evidence of what actually works to improve student outcomes:

> Our ongoing evaluation against the principles of Visible Learning forms the basis of our whole-school strategy. It impacts on all we do, from providing an engaging curriculum, to creating high expectations, to closing the feedback loop through formative assessment that promotes individual growth, to maximizing attendance, and to creating a shared vision that raises enthusiasm for learning.
>
> (Guiding coalition)

Teachers have had multiple opportunities to learn through small groups, each supported by a member of the guiding coalition. The guiding coalition deliberately constructed the teams to ensure each included at least one teacher at the "butterfly" stage, who was likely to have a positive influence on others. Teachers also received individual modeling and coaching tailored to their particular needs.

An important strategy for knowing thy impact is to be observed by colleagues and have follow-up learning conversations. Observations and walkthroughs by the leadership team have continued, with a new focus on the practices that the research shows to work, how well those practices are being implemented, and whether in fact they are having the intended impact. Student voice is now built into these observations.

Teachers are also visiting each other's classrooms to see what is happening and provide each other with feedback.

Figure 1.4 is a list that was developed by the Keilor Views guiding coalition to support observations. Based on the research into what works in effective classrooms, it sets out the school's expectations and provides a basis for rigorous conversations based on evidence.

Quantitative data is critical to an understanding of impact at both the classroom level and the whole-school level:

> We regularly look at and share student data of achievement and growth as a way of reflecting on the learning and the effectiveness of our professional program. We evaluate and re-evaluate based on what other support needs to be in place.
>
> (Guiding coalition)

Figure 1.5 provides another example of the teacher benchmarking data that is collated each term in order to analyze whole-school achievement in reading. The data is shared with staff to facilitate discussions centered on the key questions, "Where are we going?" "How are we going?" "Where to next?"

Conversations centered on knowing thy impact are often challenging. When we see things through the eyes of our students, we may experience a sense of dissonance – a feeling of disequilibrium as our fundamental beliefs and assumptions are challenged. As Helen Timperley and colleagues (2007) have demonstrated, this can lead us to restructure our former beliefs and assumptions in such a way that we achieve the impact we intended. But it can also result in our shutting down, explaining the findings away in order to protect our personal sense of identity. Genuine two-way learning conversations take time and sensitivity to where individual educators are in their personal improvement journey.

As they implemented Visible Learning in their school, the guiding coalition at Keilor Views was deeply aware of the need to build relationships of trust and challenge:

> There had to be transparency in the way we operated and the default position of 'trust' was paramount: Trust in the data you are receiving from the previous teacher from year to year, trust that the intention of "educational walks" into your classroom is to identify growth and learning points in students and to provide you with quality feedback, trust that this coaching model really is reciprocal and will help build your professional capacity, trust in the research, and trust in the instructional knowledge of the school's leadership.
>
> (Guiding coalition)

STUDENTS	**Engagement**: Focused and interacting with the learning	
	Learning: Can articulate how they are learning and how they can show success	
PEDAGOGY	**Lesson Structure**: Mini lesson, independent time, share GANAG	
	Learning Intentions and Success Criteria: LI and SC, clear, written, discussed Students engage with it (read it, write it, score to it) At the forefront of the classroom Referred to during and at end of lesson	
	Turn and Talk: Used in shared thinking mini lessons Turn and Talk expectations established Use of conversation stems	
	Resources: Use of anchor charts eLearning	
	Transition: Students know the routine Transition between lesson parts is smooth	
CONTENT	**Vocabulary**: Explicit and relevant	
	Planning: Team alignment Aligned with KVFS curriculum documents	
	Assessment: Linked to learning of a lesson Formative or summative? Conferring? Self-assessment scoring?	
	Effective Learner Qualities: Posters displayed Vocabulary used	
PHYSICAL ENVIRONMENT	**Anchor Charts**: Relevant, clear and engaging Charts of need at the forefront Logical display of charts around the room	
	Classroom Library: Covers facing out Categories/labels clear 500–1000 books Range of texts Inviting space	
	Displays:	

Figure 1.4 Observation guide

Term 4

By student numbers

Year level	Below level	At level	Above level	Total students
Prep	6	12	40	58
Year 1	9	8	36	53
Year 2	7	11	35	53
Year 3	24	14	18	56
Year 4	25	6	28	59
Year 5	15	14	23	52
Year 6	25	12	37	74
Total	111	77	217	405

By percentage

Year level	Below level	At level	Above level
Prep	10%	21%	69%
Year 1	17%	15%	68%
Year 2	13%	21%	66%
Year 3	43%	25%	32%
Year 4	42%	10%	47%
Year 5	29%	27%	44%
Year 6	34%	16%	50%
Total	27%	19%	54%

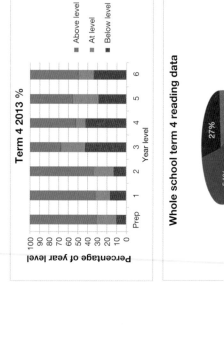

Figure 1.5 Term 4 reading data analysis

Teachers Rita and Katie provide an example of two teachers who built a trusting relationship that meant they could have challenging conversations focused on student outcomes. Both these teachers were early champions of Visible Learning who were quick to see how it would enable the school to achieve its strategic intentions, and keen to adopt its principles in their classrooms. Following expert coaching, they decided to conduct a joint inquiry into mathematics teaching. Working with matched cohorts of students, they administered a linear pre-test and then used the evidence about student strengths and needs to design a sequence of lessons. During implementation, they observed each other and provided each other with feedback, and afterwards they administered a post-test.

Rita and Katie's analysis of what happened during the teaching and learning sequence and its impact went deep. Together, they calculated the effect size for each individual student, for each class, and for the whole cohort. They unpacked where they had added value and where they had not, and looked at where there were differences. Critically, they asked "why," asking difficult questions about the expectations they had set and the ways in which they had delivered the lessons. By keeping the students and instructional practice at the core of the discussion, they avoided emotion and instead had meaningful conversations that were enriching for them both. They learnt from each other through sharing their evaluation.

What was the impact of the changed actions?

By the end of 2012, the school had completed its first impact cycle. The teacher observations and walkthroughs revealed that teacher pedagogy had become more consistent and was more in line with what is needed for both students and teachers to be assessment-capable. Changes at the school level, such as opportunities for collaborative planning using shared templates, were supporting the shifts. Visible Learning began to take on a momentum of its own:

> I began to get very deliberate about my planning and delivery of learning content. My planning documents were no longer just for compliance; they were a living, breathing reflection of what was happening in my room. The more purposeful I got, the clearer the student voice became about success and achievement.
>
> (Katie Salera, classroom teacher)

Rita reports that feedback conversations centered on knowing thy impact have become a normal part of how things are done at Keilor Views:

> As the KVPS Teaching and Learning coach, I am involved in regular debrief meetings with teachers. These discussions allow for the teacher to reflect, ask questions, and plan future goals for their own personal pedagogical practice, as well as to drive whole-school improvement. We look at the impact we have

within and across lessons using student scoring, student voice, and assessment data. It is an expectation that as colleagues, we will be involved in this feedback cycle, and it has become a critical part of the coaching process.

While it is not yet embedded practice, some teachers are collating effect-size data and using what it tells them about student learning to plan next steps. For example, Figure 1.6 shows the data collated by the year 5 teaching team to analyze the effect of a unit on division in mathematics. It compares the students' knowledge of the content and processes related to division over a term. The teachers jointly analyzed the data to make interpretations based on the following questions:

What does this mean for future planning?
How can we share practices to make the data show more consistent success across the grades?
What could be the cause of the differences among individual students?
The teachers also found that this was invaluable data to show the students themselves, as a means of giving feedback about progress and working with them to set future learning goals in mathematics.

The guiding coalition records the following impacts on the outcomes for students:

■ student voice about the learning intention and success of their own learning has become clearer;
■ students are seeing themselves as the key to their success;
■ students now discuss what they are learning, not what they are doing;
■ the Student Opinion Survey results for years 5 and 6 improved; and critically
■ achievement data shows accelerated improvement in academic outcomes for the majority of students, with an average effect size above 0.4.

In its first two years, the school exceeded its target for year 5 students. These students, who had been part of the Visible Learning journey through two years of implementation, achieved effect-size gains in NAPLAN of 1.11 for reading and 1.35 for numeracy over two years. The gains were especially impressive for the students who began at "below expected level," with effect sizes ranging from 1.2 to 3.58. Figure 1.6 provides an insight into this for mathematics, and Figure 1.7 shows the improved NAPLAN data for reading.

The improvements are clearly evident in the way students talk about their learning:

Now when students are asked about the disposition of being determined, they respond with:
"I use the learning intention to focus my learning."
"I have strategies for when I get stuck!"
"I know that learning can be tricky."

(Guiding coalition)

Effect Sizes

Assessment Titles Division   **Grade: 5**

Grade	Name	Score 1	Score 2	Effect size
5G	Student	0	20	2.35
5G	Student	12	20	0.94
5G	Student	9	22	1.53
5G	Student	24	25	0.12
5G	Student	1	22	2.47
5G	Student	0	18	2.12
5G	Student	26	25	-0.12
5G	Student	1	22	2.47
5G	Student	26	26	0.00
5G	Student	1	14	1.53
5G	Student	1	23	2.59
5G	Student	2	22	2.35
5G	Student	5	26	2.47
5G	Student	0	20	2.35
5G	Student	25	26	0.12
5G	Student	19	26	0.82
5G	Student	0	21	2.47
5G	Student	0	17	2.00
5H	Student	7	24	2.00
5H	Student	23	26	0.35
5H	Student	2	24	2.59
5H	Student	26	26	0.00
5H	Student	3	24	2.47
5H	Student	0	2	0.24
5H	Student	0	0	0.00
5H	Student	4	24	2.35
5H	Student	24	26	0.24
5H	Student	0	22	2.59
5H	Student	6	25	2.23
5H	Student	2	26	2.82
5H	Student	26	26	0.00
5H	Student	2	24	2.59
5H	Student	0	1	0.12

Figure 1.6 Effect size data for unit on division (*continued overleaf*)

Assessment Titles Division assessment   **Grade: 5**

Grade	Name	Score 1	Score 2	Effect size
5H	Student	0	21	2.47
5H	Student	1	24	2.70
5H	Student	6	23	2.00
5H	Student	3	11	0.94
5H	Student	0	2	0.24
5H	Student	26	25	-0.12
5S	Student	1	20	2.23
5S	Student	25	24	-0.12
5S	Student	23	25	0.24
5S	Student	1	4	0.35
5S	Student	0	25	2.94
5S	Student	0	10	1.18
5S	Student	0	11	1.29
5S	Student	4	16	1.41
5S	Student	0	25	2.94
5S	Student	1	25	2.82
5S	Student	2	22	2.35
5S	Student	26	24	-0.24
5S	Student	6	24	2.12
5S	Student	1	23	2.59
5S	Student	1	25	2.82
5S	Student	3	18	1.76
5S	Student	2	19	2.00
5S	Student	1	16	1.76
5S	Student	1	2	0.12
5S	Student	1	21	2.35
5S	Student	2	25	2.70
5S	Student	22	24	0.24

Average	7.15	20.15	
STDEV	9.79	7.22	
Average STDEV	8.50		
Effect size	1.53		

Figure 1.6 (*Continued*)

	Name	2011	2013	Effect Size
1	Student name	247	418	2.38
2	Student name	247	436	2.63
3	Student name	305	445	1.94
4	Student name	305	462	2.18
5	Student name	305	454	2.07
6	Student name	305	462	2.18
7	Student name	318	462	2.00
8	Student name	341	523	2.53
9	Student name	352	471	1.65
10	Student name	363	445	1.14
11	Student name	363	409	0.64
12	Student name	374	479	1.46
13	Student name	394	532	1.92
14	Student name	394	399	0.07
15	Student name	405	389	-0.22
16	Student name	405	495	1.26
17	Student name	405	471	0.92
18	Student name	415	436	0.29
19	Student name	415	488	1.01
20	Student name	415	532	1.63
21	Student name	415	542	1.76
22	Student name	426	551	1.74
23	Student name	426	523	1.35
24	Student name	426	427	0.01
25	Student name	426	532	1.47
26	Student name	436	488	0.72
27	Student name	436	532	1.33
28	Student name	436	542	1.47
29	Student name	436	505	0.96
30	Student name	447	523	1.06
31	Student name	447	479	0.44
32	Student name	447	495	0.68
33	Student name	447	532	1.18
34	Student name	458	585	1.76
35	Student name	481	585	1.44
36	Student name	494	532	0.53
37	Student name	507	599	1.28
38	Student name	507	514	0.10
39	Student name	536	551	0.21
40	Student name	536	632	1.33
41	Student name	536	614	1.08
42	Student name	536	505	-0.43
43	Student name	554	551	-0.04
44	Student name	573	551	-0.31
45	Student name	573	562	-0.15
46	Student name	597	614	0.24

Average	426.35	506.00
STDEV	84.68	59.29
Average STDEV	71.99	
Group Effect Size	1.11	

Figure 1.7 NAPLAN reading data for 2013

Student ownership of the learning is reflected in the fact that it was the student leadership team who presented the school community with the new *Keilor Views Primary School Effective Learner Qualities Student Handbook*[2] at an assembly in April 2014.

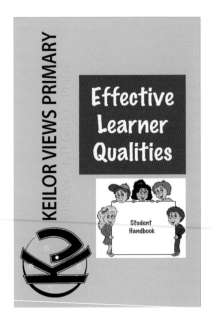

Figure 1.8 The student handbook

Today, Keilor Views is regarded as an exemplar school by other school communities who visit on a regular basis to see the shifts that have taken place.

Continuing the cycle

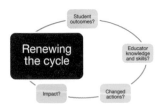

Keilor Views understands that the journey is never over. Ongoing inquiry into impact means that there is always something new to learn and improve:

By early 2013, our pedagogical consistency across the school was at its best. The use of learning intentions and success criteria had become a fundamental aspect of all lessons, assessment practices had become more streamlined and purposeful, and school-level planning and curriculum documents had been refined to suit school priorities. However, we could still see the gaps and needed to continue this journey.

During 2013, we collected evidence of where we were at with our Visible Learning priorities. It opened our eyes to a whole new set of goals and targets.

Our follow-up Visible Learning Plan paved the way for future work. 2014 has seen Keilor Views create our own set of 'Effective Learner Qualities' that will support the explicitness of what we do, each and every lesson. Furthermore, I am working with the rest of the leadership team to make the use of effect sizes more commonplace when analyzing assessments, as well as shifting the way we give feedback to students and each other as a learning community.

(Rita Scuteri)

The school has a plan in place that includes specific targets and strategies for achieving those targets. The plan sets out the learning and change that is needed for all groups – students, teachers, leaders, and families/communities. It explains how the learning will be undertaken, how it will be monitored, and how the school will know it has achieved its targets.

There is joy in this journey:

When I am lucky enough to take school tours of prospective families or visitors to our school, I can't wipe the smile off my face. It is only when I step back and observe where we are at that I realize the extent of our journey and all that we have been able to achieve. The key to our success is attributed to many factors, but the standout aspect for me, coming from a teaching and learning perspective, is the goal congruence of the leadership team. Everything we do leads back to "How will it help students learn?" and "What is best for our students?" This is our core business and this is what we should be spending time on. We have come a long way in recent years and I look forward to seeing what lies ahead!

(Rita Scuteri)

Charles warns that there is danger in becoming comfortable and that it is important to continue to observe, learn, and constantly stretch your boundaries. But that said, he makes the following observation:

Recently at the Visible Learning Conference, Professor John Hattie stood up in his opening address and said, "I'm looking at you all and thinking 'What if I got this wrong?'" I feel the same way when educators ask to visit and I always end up in the same place – that Keilor Views is a living, breathing example that he didn't.

Notes

1   These welcome signs, erected outside the school entrance, are written in all the languages spoken by the families who are a part of Keilor Views Primary School. The 2013 student leaders drove the fundraising that allowed the welcome sign to eventuate.
2   You can access the handbook from the school's website at www.kvps.vic.edu.au/page/228/Effective-Learner-Qualities

2

Discovery College

Hong Kong

Our hope was to create a detailed internal understanding, based on student voice and internal assessments, that was triangulated with external data to create an informed, mutually understood, and rich picture of where every learner was at any point in their learning journey. That picture would be the basis for understanding what we could do to help them grow individually and to plan accordingly.

Discovery College guiding coalition

At Discovery College, knowing thy impact is the central theme of a staff development process that has driven improved student outcomes across a large, multi-leveled student population that had already been doing well by international standards prior to undertaking professional learning with Visible Learning.

Context

Discovery College is a private, independent school situated on Lantau Island in Hong Kong. The school is run by the English Schools Foundation (ESF), a not-for-profit organization that also runs a number of other schools and kindergartens in the region. It opened in 2007 and moved to its current, purpose-built campus in 2008.

Discovery College is what people in Hong Kong call a 'through-train' school, meaning that it combines a primary and secondary school. It currently caters to approximately:

- 630 students at the primary school level (the five- to 11-year-olds in years 1–6);
- 500 students at the middle school level (the 11- to 16-year-olds in years 7–11); and
- 130 students at the senior school level (the 16- to 18-year olds in years 12 and 13).[1]

The student body is made up of young people from over 40 different countries and over 70 ethnicities. Students speak over 15 unique mother tongues. Learning is in English, but all students receive additional tuition in Mandarin. While many are the children of expatriates, 70% are permanent Hong Kong residents, meaning that their families have resided in Hong Kong for over seven years or are Hong Kong citizens. A significant minority are local Chinese.

A large student body requires a large staff and a carefully organized structure. Principal Mark Beach is supported by deputy principal Peter Lasscock. Andy Kai Fong and Vania Tiatto are the respective heads of the secondary and primary schools, and they are in turn supported by three vice principals. Along with business manager Pat Romano, this group forms the college leadership team. The secondary school is structured into departments, each with its own head, and teachers in the primary school work in year level teams, each with a team leader.

Discovery College offers the International Baccalaureate curriculum through the Primary Years Program (PYP), Middle Years Program (MYP), and Diploma Program (DP). Its vision statement is "Grow, Discover, Dream."

Overview

In 2013, Discovery College had successfully addressed many of the challenges of establishing a new school, including achieving accreditation to offer the International Baccalaureate curriculum. The College leadership team regarded this as an opportune time to reflect on what had been achieved and what the school could do better. The team undertook a retreat where they considered three issues in particular. First, the team was aware that many teachers saw the school's strategic planning as too complex and too focused on the logistics of establishing a new school. Consequently, many teachers did not feel that they had 'owned' the school's annual plans. The leadership team saw that there was an opportunity to move to a much more conceptual annual plan that was more directed at learning and was built with whole-staff support and input. The second issue was that while the school's student achievement data indicated that on international comparisons many students were doing well, the team recognized some significant faults in the quality of the data they were looking at and the extent to which it could be used to inform a learning-focused environment. Third, the leaders did not want to lead a school that was just doing well. They wanted to lead an improving school where all students were extended, including those who were already achieving two or three years ahead of expected levels.

In this story, we look at how the leaders of a large and successful school reoriented staff to the use of evidence-based inquiry as a means to improve their practice and thus their impact on students.

Featured teachers and leaders

This story is illustrated with vignettes and quotes from the following members of the Discovery College staff:

Deputy head of college **Peter Lasscock** is an Australian whose teaching experience includes six years as a consultant in schooling improvement. His areas of specialist expertise include student engagement, personalized learning, evidence-based practice, and the authentic use of digital technology.

Vania Tiatto is head of primary education. Previously, she was a teacher and educational leader in Australia and held various consultancy roles across the Asia-Pacific. She has specialist expertise in educational leadership, curriculum design, and professional learning.

New Zealander **Sarah Bennett** has taught at Discovery College since its inception. She has special interests in student well-being, middle leadership, and inquiry-based learning.

Matt Baron is an Australian who has spent the past 12 years teaching in Asia, including three years as a vice principal at Discovery College. His professional interests are in educational leadership, technology, evidence-based inquiry learning, and student well-being.

Kim Cassel is an Australian who has taught in Asian schools for most of her 17 years in the profession. Her current professional interests are in student well-being, literacy teaching and learning, and student assessment capability.

Flora Mather teaches English and is head of the English Department. A foundation teacher at Discovery College, she previously taught in New Zealand. Her professional interests are in critical literacy and teacher inquiry.

Annette Garnett is dean of year 7 and teaches English to students in years 7 and 8. She has been at Discovery College since its inception. Most of her previous teaching experience was in New Zealand, and she has also had consultancy roles. Her professional interests include gifted and talented education, student well-being, and teacher inquiry.

Alan Kirk is a British citizen who previously taught in the United Kingdom, Turkey, and the Philippines. He currently teaches English and Theory of Knowledge and is the Theory of Knowledge coordinator at Discovery College.

Discovery College's Visible Learning story

What were the desired student outcomes?

Academic achievement is prioritized at Discovery College. At the school's inception, the ESF mandated a set of assessment tools from the United Kingdom. These included the Middle Years Information System (MidYIS), a tool for use with students in year 7, and the Advanced Level Information System (ALIS), a tool for use with year 11 students.[2] Data from these instruments demonstrated that in comparison to a general cohort of students in the United Kingdom, the vast majority of Discovery College students were performing above what could be expected. These were salutary results, but the school's leadership team had a number of reservations about the value of the data provided:

1   The data provided a comparison based on achievement but not progress, and so it could not be used to get a true measure of the effect teaching practice was having on learners.
2   Testing only occurred once per year, which limited the opportunity to use it to inform everyday teaching.
3   When correlated with internal data, the external standardized data was useful for identifying students with additional learning needs, but provided little information about how to extend high achievers.
4   The data was not provided in a way that made it informative for the students themselves.

The school's Visible Learning guiding coalition recalls:

> At one level we could have sat back and relaxed and said we were doing very well based on the information we had, albeit from what we felt was an inappropriate tool-set. We chose not to do this. We felt we did not have the information we needed – for our students in our context – to allow us to make informed decisions around improving learning and teaching for each and every student.

In 2012, the leadership team began a search for tools that were more suitable to their context, students, and curriculum. At the same time, they were looking at how internal qualitative and quantitative measures could richly and meaningfully build the data picture around individual students, classes, and cohorts. Table 2.1 shows the external tools they selected and the purpose to which they were put.

Table 2.1 External assessment tools used at Discovery College

Purpose	Tools
Assessment for learning.	Student voice is employed at all levels, e-asTTle[3] is used with students in years 4–13, and other tools are used that are specific to particular levels.
Determining growth – the value the school adds for its students.	e-asTTle and the International Schools Assessment (ISA[4]) for students in years 4, 6, 8, and 10.
Benchmarking against similar schools.	The International Schools Assessment.
Measuring achievement against a UK cohort.	MidYIS (year 7) and ALIS (year 11).

The leadership team understood that to get the complete picture they were seeking, the school also needed to improve its use of internal assessment and, in particular, the attention it paid to students' own aspirations and perceptions. To this end, the 2012 Annual Plan included the priority "student voice." The leadership team hoped that these shifts would support improved achievement outcomes for all students, regardless of their starting point. These are the aspirations expressed in the introductory quote (page 42).

What knowledge and skills did the teachers and school leaders need to support these outcomes?

Along with its inquiry into assessment tools, the leadership team was also inquiring into teacher planning and practice. This revealed limited differentiation to student needs and strengths, indicating that the issue with assessment was not just about the quality of the tools but about teacher understandings about the purpose of assessment.

The school's search for more appropriate assessment tools led to its participation in a workshop on the use of e-asTTle. Teams from both the primary and secondary sectors of the school attended, as did teams from other schools in the ESF. This workshop, led by Deb Masters and Julie Schumacher of Cognition Education, was the catalyst for the school's entry into Visible Learning.

In September 2012, all staff attended a Visible Learning[plus] Foundation Day led by Deb Masters and John Hattie. Leaders and a number of the teaching staff recognized this as the opportunity they were seeking to discover how they could gather and use a range of data to improve teaching and learning for their students. They were particularly excited by what they were hearing about the use of student voice as a critical tool for improving practice:

We had the rhetoric but in hindsight, we did not have the practice. We quickly realized that with the right mindframes, questions, and strategies, what students could tell us could have a profound impact on practice … and it has.
(Vania Tiatto, head of primary)

While at least some members of staff were clearly on board, the leadership team realized that it needed to plan for transformational change. A leadership retreat held early in 2013 provided an opportunity to reflect on where the school was, where the team wanted it to go, and how they might take the whole staff with them. The team was aware that many staff felt that in the past the school's planning had been too distanced from the central business of teaching and learning. They realized that the development of the 2013 Annual Plan provided an opportunity to invite staff into the change process. Consequently, the retreat was followed by an externally-facilitated session where staff were invited to help identify the school's priorities for 2013–14. The team was encouraged by the fact that, though voluntary, the session was attended by one-third of staff.

The new priorities were informed by the evidence of need that was emerging from the school's participation in the Visible Learning[plus] Evidence into Action series of workshops. This evidence confirmed the importance of supporting teachers to know thy impact … and to act on that knowledge.

Staff at the voluntary session agreed on the following four priorities for teaching and learning at Discovery College:

1 Build shared understandings of what an assessment-capable visible learner does.
2 Build a culture of professional learning that is rigorous, evidence-based, collaborative, and autonomous.
3 Embody international-mindedness.
4 Nurture student, staff, and community well-being.

Priorities 1 and 2 are those that relate to Visible Learning. They are connected: it was necessary to achieve Priority 2 in order to achieve Priority 1. Table 2.2 sets out the aspirations for each of these priorities and the success criteria (or "next steps") for achieving those aspirations.

Table 2.2 Visible Learning priorities at Discovery College

Priority	Aspirations	Success criteria ('next steps')
Build shared understandings of what an assessment-capable visible learner does.	Learners understand: • what they are learning (goals/learning intentions); and • where they are at (using success criteria/assessment/ evidence/feedback).	• Learners can articulate/explain their learning intention/goal (what). • Learners understand the progression of learning in relation to the goal (where). • Learners understand where they are on the progression of learning (where). • Learners understand where and how to make further progress ("next steps").
Build a culture of professional learning that is rigorous, evidence-based, collaborative, and autonomous.		Professional learning is: • rigorous – asking challenging questions of and providing feedback for each other; • evidence-based – using student achievement data to inform 'next steps'; • collaborative – sharing and critically interrogating practice in an ongoing, reflective, and growth-promoting way; and • autonomous – providing opportunities to determine what you do, how you do it, and who you do it with.

What new actions did the teachers and school leaders try?

Discovery College enacted its plan through conducting collaborative professional inquiries in teams across the school. The inquiries were connected by the priorities set out in the annual plan and by the learning that took place through the school's ongoing participation in Visible Learning[plus] workshops. The focus of that learning was on:

- learning intentions and success criteria;
- collecting, analyzing, and sharing student voice;
- assessment for learning (formative) shared with students (including e-asTTle); and
- supporting the calculation, sharing, understanding, and learning implications of effect sizes (initially in the upper primary school).

In this part of the story, you can read some brief vignettes describing inquiries undertaken by teachers at different levels of the school. They are placed here as part of the whole-school story but it is important to understand that each was a complete inquiry in its own right. In each instance, the teacher, along with his/ her colleagues, and supported by a professional leader:

- identified a specific student outcome that was the priority focus;
- identified an aspect of their own knowledge and skills where a change might lead to improved student outcomes;
- made a change to practice on the basis of that hypothesis;
- checked whether the change had had its intended impact; and
- reflected on where their inquiry might take them next.

Inquiry into impact at the primary level

Sarah Bennett, year 5

Figure 2.1 Sarah Bennett

Sarah Bennett's inquiry was focused on a group of eight students in her year 5 class who needed to strengthen their fluency in reading. Sarah felt that a barrier for these students was that they lacked independence as learners. She asked primary vice-principal Matt Baron to support her inquiry by observing a lesson and then asking the students the following questions:

- Do you have a reading goal? What is it?
- How will you know if you've achieved your goal?
- What feedback have you had from your teacher about your reading lately?
- What do you do if you get stuck?
- How do you feel if you get something wrong or if you don't understand something? What do you do?

Matt made transcripts of the students' responses which he then shared with Sarah. Matt and Sarah analyzed the transcripts independently and then compared their thoughts to come up with agreed understandings. They agreed that:

- two out of the eight students had an identified reading goal that had been set with the teacher;
- none of the students could explain criteria that would indicate when they were successful;
- six of the eight students knew they were learning about fluency and could describe what this meant;
- half the students could recall feedback from the teacher about their reading; and
- all students had at least one strategy for what to do if they got stuck in their reading.

A particular puzzle was that Matt had observed Sarah providing a student with feedback about his strengths and an area for development, and yet when that student was asked about whether he had recently received feedback on his learning as a reader, he answered that he had not. Sarah realized that if students could not even recognize that they were getting feedback, they were in no position to use feedback for improvement:

> The student voice highlighted for me the importance of making everything explicit to the students – learning outcomes, criteria for success, what feedback is, and how it supports our learning.
>
> (Sarah Bennett)

On the basis of this insight, Sarah and her year 5 teaching colleagues developed a six-week unit that sought to improve the students' reading fluency through processes and activities that simultaneously built their capabilities as independent learners:

> We started by including the students in developing success criteria for reading fluency. Students trialled and observed a variety of different reading fluencies and then collaboratively developed their own criteria for what they believed a fluent reader looked and sounded like. They then selected the areas within this where they were already doing well and decided on their personal target or reading goal. They were explicitly taught what feedback is, the purpose of it, how to give and receive feedback, and how to act on feedback once it has been received.
>
> (Sarah Bennett)

Retesting at the end of the unit, through teacher observations using the co-constructed success criteria, revealed that the focus students had achieved the target of "reading a range of texts fluently at an appropriate level for year level." When Matt observed Sarah again, it was clear that she had become more explicit in identifying the learning outcomes and sharing the criteria for success, and that feedback was clearly related to those criteria. Interviews with students revealed that they understood enough about their expected progress, how they were doing, their next steps for learning, and the nature and practice of effective feedback that they could both self-assess and give each other feedback on their learning.

Sarah concluded that collecting data that reflected student voice had proven useful in setting new directions for student learning and empowering her students in their own learning. She has since replicated the process in other parts of the curriculum and in relation to other valued student outcomes, including student well-being. Based on her own journey, Sarah offers the following advice to her colleagues around the world:

> Involve students in the decision-making so they have ownership of their own learning. Develop a common language for learning. Develop small steps so students can see a clear pathway to their learning goal. Involve students in creating success criteria. Provide opportunities for self-monitoring so students can make decisions about their own learning.

Kim Cassel, year 6 teacher

Figure 2.2 Kim Cassel

Kim's inquiry was undertaken collaboratively with the year 6 teaching team. In the past, these teachers had linked their teaching of reading to genre and text-types. The teachers had a hunch that their students would achieve greater success if their teaching became more targeted on developing the skills and strategies of successful readers. After being introduced to the e-asTTle reading tool, they saw an opportunity to use the data it provides to target those skills and so improve their students' reading outcomes.

The first action was to use diagnostic tools, including e-asTTle, PROBE[5] and the Developmental Reading Assessment (DRA)[6] to identify the specific strengths and needs of each individual student and what their next steps should be. Kim explains:

> In our collaborative planning and shared teacher inquiry times, the year 6 teachers analyzed the data provided by e-asTTle. We compared the next steps for each of our classes and looked for patterns among them. This enabled us to identify specific reading strategies that our students needed to develop. These included inferencing, finding key information, and skimming and scanning.
>
> The question then became "How do we meet the needs of the readers?" We laid out a plan for our year's reading program that included the explicit teaching of the reading strategies identified in our analysis. We explored different resources to help support the teaching and learning of those strategies and decided to use ASCD Reading for Meaning, First Steps in Reading, and PROBE. We used those resources to plan reading units that explicitly targeted the strategies we'd identified.
>
> (Kim Cassel)

The teachers wanted their students to be able to articulate their strengths, challenges, and goals in order to be active participants in improving their reading. Therefore, they shared the e-asTTle data with their students, using the e-asTTle Individual Learning Pathway reports, which the program generates to specifically help students to understand where they are in their reading, where they need to go next, and to know how they will get there. However, they were not so sure that their students understood what a good reader was, so they sought the students' perspectives:

> We asked the students, "What do you need to do to become a better reader?" Most students said "read more" or "read harder books," so we knew that we had to develop their understanding of the traits of good readers. We then developed a planner for the students that set out the skills, knowledge, and attitudes of good readers. We had the students use the planner to create weekly learning intentions for their reading.
>
> (Kim Cassel)

Kim says that there has been a noticeable, ongoing change in classroom relationships, with teachers feeling less responsible for "delivering" the learning and instead working more collaboratively with their students on clearly identified skills. There has also been a marked change in professional conversations. Rather than discussing how to "fit" the reading program into classroom units of inquiry, the focus is now on reading strategies that students would authentically need to use within a particular unit (for example, using skimming and scanning to quickly access information in a non-fiction text during a unit on science).

There are also noticeable changes in the ways students think and talk about their reading:

> Students started referring to specific reading strategies in all areas of the curriculum and also making choices about which strategy best suited the purpose of their reading. Students also thought about themselves as readers beyond the classroom and realized that the key to their reading success was simply finding books that they enjoyed reading.
>
> (Kim Cassel)

Critically, the rate of student progress has increased, with an average effect size for Kim's class of 0.75 over a teaching period of three months.

Kim and her colleagues are enthusiastic about their learning so far and keen to take their inquiry further. Next steps include developing a common terminology for reading strategies so that it is easier for students and teachers to talk to each other about progress, setting up more explicit processes for teacher self-reflection, and developing tools to better understand students' attitudes towards reading.

Matt Baron, vice-principal at primary level

Figure 2.3 Matt Baron

All teachers in the upper primary school used effect sizes to check whether and to what extent students had progressed in response to their changed practices. In year 4, the average effect size was an extraordinary 0.9 over an average of six months.

Matt explains the value of this approach from his perspective as a leader of professional learning:

> Measuring student growth has become an important process in the upper primary. It allows students and teachers to identify what might be going well or what might need changing in terms of approaches to learning. The use of effect sizes also allows us to look at students in a different light other than pure attainment. Students with low attainment levels may have shown significant growth that can be shared and celebrated with the student. Effect sizes allow teachers to identify students with high attainment but low growth and determine why this might be. Is it the level of challenge? Is it attitudinal? Is it something else that needs changing?

Inquiry into impact at the secondary level

In the English department, specific teacher inquiries were initiated by teams of teachers at each year level but the change process and reconstructed pedagogy were developed across the department. In this way, the learning and change was tailored to the specifics of each teacher and group of students, but simultaneously shared with the wider group.

Flora Mather, English head of department and teacher of year 11 English

Figure 2.4 Flora Mather

Flora selected several strategies to find out about her students' strengths and needs in terms of reading and writing:

- e-asTTle reading and writing;
- interviews with students around a specific piece of writing;
- student self-assessment around the same piece of writing.

Flora triangulated the data to identify the following priorities for students:

- to use reading strategies that encourage empathy, visualization, and critical engagement with the purpose and audience of a text;
- to articulate a range of strategies that authors use to shape their writing (using vocabulary and sentence types) for specific purposes and audiences;
- to use these strategies;
- to self-monitor their reading and their writing to ensure that these strategies are being used.

Along with her colleagues, Flora engaged in professional learning that included the use of e-asTTle, an understanding of effective feedback and the concept of Know Thy Impact, and the co-design of success criteria. On the basis of this learning and what she understood about the priorities for students, she identified the need to make the following changes to her practice:

> I needed to help students build success criteria so they would know when they were successful.
>
> I needed to plan for opportunities for students to learn clear and easy strategies for achieving sentence variety for effect. Questioning of the students quickly revealed that their knowledge of sentence types, use of conjunctions, etc. was very limited. I needed to go back and fill these gaps.
>
> I needed to develop a system whereby students could identify inferred ideas in what they were reading so they could begin to describe the ways in which writers use language and syntax for specific purposes and audiences.
>
> I needed to ensure that my feedback on student writing was focused on the main goals students had set, as well as broadening their perspective on vocabulary, sentence starters, and lengths.

Flora then developed and implemented an eight-week unit that integrated these goals for student outcomes and her own practice. Features of the teaching and learning approaches included:

- the selection of texts that lent themselves to developing the targeted reading strategies;

- explicit teaching and modeling of the targeted reading strategies;
- reciprocal reading groups;
- opportunities for guided reflection as individuals, in pairs and groups, and as a class;
- student-generated guides and glossaries;
- explicit teaching of vocabulary, sentence types, and word classes;
- the use of exemplars to build an understanding of the assessment criteria for writing tasks in the International Baccalaureate's Middle Years Program (MYP);
- the co-design of success criteria for creative writing;
- focused work on sentence starters that students self-assessed using the agreed success criteria and for which they received teacher feedback both verbally and via Google Docs.

At the end of the unit, student self-assessment showed a significant increase in confidence and understanding. Flora judged all the students to have achieved an outstanding standard in the final piece of work and was delighted to observe the changes in student talk – their ability to articulate the concepts and strategies they had learnt and to describe and reflect upon their learning journey. Likewise, retesting with e-asTTle confirmed a notable improvement in the target outcomes for reading and writing.

Student voice and e-asTTle are now a regular part of Flora's practice. She and her colleagues are now seeking to broaden the arsenal of "nimble" formative assessment tools that they can use in their continuing professional inquiries.

Annette Garnett, year 7 English

Figure 2.5 Annette Garnett

Annette's inquiry focus was on a group of four year 7 students who did not enjoy writing and lacked independence as learners. She wanted to find out what these students thought about their writing and what their personal goals for writing might be. In particular, she was interested to know about their understanding of the purpose of feedback in its various forms and how they could use feedback to move their learning forward. This necessitated finding out how well the students understood the rubrics that the MYP uses to measure the growth of a student's knowledge and skills.

Annette conducted her inquiry in collaboration with a colleague who also taught year 7 English and had similar concerns. The teachers used e-asTTle to identify the next steps for the students' learning as writers. They shared this data with the students and their parents. They then collected data from a variety of sources to find out what their students were thinking about their learning as writers.

The two teachers invited head of department Flora Mather into their classes to ask their focus students a similar set of questions to those Matt Baron had asked the students in Sarah Bennett's class. The group's analysis of the interview transcripts revealed gaps in the students' understandings about their own learning and about how skills learnt during writing lessons could be transferred to other written tasks.

Annette and her colleague checked their students' understandings of the MYP rubrics by asking the group to discuss and agree on the evidence that would be required to demonstrate success in each of the relevant rubrics. When the teachers evaluated the students' responses, they could see that the students needed further support to understand the criteria for success.

The teachers checked students' individual understandings by having them complete a writing self-assessment form that had first been explained to them. On the basis of that process, the students set personal writing goals that were recorded in a departmental document.

Supported by Flora, the teachers reflected on their findings and the patterns that had emerged. Their overall conclusion was that the students needed the skills to better self-regulate their personal learning journeys as writers. To support them in this, the teachers realized they needed to adopt more effective feedback strategies, provide their students with the tools and understandings they needed to make good use of that feedback, and reflect on messages from the students about how the changes were impacting on their learning. They also wanted to provide opportunities for parents to build their understandings of expectations for their children's writing so that they could better support their learning at home.

The teachers applied their professional learning to become more explicit in their teaching of the skills and strategies of effective writers and to provide more effective feedback that was clearly related to the learning intentions and the criteria set out in the MYP rubrics. In order to support their students to make use of that feedback, they knew that they needed to further unpack the rubrics. They supported this by providing exemplars of student work at various levels of achievement and having the students work collaboratively to determine the features of writing sought by the rubrics and the evidence needed to establish where each piece of writing sat. The students then co-designed task-specific clarifications and constructed feedback for the authors of the exemplars. They transferred this to their own interactions, developing prompts for peer feedback. These experiences provided the language and understandings the students needed to interpret the more directed feedback they were getting from their teachers. At the same time, Annette and her colleagues used the conversations around learning intentions and success criteria to raise the students' expectations of what they could achieve and their awareness of the progress they were actually making.

Parents were included in this learning. Early in the academic year, the vice-principal of the secondary school ran a parent workshop to further reinforce the understandings around the rubrics. Parents were informed of progress through discussions with their own child, in formal conferences with the teacher, and through the written feedback their child received in relation to each new task. The teachers made video recordings of some formative and peer feedback, which they shared with parents. They also emailed parents to share and celebrate success.

When the students were retested at the end of the unit, using both e-asTTle and the MYP rubrics, they had made significant progress in their development as writers. The effect size for content was 1.83, and for style and language mechanics it was 1.35.

Annette finds that her students are now far more confident as writers. They enjoy writing and are articulate about their development as writers. This is evidenced in the students' responses when Flora repeated the interview processes at the end of the teacher-led inquiry. For example, these are the responses when she asked, "How are you going to work on [your goals] for the remainder of this year? What are your next steps?"

> Mrs Garnett has run goal workshops – I'm able to use a thesaurus and make good choices. Mrs Garnett helps me make choices in the library for books with harder words.

> Refer to the rubric and writing checklists. These include the ways I can make improvements to my writing.

> The TEEL [Topic sentence, Explanation, Example, Link] structure is up on the board. I can look at it. I can color code it to make sure that I have each part in my paragraph. I can ask Mrs Garnett.

> Include more written devices and follow the rubric more.

One particularly reluctant writer improved to the extent that he was selected to read his work at the final assembly of the school year. His delighted parents wrote to thank Annette and the school principal: "You are doing such an amazing job inspiring our kids to be the best they can be."

Looking back on the journey so far, Annette believes:

> What has been the most significant aspect of this process is that teaching is more visible to the student, and that the learning is more visible to the teacher. With such transparency, students do not have to 'guess' what the teacher is looking for. Successful outcomes have come from students being more aware of themselves in their learning journey. ... It was exciting to see students using the language of Visible Learning – "Where is your focus?" "Where are you now?" "What are your next steps?" – when working independently, in pairs, or in small groups.

Alan Kirk, year 8 English

Figure 2.6 Alan Kirk

When the year 8 teachers at Discovery College used e-asTTle to test their students' reading and writing achievement, a puzzle emerged. As a group, the students did well in e-asTTle reading, but not so well in writing. Inquiry into the final assessment task from the previous academic year raised further concerns, with marked disparities in student achievement. More worryingly, in Alan's opinion, was that when Flora Mather interviewed the students, their responses revealed a wide variety of interpretations as to what the task was designed to evaluate and what "success" would look like. In particular, few students were able to clearly describe the next steps for their learning with regard to the specific genre, which had been travel writing.

These findings prompted Alan to look more closely at the assessment criteria. Alan realized that they had been too linguistically complex and too distanced from the specific features required for successful travel writing to work well as success criteria. He also realized that the students needed to participate in constructing the criteria for the task if they were to truly understand the strategies and techniques they were supposed to be learning.

Initially, Alan shared these reflections at the year 8 team meetings where the team considered them in relation to their own students and teaching practice. Together, they agreed to focus on the construction and application of success criteria and the provision of teacher and peer feedback. Through this, they hoped their students would increase their effectiveness and independence as writers.

The context for the new learning was a new unit on travel writing that included an extensive array of activities. These included:

- an introduction to the concept of writing about experiences while abroad or in out-of-the-ordinary situations;
- opportunities for the class to explore specific examples of effective travel writing by students and professional writers and to use this as the basis for co-constructing a list of the features of a great travel recount;
- reworking the list of features into a new list that was renamed "My Destination Success Criteria" (for example, "I can incorporate dialogue to give my writing a sense of realism and impact");
- the students' creation of posters setting out the success criteria in a colorful and memorable way;
- further analysis of exemplars, along with opportunities for students to practice and perfect their own writing with respect to specific success criteria;
- the provision of timely and appropriate feedback from both teacher and peers;
- a summative assessment task that the students self-assessed using the co-designed success criteria;
- support for students to evaluate where they felt they had done well and where they needed more work; and
- teacher provision of summative assessment grades and written feedback.

The most significant impact on students was the growth in their autonomy and sense of confidence. Alan also observed that his students:

- were more aware of the importance of employing a range of strategies in their writing to increase its impact;
- had a greater understanding of the conventions of the genre they were analyzing and attempting to emulate;

- had a clearer understanding of the meta-language of literary analysis; and
- had significantly improved their mastery of the travel writing genre.

Alan's inquiry was initiated by his realization that the teacher-developed rubric did not provide students with the criteria they needed to direct their learning. Part of his own learning, then, was that:

> An assessment rubric is ten times more effective if the students themselves have an input into its construction and it is not imposed from outside. By doing so it has meaning for them and their understanding of the artistry of literary or non-literary narratives is enhanced.
>
> (Alan Kirk)

What was the impact of the changed actions?

Discovery College reports that evidence-based inquiries are now the basis for its whole-school approach to internal teacher development. Key features of these inquiries include the use of:

- student voice through purposeful student interviews;
- photographs of learning spaces, activities, and students that are used as the basis for discussion;
- rigorous professional discussions about changed practices and the evidence that points to these changes; and
- the ongoing collection of evidence to check whether the changes result in improvements in student learning.

The school leaders observe that learning intentions and success criteria are explicit in the majority of classrooms. When they interview students, they find that they are able to more clearly articulate their understanding of what they are learning and how they know if they will be successful.

The leaders believe that adherence to two golden rules led to their success:

- set a realistic timeframe involving stages of professional development (multiple times over extended period), implementation, and evaluation; and
- involve a coalition of teacher leaders that outnumber administrators.

Deputy head Peter Lasscock recalls that some false starts occurred with inquiries where the goal or aim was not clear and it was therefore not possible to clearly measure the impact. However, the evidence of impact in the data below demonstrates Peter's point that "Students can have profound impact on learning and our teaching … if we just listen."

The results in Figures 2.7, 2.8, and 2.9 are from the external International Schools Assessment showing cohort growth over time. These support the evidence of impact claimed in the stories from the secondary school teachers. They follow PISA grade standards: the year groups at Discovery College are one ahead but the same age (for example, Grade 9 is Discovery College's year 10).

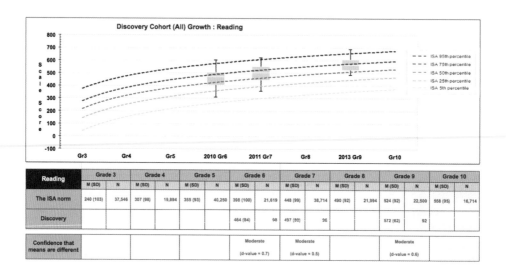

Reading	Grade 3		Grade 4		Grade 5		Grade 6		Grade 7		Grade 8		Grade 9		Grade 10	
	M (SD)	N	M (SD)	N	M (SD)	N	M (SD)	N	M (SD)	N	M (SD)	N	M (SD)	N	M (SD)	N
The ISA norm	240 (103)	37,546	307 (98)	19,894	355 (93)	40,250	398 (100)	21,619	448 (99)	38,714	490 (92)	21,994	524 (92)	22,500	558 (95)	16,714
Discovery							464 (84)	98	497 (90)	96			572 (62)	92		
Confidence that means are different							Moderate (d-value = 0.7)		Moderate (d-value = 0.5)				Moderate (d-value = 0.6)			

Figure 2.7 Reading

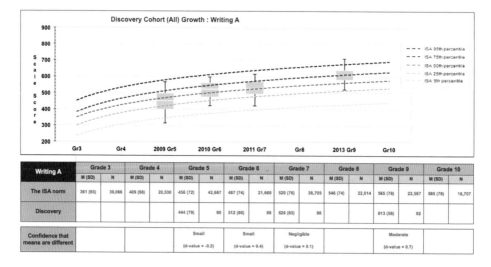

Writing A	Grade 3		Grade 4		Grade 5		Grade 6		Grade 7		Grade 8		Grade 9		Grade 10	
	M (SD)	N	M (SD)	N	M (SD)	N	M (SD)	N	M (SD)	N	M (SD)	N	M (SD)	N	M (SD)	N
The ISA norm	361 (65)	39,066	409 (68)	20,530	456 (72)	42,667	487 (74)	21,660	520 (76)	38,705	546 (74)	22,014	565 (78)	22,567	585 (78)	16,707
Discovery					444 (79)	90	512 (60)	99	526 (65)	98			613 (56)	92		
Confidence that means are different					Small (d-value = -0.2)		Small (d-value = 0.4)		Negligible (d-value = 0.1)				Moderate (d-value = 0.7)			

Figure 2.8 Writing A (narrative)

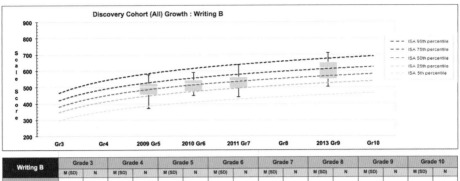

Figure 2.9 Writing B (narrative)

Writing B	Grade 3		Grade 4		Grade 5		Grade 6		Grade 7		Grade 8		Grade 9		Grade 10	
	M (SD)	N	M (SD)	N	M (SD)	N	M (SD)	N	M (SD)	N	M (SD)	N	M (SD)	N	M (SD)	N
The ISA norm	403 (55)	38,924	435 (58)	20,532	476 (61)	42,621	498 (63)	21,612	529 (65)	38,660	556 (67)	21,958	574 (71)	22,401	597 (71)	16,620
Discovery					488 (55)	90	516 (51)	98	531 (61)	96			608 (59)	92		
Confidence that means are different					Small (d-value = 0.2)		Small (d-value = 0.3)		Negligible (d-value = 0)				Moderate (d-value = 0.5)			

Continuing the cycle

The "early adopters" at Discovery College, both individuals and teams, now have credible evidence of the improvements that arise from knowing thy impact and encouraging students to be visible learners. The next big step is for them to use their success to help others adopt and own the Visible Learning ideas and strategies. Specifically, the school seeks to further embed teachers':

- understanding of the factors that have the most impact on learning;
- strategic use of formative data to inform their teaching; and
- understanding and application of tools to ascertain impact, especially in areas outside of mathematics and English.

Notes

1 These levels relate to the International Baccalaureate curriculum.
2 These tools were developed by Durham University's Centre for Evaluation and Monitoring – see www.cem.org
3 e-asTTle was developed by a team at the University of Auckland, led by John Hattie and sponsored by New Zealand's Ministry of Education – see http://e-asttle.tki.org.nz/
4 ISA was developed by the Australian Council for Educational Research – see www. acer.edu.au/tests/isa

5   A tool for assessing reading comprehension developed by Triune – see http://comprehenz.com/probe-2-reading-comprehension-assessment/

6   A formative reading assessment system developed by Pearson – see www.pearsonschool.com/index.cfm?locator=PSZw5u&PMDb

3

Sadadeen Primary School

Australia

As soon as I learnt about the different mindframes and how they work, it changed the way I teach and the way I approach everyday situations. When I am having a tough day, I go home and reflect and evaluate. I question if I could've done anything differently. I wonder, "If I had changed my frame of mind and responded differently to the child, would the way the child reacted have been different?"

Thanks to this approach, I now see myself as a change agent. I am able to consciously shift my way of thinking, and "come at it" with a different attitude. I believe this has had a positive impact on my relationship with the students and has increased the learning conversations in the classroom. The evidence tells me this is true. Talking to my students and colleagues and looking at the achievement data ... student engagement is up and so is their achievement.

Pippa North, teacher, Sadadeen Primary School

Teachers at Sadadeen School have transformed themselves from a mindframe where issues of student behavior and achievement were externalized to one where they perceive themselves as change agents who take responsibility for leading the learning in the classroom. As change agents, they closely monitor what they are doing, its impact on students, and where they could change to do better.

Context

Sadadeen Primary School is situated in the heart of Australia, in the famous outback town of Alice Springs. It is a small school with around 30 students in the transition (school entry) class and around 100 students in years 1–6. The school is also attached to three small preschools, one of which is located onsite.

After a period of decline, Sadadeen School has entered a phase of sudden and rapid growth. Most of the new students are Indigenous Australians, with many living in town camps[1]. Today, 92% of students are Indigenous Australians. A high percentage are disadvantaged in terms of family income and educational background. For example, 50% of families do not have a parent or carer who attended school beyond year 9, and over 80% of families receive welfare payments.

The teaching staff combines highly experienced and beginning teachers. There tends to be a high turnover rate, as reflected in the fact that four of the five-member senior leadership team joined in 2012, with the remaining one joining in 2014. While many members of staff were intensely interested in the education of Indigenous children, few were from the community and none were Indigenous Australians themselves. This hampered teachers' ability to connect with their students and understand how their culture was a resource for learning.

Overview

When Julie McLaren joined Sadadeen Primary School as its new principal in January 2012, she found a school characterized by high levels of student disengagement matched by very low levels of achievement. Long and frequent student absences were common, as was disruptive behavior. Teacher James Pollard recalls his first impression that this was a "tough" school, with verbal and physical aggression permeating many students' relationships with each other, their teachers, and their families. This was a particular issue with Aboriginal students. Tellingly, two of the school's eight classes were Indigenous Education Units (IEU) where students were placed on the basis of their poor behavior and achievement.

It is understandable that in this situation many teachers felt a sense of helplessness, but this is not an attitude that enables change for improvement. It is admirable that in just one year, teachers at Sadadeen shifted their stance from a deficit mindframe to one where they saw themselves as change agents who can and do improve the learning opportunities for their students. The proof is in the data – extraordinary shifts that have dramatically improved the lifelong prospects of students who had previously made little or no progress at school.

This story shows how a clear and determined focus on teacher mindframes and on relationships with students, accompanied by close attention to the impact on learning, can transform a school and the outcomes for its students.

Featured leaders

This story is primarily based on the reflections of the school's guiding coalition, which consists of the entire leadership team. All are relatively new to the school.

Principal **Julie McLaren** was appointed in January 2012.

The assistant principal, **Ailsa Moyses**, arrived in Term 1 2012.

Senior teachers **Ali Hood** and **Kate Kennedy** arrived at the start of Term 3, 2012, and **Claire Perrott** joined at the start of 2014. Ali is also the Visible Learning impact coach.

The school's Aboriginal and Islander Education Worker (AIEW), **Carmy McLean**, was also part of the delivery team. Her role is to work with classroom teachers to help support the learning of Indigenous students and to help liaise with these students' families and community.

The leadership team is committed to making a positive difference to all children in the school. The leaders share a strong commitment to social justice and to the belief that all children can learn given the right support. They bring a wealth of experience in a range of settings, both locally and interstate.

Sadadeen Primary School's Visible Learning story

What were the desired student outcomes?

In 2012, overall student outcomes at Sadadeen Primary School were poor on any measure. In terms of student behavior and engagement:

- 9% of students were referred to Student Services for behavior support;
- 18% of students were placed in the Indigenous Education Units (IEU) on the basis of behavioral and academic issues;
- Indigenous students attended only 50% of the sessions at the (onsite) Natalie Gorey Preschool; and
- T(transition)–6 students attended only 70% of their classes.
- The NAPLAN[2] data for 2012 demonstrates the picture in terms of academic achievement:

In year 3:

- 78% of students were at or below the national minimum standard for numeracy;
- 70% were at or below the minimum standard for reading; and
- 58% were at or below the minimum standard for writing.

In year 5:

- 69% of students were at or below the national minimum standard for numeracy;
- 71% were at or below the minimum standard for reading; and
- 64% were at or below the minimum standard for writing.

In October 2012, the Northern Territory Department of Education offered Central Australian schools the opportunity to hear Professor John Hattie speak and then engage in a Visible Learning project. Inspired by John's presentations, Sadadeen School's leaders were keen to join the initial cluster of ten schools that were surveyed in preparation for the program's rollout across Central Australia in 2013. Supported by consultants Deb Masters and Mary Sinclair, the team conducted a review to deepen their understandings about what was happening at their school in terms of both student outcomes and teacher understandings and skills.

A key finding of this inquiry was that students did not see themselves as learners and did not understand what made for a good learner. A video recording of interviews with 19 students made this very clear:

> Most of the students indicated that behavioral characteristics such as being quiet, listening, being good, finishing your work, and doing what the teacher says were indicative of a good learner. Some students had no response.
> (Extract from Sadadeen School Visible Learning video diary)

On the basis of their analysis, the school identified the following desired outcomes for students:

- Students to be involved in goal-setting and celebrating their learning – students who have high expectations and expect success!
- Students to be settled, connected to the learning, excited, and eager to come to school.

Staff participated in establishing a set of targets that the school could use to specify its goals and measure progress towards those goals. These were ratified by the school council, committed to in the Annual Operating Plan (AOP), and used as the basis for reporting to the community at the end of the school year. Some of these targets are set out in Table 3.1.

What knowledge and skills did the teachers and school leaders need to support these outcomes?

The review of teacher understandings and skills confirmed that teachers were in a state of some crisis. They spent the majority of their time dealing with behavior management and spent very little time on learning. Teachers worked hard, but they tended to work in isolation and grab at quick fixes without testing whether they were working. A deficit culture had developed, where teachers felt that despite their best efforts, the challenges were too great for them to overcome. Early in the self-review process, the leaders recognized that they needed to focus on changing these mindframes.

Table 3.1 Knowing thy impact: Student targets at Sadadeen Primary School

Outcome focus	Targets for 2012–2013
Reading	70% of students with 85% or greater attendance making expected or greater year level gains in reading (using PM benchmark levels): transition = 3 levels; years 1, 2, & 3 = 6 levels; years 4 & 5 = 4 levels.
Mathematics	70% of year 1 & 2 students with 85% or greater attendance making expected or greater gains in number (using I Can Do Maths). 70% of year 3–6 students with 85% or greater attendance making expected or greater gains in number (using PAT mathematics).
Attendance	Increase preschool attendance of Indigenous children from 50% to 70%.
	Increase T–6 attendance of Indigenous children from 70% to 80%.

> Staff needed to let go of the "Yes but" approach/barrier and believe that all the children could learn – to focus firmly on learning.
>
> (Sadadeen Primary School guiding coalition)

A whole-school professional learning day – including classroom assistants as well as teachers – played an important role in getting people to think about where the school was and what staff could do to improve. It began with the creation of a "human graph." Principal Julie McLaren asked staff to stand on a line to indicate where they thought the school was with regards to each mindframe. She then invited people situated at the "high," "middle" and "low" points on the line to explain the reasons for the judgment they had made.

One of the lowest scores on the graph was for "I am a change agent." Fundamentally, a teacher who is a change agent believes that they can change their practice in such a way that the outcomes for their students will improve. The leaders were concerned because without this belief, nothing else is likely to happen. They graphed the "positive beliefs" of a change agent listed in the Foundation Day workshop[3] identifying this factor as one they needed to concentrate on. They also included staff in this analysis, using the same list to have them think, pair, and share the beliefs they thought were critical in achieving the mindframe of a change agent. This inclusive process led to staff identifying the following ideas as areas for improvement:

- It is important to develop high expectations for all students relative to their starting point.
- Developing peer interactions is powerful for improving learning.
- Critique, error, and feedback are powerful opportunities for improving learning.

The school's inquiry also identified that the school needed to focus on the mindframe "I develop positive relationships." This was manifest in the school's issues with behavior management and especially the large numbers of Aboriginal children located in the Indigenous Education Units. Because this was so significant, the school was glad to link their Visible Learning inquiry with the Culture Counts workshops' inquiry into Relationships-based Learning. The concept of Relationships-based Learning[4] is drawn from Professor Russell Bishop's research, which focuses on the importance of relationships in bringing about educational success for students from Indigenous or minority groups. For some staff at Sadadeen, this meant a significant shift in thinking. Where their focus had been upon their right to teach, they needed to think about their students' right to learn, and their own responsibility to enable that learning. They needed to recognize and build on the strengths their students brought to their learning, rather than focus solely on gaps and weaknesses.

The leadership team decided on the following priority outcomes for staff:

- Staff to see all students as capable learners.
- Staff and students to be inspired and passionate teachers and learners who enjoy the challenge.

Carmy McLean helped lead conversations to find out how parents and families viewed the school. Through her inquiry, the leaders came to realize that along with the work to raise the expectations of students and staff, they also needed to ensure families could see a learning-focused school in which their children were enjoying success.

What new actions did the teachers and school leaders try?

Sadadeen's professional learning included many of the same foci as other schools, with work undertaken to "make learning visible" through introducing evidence-based practices such as the construction of clear learning intentions and success criteria, the design of tasks that were aligned with the learning intentions, and the use of feedback processes that enabled students and teachers to measure, monitor, and manage student progress. However, the dominant message was the need for teachers to take on the mindframes of change agents and for students and their families to likewise raise their expectations and believe in the innate capability of all students. Some of the actions the school undertook to make these changes are outlined below.

Defining the mindframes

While the mindframes are supported by empirical research, they needed to be translated into the practical realities of this small community in the desert.

Unpacking each of the mindframes in relation to their particular context helped build staff understanding of what they meant in terms of their personal learning and practice. The mindframes are kept on display in the staffroom as a constant reminder of the expectations for staff. Figure 3.1 shows the school's definition of "we are change agents."

Mind Frames: Visible Learning

Mind Frame: As educators we believe we are change agents.

- We see ourselves as change agents, we are enablers NOT barriers
- It is about raising the self-esteem of our kids, ourselves and our school community
- We need to be flexible in regards to the different cultural groups in our school community, the diversity of groups

In our context this means:

- Explicit teaching of the Mind Frames and practice of the MF, sharing and documenting experiences
- Things we are doing: SLIC, drumming, Girls Group, HIP and HOP, G&D, PLC, Yarning Sessions, FAST, Passport Programme, incentive awards, Sadadeen Smileys, attendance incentives, Individual Learning Programmes
- Staff PD – Cultural Awareness, understanding students' environments, celebrating NAIDOC, catering for and PD related to EAL/D learners

Sadadeen Primary School August 2013

Figure 3.1 Mindframes at Sadadeen (excerpt)

Learner qualities

The school's set of learning qualities evolved naturally out of the mindframes. Staff agreed that strong learners:

- work as a team;
- aim high;
- are proud; and
- question and wonder.

Making learning connections with parents

Teachers now send home two pieces of work each term to show parents and families concrete evidence of their children's learning. The preschools have initiated "brag books" – a photographic record of each child's achievements that they can share with their families and keep when they move on to a new school. The school invites parents on "learning trails" where their children take them on a tour through the school, visiting all of the sites where learning takes place. The child leads their parent on a learning activity in a practical demonstration of their success. These activities are intended to build pride and a positive attitude, as well as being opportunities to share the language of learning with the wider community.

Sharing stories of impact

Teachers and leaders are not keeping their observations to themselves: they are sharing stories of impact with each other so that they constantly inform new learning and change across the school.

One way of sharing these stories is through the creation of a data wall (Figure 3.2) that lets teachers clearly see the progress of individual students. This provides a ready starting point for conversations focused on how learning opportunities are impacting on student-valued outcomes. Photographs of the students are clearly displayed to reinforce the notion that they are "our students" and not just nubmers on a spreadsheet.

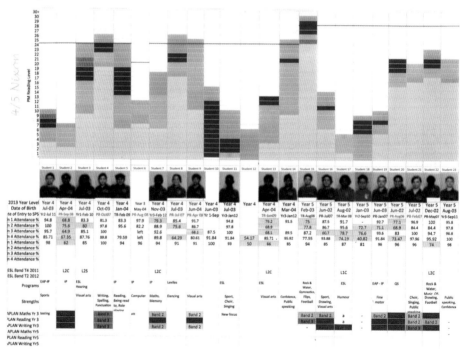

Figure 3.2 Data wall

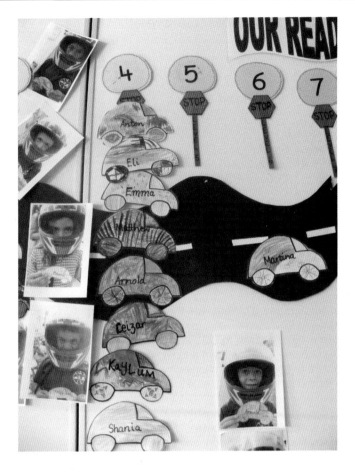

Figure 3.3 Exemplifying and celebrating progress

Likewise, teachers display student reading progress on their walls (Figure 3.3), demonstrating both their expectations for student achievement and the happy fact that students are now progressing at a greatly improved rate!

Another approach has been for teachers and leaders to write and share stories of success when they have met and overcome a challenge. This has proved to be powerful: teachers now theorize that "If we can do it with these students, then we can do it for all our students." Figure 3.4 provides an example of such a story.

Notice how the template prompts teachers to structure their story according to the phases of the impact cycle. Even at this early stage of implementation, there are examples of teachers returning to students' stories to construct the moving picture.

Sadadeen Stories

Student name: Shania
Year level: Grade 2
Date: October 2013

Prior behaviors/concerns about learning:
- Shania had little confidence to learn
- She would not participate in group work
- Was very low in reading/writing/numeracy
- She was using actions of Jolly Phonics without understanding
- Sat in the background and not with other students

What was implemented? What was the change in structure, routines or practice?
- Has joined SLIC
- Looks forward to coming to SLIC each day
- She has become very confident and knows she is learning
- Works a lot better and isn't "shamed" when wrong
- Enjoys challenges now and is able to have a go

Changes/impact on the relationship and learning:
- Shania has experienced success with her learning
- She is very keen to do the work and complete it
- She has improved with her reading/writing/numeracy
- Is now reading PM level 4/5, began as a pre-reader
- Boost in her confidence to learn
- She is happy and joins in all group work
- Shania sits right up the front and engages with lessons
- Shares her learning with her family
- Uses her individual learning folder to show work to family

Figure 3.4 Shania's learning story

Other stories are more anecdotal and informal. They include brief recounts in the weekly newsletter of the positive changes the leaders have seen taking place in classrooms. The leaders have found that this helps build a sense of optimism when the going gets tough.

Disbanding the Indigenous Education Units

All students are now included in the mainstream classes. The school provides additional scaffolding for students who find school challenging through two new programs: the Strong Learners Intensive Centre (SLIC) and the High Interest

Program (HIP). SLIC is designed to provide small group intensive support for students who are operating below or well below their peers. HIP is a practical, hands-on program that is often run in the outside teaching area during the second half of the day.

This does not mean overlooking the specific strengths and needs of Indigenous learners. Instead, all teachers are taking part in cultural awareness training and the school is deliberately seeking to employ more Indigenous staff, especially people who can speak the local languages. As Figure 3.5 demonstrates, changes have been made to the look of the school to communicate to the mostly Aboriginal students and their families that their language and culture are valued.

Figure 3.5 Learner qualities at Sadadeen (excerpt)

Creating a village

We are all familiar with the proverb "It takes a village to raise a child." However, for this to work, it requires the adults in the village [i.e. the school] to have real relationships with children. Only then can they know and respond to their needs. One way of achieving this is to start each day with a whole-school 15-minute fitness session. Another is through taking students on whole-school excursions and holding special events to share and celebrate learning success. The relationships that this builds mean that when a student is having a bad day and needs a change of setting, it is much easier for them to move to a different place with a different teacher.

What was the impact of the changed actions?

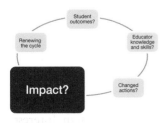

The impact of the changes is clearly visible in the teachers' stories. One that is telling is written by James Pollard. When James instigated a "learning garden" program early in 2013, colleagues commented, "These garden drums will not last for more than a week before the students have destroyed them" or "It's a nice idea, just not right for this school." In reality, the gardens have been a great success. For some students, they have been the switch that made school a safe and enjoyable place to be. Their pride in the gardens has translated into pride in school and therefore a greater willingness to engage positively with teachers, peers, and learning. An unexpected consequence is that a family with a child at the preschool approached James about their interest in connecting the work being done at school with their own work in establishing a community garden in the town camp. This is a powerful indicator that the school is being successful in the creation of more constructive relationships, not just with students, but also with their families.

Today, teachers at Sadadeen have remarkable proof that they are indeed agents of change who have the power to improve learning and well-being outcomes for their students. As Table 3.2 indicates, virtually all of the targets they set in 2012 were achieved in 2013.

Table 3.2 Knowing thy impact: Student outcomes at Sadadeen Primary School

Outcome focus	2012: Targets	2013: Achieved/not achieved
Reading	70% of students with 85% or greater attendance making expected or greater year level gains in reading (using PM benchmark levels): Transition – 3 levels; years 1, 2, & 3 – 6 levels; years 4 & 5 – 4 levels.	Achieved. Effect size of 0.45.
Mathematics	70% of year 1 & 2 students with 85% or greater attendance making expected or greater gains in number (I Can Do Maths)	Achieved. Effect size of 0.66 in PAT mathematics. 44% of students had at least 2 years' growth in Maths in 1 year.
	70% of year 3–6 students with 85% or greater attendance making expected or greater gains in number (using PAT mathematics)	70% of students improved in excess of 1 year's growth. NB: Of 22% with negative growth, half of the students in the cohort have had significant, multiple, traumatic or socially detrimental incidents in their personal lives within the testing period. The other half, along with the 7% with less than 0.39 growth, have been highlighted for further assessment and monitoring.
Attendance	Increase Indigenous pre-school attendance from 50% to 70% in 2013.	Achieved – reached 72%
	Increase T–6 Indigenous attendance from 70% to 80% in 2013.	Not achieved – increased to 75%

Continuing the cycle

The first year's impact cycle showed much progress but the work is ongoing. Sadadeen's commitment to Visible Learning is manifest in the plan it developed for 2014 (Figure 3.6). This document clearly sets out and integrates the school's beliefs and aspirations, the actions it will take to meet its targets, and the ways in which progress will be measured. It makes visible the leaders' shared beliefs that "mindframes are a critical lever for change, that the focus must always be on learning, and that we can always challenge ourselves to do better."

Baseline statements
- From the work we did in 2013 around Relationship Based Learning, we understand the importance of positive teacher/student relationships.
- Student surveys indicate our students are beginning to articulate what they are learning (instead of what they are doing).
- Effect size data indicates that with explicit targeted teaching our students show improvement regardless of current attainment.
- Behavior data indicates that when the teaching programme and classroom climate meet learner needs, there are fewer behavior issues.

Focus area: THE VISIBLE LEARNER – developing assessment capable learners
- Developing a shared language of learning across the school using our Sadadeen Learner Qualities
- Developing the use and understanding of the nine Mindframes so students and staff are actively involved in the learning process

---

Aspiration
Our Sadadeen students demonstrate the four Learner Qualities through their actions in the classroom. They describe the qualities and give examples of classroom behaviors that exemplify the qualities. The Mindframes underpin classroom practice to give students the strategies and self-talk to achieve their learning goals. Students are active in their learning; they know about their learning and can plan personal targets.

VL Focus Area	Mindframes	Targets	Who is responsible?	How will we achieve this?	How will we measure?
The visible learner	I inform all about the language of learning	All students T-6 can articulate the Sadadeen Learner Qualities, what they are and give examples of what they look like, by end of Term 1. We begin to see and hear examples throughout learning time across all classes	Leadership team All teachers	Continual embedding of LO language across the school, with visual prominent in all learning areas	• Student Interviews • Classroom observations

Figure 3.6 Sadadeen School T–6 Visible Learning Plan, 2014 (*continued overleaf*)

We work as a team	I develop positive relationships	At least 90% of our students participate in reward excursions based on them "working as a team"	All school staff	Students are given multiple opportunities to practice "working as a team"	• Data collected on number of children who participate in excursions
We aim high	I enjoy the challenges I see learning as hard work I am a change agent	All classrooms refer to LI for two main lessons per day by end Term 3 Every student has a learning goal displayed and can explain their personal goal to peers/staff commencing Term 3	Impact Coach	Staff PD on writing LI and using SOLO taxonomy	• Data collected via random student interviews indicate they can articulate the LI and verbally share their goals
We are proud	I am an evaluator I see assessment as feedback to me	All students can articulate a strategy they are working on for reading by end of Term 3	Classroom teachers Leadership team	Staff PD on promoting the use of reading strategies	• Classroom observations and student interviews to check references and use of strategies during MGR sessions
We question and wonder	I talk about learning not about teaching I engage in dialogue not monologue	Conversation about learning is evident in classrooms. Observations show that a higher % of feedback to students is moving away from praise into the three other areas	Impact coach and teachers who attend Headstart on feedback	Staff PD on the four types of feedback	• Peer and Exec: 10 minute observations give information to teachers on the type of feedback they are giving children

Figure 3.7 (*Continued*)

Notes

1   A town camp is a small community of Aboriginal people who live on the fringe of an urban community. Residents tend to share language and/or geographical origins.

2   The National Assessment Program – Literacy and Numeracy (NAPLAN) is Australia's annual assessment for students in years 3, 5, 7, and 9. See www.nap.edu.au/naplan/naplan.html

3   Cognition Education/Macmillan Professional Learning (n.d), p. 55.

4   To learn about Relationships-based Learning and its communication through the Culture Counts[plus] program, see http://cognitioneducation.com/services/teaching-and-learning/culture-counts

Part I
Appendix 1

Active reading guide

In *Visible Learning for Teachers: Maximizing Impact on Learning*, John Hattie (2012) sets out eight mindframes or "ways of thinking" that he argues should underpin every action and decision in schools and systems. John says that teachers and leaders who adopt these mindframes are more likely to have a positive and significant impact on student learning. Now that you have read the stories in this chapter, you may like to use the table below to record what you noticed about the mindframes of teachers and leaders at Keilor Views Primary School and Sadadeen Primary School, and how they impacted on student learning and behavior.

Visible Learning mindframes	Examples observed in the learning story	The impact on learners
Mindframe 1: Teachers/ leaders believe that their fundamental task is to evaluate the effect of their teaching on students' learning and achievement.		
Mindframe 2: Teachers/ leaders believe that success and failure in student learning are about what they, as teachers or leaders, did or did not do … we are change agents!		
Mindframe 3: Teachers/ leaders want to talk more about the learning than the teaching.		
Mindframe 4: Teachers/ leaders see assessment as feedback about their impact.		
Mindframe 5: Teachers/ leaders engage in dialogue, not monologue.		
Mindframe 6: Teachers/ leaders enjoy the challenge and never retreat to 'doing their best'.		
Mindframe 7: Teachers/ leaders believe that it is their role to develop positive relationships in classrooms/ staffrooms.		
Mindframe 8: Teachers/ leaders inform others about the language of learning.		

Part I
Appendix 2

Theory to practice

The stories in this chapter look at the concept of Knowing Thy Impact. We began by looking at the mindframes that sit beneath that concept. As you read, you may have used the template in Part I: Appendix 1 to see how those mindframes played out in the improvement journeys of the exceptional educators in these stories. Here you may like to take some time to contemplate your own practice, either by yourself or with a trusted colleague. This may lead to your planning a personal inquiry journey as you consider how your ways of thinking may be impacting on those for whose learning you are responsible, be they students or teachers.

Visible Learning mindframes	Self-evaluation: How do I think I'm doing? What stories can I recall about how my way of thinking impacted on the learners for whom I am responsible?	Next steps: If I feel a need to improve, what might this look like? What is the first step I could take?
Mindframe 1: Teachers/leaders believe that their fundamental task is to evaluate the effect of their teaching on students' learning and achievement.		
Mindframe 2: Teachers/leaders believe that success and failure in student learning are about what they, as teachers or leaders, did or did not do … we are change agents!		
Mindframe 3: Teachers/leaders want to talk more about the learning than the teaching.		
Mindframe 4: Teachers/leaders see assessment as feedback about their impact.		
Mindframe 5: Teachers/leaders engage in dialogue, not monologue.		
Mindframe 6: Teachers/leaders enjoy the challenge and never retreat to 'doing their best'.		
Mindframe 7: Teachers/leaders believe that it is their role to develop positive relationships in classrooms/staffrooms.		
Mindframe 8: Teachers/leaders inform others about the language of learning.		

Effective Feedback

4

Monmia Primary School

Australia

In the synthesis of international research that underpins Visible Learning, Hattie (2009) showed that feedback can be very powerful in enhancing learning. Effective feedback, combined with effective instruction, has an average effect size of 0.70. This is twice the average effect.

> If feedback is directed at the right level, it can assist students to comprehend, engage, or develop effective strategies to process the information intended to be learnt. To be effective, feedback needs to be clear, purposeful, meaningful, and compatible with students' prior knowledge, and to provide logical connections. It also needs to prompt active information processing on the part of learners, have low task complexity, relate to specific and clear goals, and provide little threat to the person at the self level. The major discriminator is whether it is clearly directed to the task, processes, and/or regulation and not to the self level. These conditions highlight the importance of classroom climates that foster peer and self-assessment and allow for learning from mistakes.
>
> *Hattie & Timperley (2007, p. 104[1])*

This is the story of how Monmia Primary School implemented the Visible Learning feedback model.

Context

Monmia Primary School is situated in Keilor Downs, a suburb 17 kilometers north west of Melbourne, Victoria. The school has 418 students, ranging from the preparatory level (five years old) to year 6 (11–12 years old). Aside from the two preparatory classes, students are placed in composite classes, each comprising two year levels.

The school is characterized by diversity, with students from over 30 countries and language groups. Two-thirds of students are from low socio-economic backgrounds. Interestingly, 66% of students come from outside the school zone, a fact that staff ascribe to the large number of students whose primary daytime carers are grandparents who live within the zone.

Monmia is committed to providing innovative programs that stimulate and challenge each student to develop lifelong learning skills and strategies. It is a participant in KidsMatter,[2] a nationwide mental health initiative, and is nationally recognized for having embedded a whole-school approach to improving mental health, wellbeing, and learning outcomes for all students. Leaders foster a school culture that is family-centered and where people have a sense of belonging.

The school leadership team is headed by principal Lorraine Bell and assistant principals Vineta Mitrevski and Lucy Vorpasso. They are assisted by Natalie Creasey, Deb Hicks, and Dean Squires, the school's literacy, numeracy, and ICT coaches.

Overview

Professional learning has long been a priority for staff at Monmia Primary School, with a five-year whole-school focus on literacy and numeracy. A primary means for improvement has been the construction of five internal professional learning communities, an approach that was based on the work of Dufour.[3] The school employs two external literacy consultants and has its own school-based literacy and numeracy coaches. Professional learning time is protected in the school timetable, with teaching teams released for two-hour planning meetings where they use student data to make collaborative decisions about "next steps." (There are five such teams, one for specialist teachers, and one each for teachers at the preparatory, years 1–2, 3–4, and 5–6 levels.)

The school has long engaged in inquiry into the impact of changed practice on student outcomes, and this has seen a number of new initiatives. The most recent shift in focus took place in 2012 when the leadership team took the opportunity to participate in a study tour to New Zealand organized by the Keilor/St Albans Network. The tour provided an opportunity for school leaders to visit New Zealand schools that had successfully implemented the principles of Visible Learning. Inspired by what they saw, Monmia's leadership team went home with a vision that their students should become assessment-capable visible learners. Alongside other schools in the network, the school embarked on a Visible Learning journey that has seen impressive gains in student achievement in reading, writing, and mathematics.

This story is primarily focused on the school's implementation of the Visible Learning feedback model. It looks at how teachers are learning to give effective feedback to students and to check whether the students have understood and applied that feedback. It also shows the growing attention to student voice.

Featured leaders

This story is based primarily on the reflections of the guiding coalition as a whole, but three leaders are quoted directly:

Lorraine Bell became principal of Monmia Primary School in 2006, following a 21-year career as a teacher and school leader. Lorraine is adamant that all students can succeed given a committed, caring, and effective teacher, and that effective teaching requires us to engage in continuous learning. She is an instructional leader who believes in the wisdom of distributed leadership and that "change can only come through collective understanding and dedicated collaboration."

Assistant principal **Vineta Mitrevski** leads schooling improvement at Monmia. She says that "John Hattie's research has stretched my thinking. I realize now that as an educator, it is crucial to hear and feel the voices of the learner and ensure I see myself as a learner, too."

In her role as literacy coach, **Natalie Creasey** coaches and mentors teachers across the school, using a "gradual release of responsibility" model. She is careful to differentiate her coaching and the feedback she provides to target the specific strengths and needs of teachers and students in different classrooms.

Natalija Caridi has taught at Monmia since she began teaching in 2001. She is the teaching and learning leader of the years 5–6 professional learning community. She is an eager participant in professional learning who actively seeks to make links between the aspects of interventions that she knows to work.

Monmia Primary School's Visible Learning story

What were the desired outcomes?

Four years ago, Monmia Primary School's leadership team developed and implemented a theory of action[4] for school improvement. Along with other schools in its regional network, the school decided to tackle both literacy and numeracy pedagogy through professional learning that incorporated one-on-one coaching. Senior and middle-level leaders went on to collectively build the instructional capacity of teachers and support staff, taking an action research approach that included reorganizing the teaching teams into professional learning communities, each with its own leader.

Evidence from assessment data showed that the school was successful in improving literacy and numeracy outcomes through this approach. The NAPLAN[5] data showed the average effect size for the entire group over 2011–2013 was 1.31 (Figure 4.1), well above the expected effect size of 0.8.[6]

Student	Pre-test	Post-test	Growth effect-size
1	458	445	-0.21
2	436	436	0.00
3	573	573	0.00
4	573	585	0.19
5	394	409	0.24
6	554	573	0.31
7	415	436	0.34
8	521	542	0.34
9	352	378	0.42
10	554	585	0.50
11	436	471	0.56
12	363	399	0.58
13	469	514	0.73
14	363	409	0.74
15	415	462	0.76
16	405	454	0.79
17	447	496	0.79
18	481	532	0.82
19	436	496	0.97
20	374	436	1.00
21	426	488	1.00
22	415	479	1.03
23	405	471	1.06
24	447	514	1.08
25	447	514	1.08
26	481	551	1.13
27	374	445	1.14
28	415	488	1.18
29	405	479	1.19
30	405	479	1.19
31	447	523	1.23
32	394	471	1.24
33	405	488	1.34
34	458	542	1.35
35	458	542	1.35
36	394	479	1.37
37	341	427	1.39
38	384	471	1.40
39	330	418	1.42

Figure 4.1 NAPLAN reading matched cohort data sample, 2011–2013

These are impressive results, but when the leadership team inquired more deeply into what was happening in classrooms, they found that while students had grown in their ability to articulate their knowledge of comprehension strategies and their understanding of numeracy, their learning was still under the control of the teacher. Teachers were planning instruction around a specific learning purpose, but were not sharing that purpose with their students. Furthermore, despite their participation in professional learning communities, instructional practice varied from teacher to teacher.

Literacy coach Natalie Creasey recalls that the leadership team had many questions:

> We had great depth to what we were teaching in literacy and numeracy – we were doing this really well! But was the teaching focused enough? Was it specific enough? Did the students really understand what they were learning or where they were at in their learning? What evidence did we have? Did they understand what their needs were and what they had to learn? How would they know they had learnt it? And if they did, where to next? Were we providing them with the best tools to learn without us spoon-feeding them absolutely everything? Where could they go if they did not know what to do? How could we make them more independent, particularly as we were embracing the open, flexible community learning space (rather than the traditional small, closed classroom)?

An opportunity for the leadership team to visit Visible Learning schools in New Zealand provided the answers they were seeking. In particular, the team was excited at how articulate the students at these schools were being in using the language of learning. They returned, inspired by a vision for Monmia students to be assessment–capable visible learners.

What knowledge and skills did the teachers and school leaders need to support these outcomes?

Monmia Primary School has always understood the connection between improved outcomes for students and the professional learning outcomes it needs to achieve for staff. In this instance, the team realized that if students were to become articulate visible learners, then a priority for staff would need to be the provision of effective feedback. This was the missing piece they were seeking in their drive for improvement.

After seeing how well the New Zealand students could articulate what they were currently working on and why, as well as being able to share their learning goals and strategies, we were clear that we wanted our students to be able to do the same. This meant that they needed to be exposed to the purpose for their learning and have clear success criteria explained prior to the task to allow them to monitor their progress and reflect on their achievement. Crucial to this is the importance of quality feedback to provide direction and support to students throughout their learning journey. For this to be possible, we wanted all of our staff to be skilled in providing effective feedback.

(Vineta Mitrevski)

Along with the 22 other schools in their network, Monmia's leadership team took part in the three-day Visible Learning[plus] Foundation Series. Consultant Helen Butler from Visible Learning[plus] Corwin in Australia became the school's critical friend, challenging thinking and supporting the use of data to inform 'next steps' in classrooms and across the school. The school established its guiding coalition, consisting of the senior leadership team and the leaders of the schools' professional learning communities.

The first step was to use the Visible Learning[plus] School Matrix – Stage One to get a picture of the school's strengths and needs and find out where more evidence was needed. The team then used student focus groups and classroom interview questions to fill the gaps in evidence and identify the areas of most pressing need. The data confirmed the team's perception that they needed to get students taking control of their learning. Specifically, they wanted students talking about their learning in relation to the three feedback questions. The questions and the concepts that relate to them are:

Where am I going? This is articulated in learning intentions, goals, and success criteria.

How am I going? This is explored through self-assessment and self-evaluation.

Where to next? This relates to progression and setting new goals.

As Hattie and Timperley explain:

These three questions address the dimensions of feed up, feedback, and feed forward. An ideal learning environment or experience occurs when both teachers and students seek answers to each of these questions. Too often, teachers limit students' opportunities to receive information about their performance in relation to any of these questions by assuming that responsibility for the students and not considering the learning possibilities for themselves.

(Hattie & Timperley, 2007, p. 88)

The evidence confirmed their new theory of action: that if students were to become assessment-capable visible learners, then their teachers needed to learn how to set up classroom environments in which both they and their students were able to give and receive effective feedback.

Figure 4.2 sets out the understandings and practices that the guiding coalition wanted to make routine. You will notice that the targets are for the entire school community. Visible Learning is for everyone.

All stakeholders understand that the purpose of feedback is to:
• close the gap in learning; and
• improve student progress and achievement.

Students understand that:
• everybody can give and receive feedback;
• feedback can be used to do things even better – for improvement;
• assessments/test scores are feedback to the students and teacher; and
• they should seek feedback – ask for feedback.

Teachers:
• incorporate and strategically plan for feedback in every session, including through providing reflection time;
• know about and apply the different levels of feedback; and
• build a feedback culture into every classroom.

Leaders:
• use feedback to drive school improvement.

Families/community:
• understand that feedback can be given by anyone.

Figure 4.2 Feedback targets at Monmia School

What new actions did the teachers and school leaders try?

The school began its Visible Learning journey with the leadership team seeking buy-in from staff by sharing what they observed on the study tour and inviting them to consider two questions:

What did you notice?
What does this mean for our own school?

The leadership team shared its learning from the three Visible Learning[plus] workshops with the entire staff. They also took staff along with them as they gathered and analyzed the evidence in relation to the Visible Learning[plus] School Matrix. This created much discussion as staff saw what the students thought about learning, feedback, and their teachers. There was general agreement that the school was quite good at using the feedback from assessment outcomes as a means of understanding the impact of teaching, but concern that half the teachers were not planning for feedback within regular lessons, and that student voice was not routinely listened to and used to inform decision-making. Teacher comments included:

> We need to have more student voice across the school with regards to feedback, and make sure that they feel they are listened to. On a daily basis and on school feedback.

> Do we wish to seek student feedback about the effectiveness of our teaching and use this information as "evidence" in our performance review?

The school leaders conducted professional learning sessions with all staff on clearly defining and understanding the purpose of learning intentions and success criteria. Readings were provided, with examples of what does and does not make for a quality learning intention. This included readings by Shirley Clarke, well known for her work on formative assessment.[7] The team made it clear that they expected all staff, including specialist teachers, to integrate explicit learning intentions and success criteria into their day-to-day practice.

The learning about learning intentions and success criteria was connected to the Visible Learning instructional feedback model (see the version in Part II: Appendix 1). The intention was to develop the teachers' theoretical understandings about feedback so that the new practices were not just something they had to do but something they truly understood and could apply to a wide range of teaching and learning contexts. At the same time, this shared learning provided a common language for teachers to use when talking to each other and to their students.

Figure 4.3 is a diagram that was developed by the guiding coalition. It unpacks what the four levels of feedback looked like to the members of the coalition and is accompanied by examples of their application at the school. By creating such tools, the coalition connected the generalized research principles to the particular context of their school community.

Despite the robustness of the research, teachers wanted to see the Visible Learning model for themselves before attempting any change.

> There was some reticence initially, as they assumed that this would be an "add on" to an overcrowded curriculum and their limited time. It was taking on "another new thing"! They had yet to see that this was not MORE. It was a deeper, more effective way of planning, teaching, assessing, and learning.
>
> (Monmia School guiding coalition)

The leaders addressed this by showing teachers video clips demonstrating the power of feedback in action. These clips were shared with students, too, helping them to understand the four levels of feedback and how they can be used to inform the "next steps" for learning.

Modeling by the school-based coaches provided another opportunity for teachers to see what effective feedback looks and sounds like. This was followed by coaching and opportunities to practice the four levels of feedback. The coaches monitored classroom implementation through observations and walkthroughs that were followed by debriefing sessions.

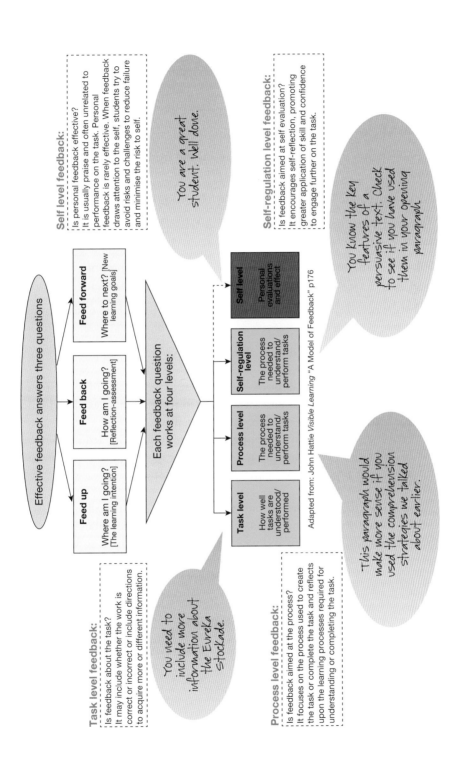

Figure 4.3 Effective feedback at Monmia School

As the following example demonstrates, the coaches used the Visible Learning[plus] tools to collect evidence that could be used as the basis of conversations about the levels of feedback being provided and the usefulness of the information being conveyed. The following examples were observed being given to students in year 1:

> What do you need to do? … Okay … fantastic, do that …

> Well done to people who have …

> Yes, fantastic, we can use the picture on the front cover to … [eye contact, nodding]

> Make sure you're listening, xx, to hear what's being said [smile] … That's fantastic.

> [smiling] What helped you make that prediction, xx? Have you been on a ride before? … Okay [smile].

> Okay, I heard you mention a zoo, so I think you're using prior knowledge … Yes, what's your prediction …? … Okay, that might happen.

> What helped you make that prediction, xx? … [smile] … Okay, hmmm … That might happen …

> xx, what have you just done? … Yes, you can confirm your prediction [smile]?

Figure 4.4 is based on an analysis of 21 examples of feedback in the course of this lesson. Notice how there is a sense of warmth in these exchanges, despite the low scoring for praise – the least effective level of feedback.

The established professional learning communities (PLCs), led by members of the guiding coalition, provided an ideal forum for exploring the new concepts and confronting issues in an environment of trust and respect:

> Early in our feedback discussions, some PLCs found it challenging to know when to use instructional feedback and when to offer praise. As a school where student self-esteem and well-being is a high priority, it was difficult for

Year 1 feedback analysis

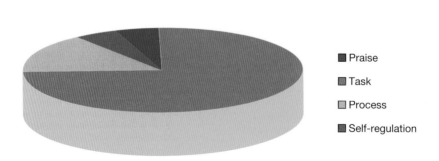

- Praise
- Task
- Process
- Self-regulation

Figure 4.4 Monitoring feedback levels

some staff to remove praise from the instructional feedback we were learning to give our students. Our staff discussions were robust and encompassing of our core beliefs around student learning. We developed a strategy that clearly explained when we would provide students with explicit academic feedback and when we would offer praise and encouragement. One team decided to record themselves working with students to provide baseline data.

(Guiding coalition)

The guiding coalition constructed a series of professional learning action plans that were tailored to the specific requirements of each community and Figure 4.5 is an example of this.

PLC Feedback Action Plans

Agreed timeline:

PLC Task: What does learning mean to you?
Action Plan for Specialists: Short timeline, end of term.

Look at the kind of feedback given and what type it is. Focus on the amount of praise given, as opposed to instructional feedback.
The specialist will record the conversations they have with students and share these with others in the team.

Long timeline: Look at what the students take away from what is said.

Preps: What is feedback? How does it help us learn?
What does it look and sound like? Explicit teaching anchor charts, etc.
Modelling. Reflect later on which feedback helped us to learn.
Focus group questions and surveys. Effect size data. End of term.

1/2: Introduce and discuss. What does feedback look like? Short-term.
Look at next maths unit on length. Create a rubric – students will self-regulate (date when they have achieved).

3/4: What is feedback? Y-chart and then move on to discussing:
What is the feedback that helps me? Survey and interview questions will be used afterwards. End of term.

5/6: Vineta will take a student focus group and question students about what they know about feedback. Next step, team will analyse information and plan what to cover – explicit teaching. Team to look at – Who will give feedback? Identify the opportunities to get feedback. Feedback section in the student writing folder – create scaffolds or prompts for peer feedback.

There was some discussion about praise and what the parents and students will think about instructional feedback.

Figure 4.5 PLC feedback action plans

The learning about Visible Learning and effective feedback builds on the school's prior work in developing a culture of collaborative professional learning focused on improving literacy and numeracy outcomes. This had included the use of "learning walks" as a process for providing ongoing feedback from leaders to teachers and peer to peer. It took the leadership team many months to set up a culture and processes that ensured teachers felt comfortable having their peers and leaders in their classrooms. It meant building a culture with strong relational trust and providing staff with professional reading related to the research on teacher formative evaluation and implications for teachers' practice. Monmia's leadership team developed protocols for learning conversations, introduced SMARTER[8] goals as a framework for observations and feedback, and provided timetabled time for debriefing with staff so the feedback was "just in time" and about the teacher's "next steps."

With the implementation of the Visible Learning intervention, these walks were refined to reflect the new understandings and practices. This included ensuring a greater focus on the learners through using the Visible Learning questions and prompts to find out about the students' perspective on what was happening. It also included a shift to ensuring that professional dialogue and learning was informed by the evidence collected, based on what was seen and heard in the classrooms. This happens at two levels: in the post-observation conversations where the evidence forms the basis for formative feedback and at the whole-school level, where conversations and professional learning are informed by the collated evidence.

What was the impact of the changed actions?

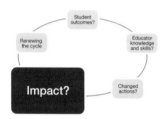

On their walkthroughs and during observations, the guiding coalition noticed an immediate change in classrooms, with teachers putting up visual prompts to support themselves and their students to give and receive feedback. You can see some examples in Figures 4.6 and 4.7.[9]

Initially, learning intentions and success criteria were new concepts to most teachers, but they are now common practice. Teachers share them with students at the beginning of lessons and actively support students to reflect upon their progress in relation to specific criteria.

Students use rubrics for both self- and peer-assessment, and the school finds them a valuable tool. They allow teachers to reiterate their expectations, and allow students to monitor their progress towards achieving the success criteria. Figure 4.8 is an example of a reading reflection rubric that students use for self- and peer-assessment.

Figure 4.9 is an example where students have shown their developing understanding of the learning intentions in their first attempt at developing their own success criteria.

Figure 4.10 shows an example of success criteria that were co-designed by the teacher and students and then crafted to have a strong visual impact.

The school has been using reading and numeracy journals to record feedback and goals for students that are regularly checked during one-on-one conferences. Students are expected to provide evidence of where they have put the feedback into practice before they can move on to a "next step" in their learning. Figures 4.11 and 4.12 provide examples of this in a student's reading journal.

Figure 4.6 What is feedback?

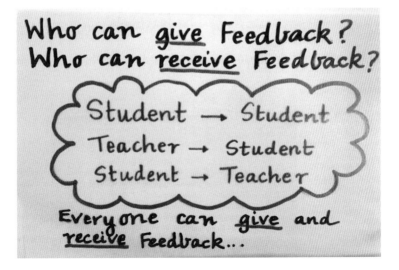

Figure 4.7 Who can give feedback?

Reading Reflection Rubric

Learning Intention: We are learning to write thoughtful reflections about texts

Success Criteria:	★ ★ ★	★ ★	★
Ideas	I used 3 or more comprehension strategies to show my ideas and thinking about the text.	I used 2 comprehension strategies to show my ideas and thinking about the text.	I used 1 comprehension strategy to show my ideas and thinking.
Evidence	I supported all of my ideas with evidence from the text (quotes, page numbers).	I supported some of my ideas with evidence from the text.	I supported one of my ideas with evidence from the text.
Clarity	All of my writing makes sense. It is easy for the reader to understand.	Most of my writing makes sense. The reader would be able to understand most of the text.	Some of my writing makes sense…
Voice	My response is very interesting to read – my own writing style is evident.	My response is somewhat interesting – my style is evident in some parts of my responses.	My response sounds boring and lacks style and personality.
Conventions	Very neat and I have edited for proper: -grammar -spelling -punctuation -paragraphing.	My writing is neat; I have done some editing for: -grammar -spelling -punctuation -paragraphing.	My writing is messy and I have obvious errors with: -grammar -spelling -punctuation -paragraphing.

Figure 4.8 Reading reflection rubric

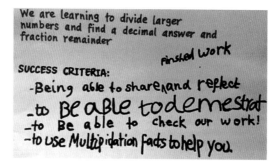

Figure 4.9 A first attempt at student-developed success criteria

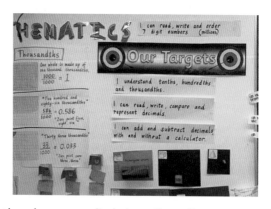

Figure 4.10 Co-designed success criteria in mathematics

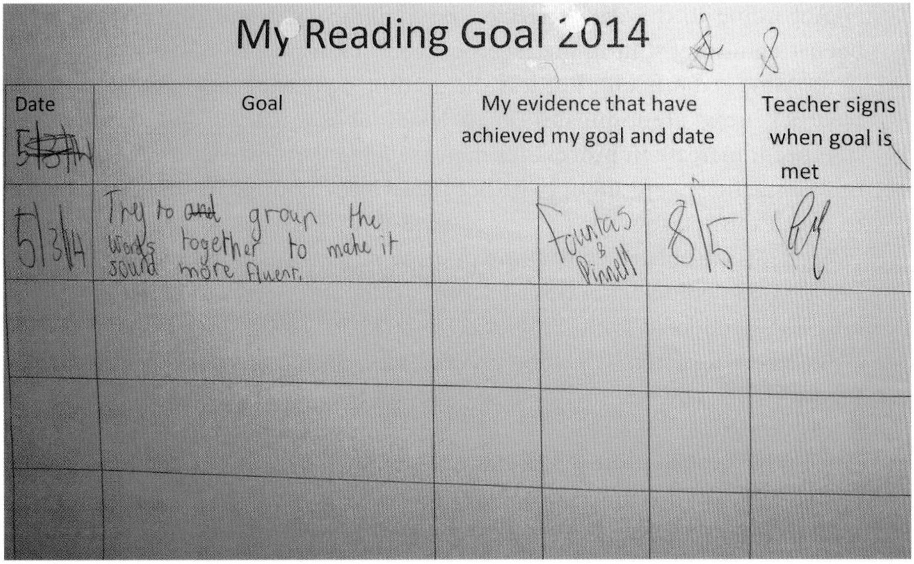

My Reading Goal 2014

Date	Goal	My evidence that have achieved my goal and date	Teacher signs when goal is met
5/3/14	Try to and group the words together to make it sound more fluent.	Fountas & Pinell 8/5	

Figure 4.11 Reading journal (a)

Reading Focus: Cohesive Ties

Learning Intention: To think about words that identify the "who" and the "what" to make it clear for us what the text is about and make connections.

Success Criteria	I do this …	I do this most of the time …	I still need help with this …
• I look for key words like *he, she, they, it, him, her* (personal pronouns).	✓		
• I go back and reread the previous sentence of paragraph to help clarify the *who* or the *what* if it does not make sense.	✓		
• I read on to clarify the *who* and the *what* and think about what makes sense.		✓	

Reflection: My goal is to read on to clarify the who and the what and think about what makes sence.

Figure 4.12 Reading journal (b)

According to the data collected on walkthroughs and observations, there has been a significant shift in the levels of feedback teachers give to students. Initially, praise was predominant, but it is the guiding coalition's impression that task-level feedback now predominates at all levels of the school and there has been a significant increase in process-level and self-regulation-level feedback. At the time of writing, they were about to gather the twelve-month comparative data necessary to check this impression.

Students are able to explain the purpose of feedback and how best to provide it. Figure 4.13 demonstrates this, drawing on the interviews members of the guiding coalition conducted with individual students.

Teachers are actively seeking processes for getting feedback from their students. Figure 4.14 shows a traffic signal system that students use to provide instant feedback to their teacher on how they are doing and the scaffolding they may need. The students place a sticky note with their name on one of the spots as feedback to the teacher about how they are going with their learning for that session or unit of work.

Year 5 Student

We have been learning about feedback and how it can help us in our learning.

What is feedback?

Feedback is when you tell someone or yourself what you need to work on/improve or what you did really well.

Who can give feedback?

Anyone in our community

Students in your class

Students in other classes

Teachers

People from the office

How has feedback helped you in your learning?

Feedback has helped me in my learning. In maths, I struggle sometimes. I know what I need to work on and what are my strengths (what I am good at…). Currently I am working on my fractions.

What does effective feedback sound like?

"I really, really like the way you…" or "You really need to improve on … so it can help you in the future." Effective feedback is when you take it in and take from it and use it in your everyday learning.

Figure 4.13 A student's understandings about feedback

Figure 4.14 Student–teacher feedback system

At the end of each term, students have the opportunity to tell their teacher what they could do to enhance learning.

> Next term, I wish my teacher could push me more and give me some harder work.
>
> (Year 3–4 student)

> Next term, I wish my teacher would explain things better e.g. model things out, use more anchor charts.
>
> (Year 3–4 student)

The leaders' vision was for students to become assessment-capable visible learners. The school now has ample evidence to demonstrate that students have grown in their ability to articulate what they are doing, why, and how they would know if they were successful. Students, teachers, and leaders set challenging personal learning goals based on a realistic understanding of their current strengths and needs and the next stage for their learning. This has translated into improved student achievement outcomes, for example, in NAPLAN, the Progressive Achievement Tests, the Fountas and Pinnell Benchmark Assessment System, and the On-Demand Adaptive Tests. Together, these assessment regimes indicate accelerated growth in reading, writing, and mathematics.

Examples of the improvement in terms of effect size include:

- On-Demand Number assessments revealed the average growth effect-size from 2012 to 2013 for the matched cohort was 0.51 in one year from year 3 to year 4;

- NAPLAN Numeracy results for the school also showed an average effect size of 1.56 for students, above the average expected effect size of 0.8 from 2011 to 2013; and
- NAPLAN Reading results also provided evidence of whole-school improvement for students, measuring an effect size of 1.33 from years 3 to 5 from 2011 to 2013. Writing and spelling also had above average effect sizes of 1.19 for the same period.

Reflecting on the changes brought by Visible Learning, Natalija Caridi writes:

> Over the last two years, I have become more confident in guiding students in talking about their learning and taking responsibility for their learning. What has empowered me is my knowledge of the curriculum and my understanding of the needs of the learners. This has come with time, but I am now at the point where I can guide students with questions such as, 'Where to next with your learning?'
>
> Another change in practice is ensuring that students are given ownership of their test results and they track their performance against their goals and give evidence to show mastery of goals. My students are comfortable with the honest feedback they receive, as it pushes them to constantly improve.

Principal Lorraine Bell is adamant that the improvements can be ascribed to the school's participation in an initiative that is based on solid research, along with a collaborative inquiry approach where evidence, committed leadership, and a culture of learning drive change and improvement:

> Over my 35 years as an educator, I have seen many initiatives come and go in education. Being a change agent myself in all my school settings, I have always looked for the most effective strategies to make the most difference to children's learning. Visible Learning has influenced a change in my leadership style, my mindset, and my understandings about the power of effective feedback. This is not "just another initiative"; it is a process based on solid research and with demonstrable evidence that it empowers students to understand their learning and articulate what they need to know and where they are going next. It is exciting for me to contemplate our successes across the school, where teachers naturally develop learning intentions and success criteria with their students; where professional learning communities discuss student data to inform their planning; where there is evidence of student-to-student feedback, teacher-to-student feedback, teacher-to-teacher feedback, and leadership-to-teacher feedback. My future aspirations are to continue to develop my own skills at effective feedback, modeling these to all stakeholders in our community. I am excited about what will come next for myself and our school community in the Visible Learning adventure.

Continuing the cycle

The school continues to work towards its vision of providing all students with the knowledge and skills to be assessment-capable visible learners. Moving into the next cycle of inquiry, the school intends to focus more deeply on:

- encouraging students to seek feedback from their teacher and peers;
- students being more actively involved in their learning through increased student voice and choice.

Helen Butler continues to support the school to go deeper into their inquiry. State funding has been approved to enable the next cycle to include close collaboration with three other schools in the regional learning network. This will involve visits between schools that will include opportunities for teaching teams to share and discuss their school data and develop common planning documents that include learning intentions and success criteria.

Notes

1 Hattie, J., & Timperley, H. (2007). The power of feedback. *Review of Educational Research,* 77(1), 81. Sage Publications. Available from http://education.qld.gov.au/staff/development/performance/resources/readings/power-feedback.pdf

2 You can learn about KidsMatter at www.kidsmatter.edu.au

3 For information about this approach, see the website All Things PLC at www.allthingsplc.info

4 An effective theory of action is an "if... then" statement that sets out a measurable goal for improvement and an evidence-based strategy for achieving that goal, and that can be improved through inquiry into impact.

5 National Assessment Program – Literacy and Numeracy (NAPLAN) is Australia's annual assessment for students in Years 3, 5, 7, and 9.

6 See Hattie (2012) Appendix E for details about how to calculate effect sizes. See also the Resource page on the Visible Learning[plus] website at www.visiblelearningplus.com

7 Shirley Clarke's website is worth visiting for more information, including video clips and case studies. You can find it at www.shirleyclarke-education.org

8 SMARTER is an acronym for Specific, Measurable, Ambitious, Realistic, Time-bound, Evaluate, and Re-evaluate.

9 If you would like to see more examples, see Monmia School's Visible Learning board on Pinterest: www.pinterest.com/taradcat/monmia-ps-visible-learning/

5

Presbyterian Ladies' College

Australia

Thirteen-year-old Sarah is a year 10 student at Presbyterian Ladies' College (PLC). Sarah is an assessment-capable learner who knows how to use feedback to improve the quality of her work.

> After getting my composition assessed by Ms Tan, I realized my piece was not very well written in terms of where the notes were sitting. This means that my melody was very jumpy and had little shape to it. After thinking about this, I changed most of my melody to give it shape. I did this by having the notes with small intervals between them and instead of having a high note, then suddenly a low note, then a high note again; it went from lower notes and higher to the high notes, then back down again, a bit like a scale but using passing notes and cadences. Also, I had the accents of my melody on the wrong words of my lyrics so I created an anacrusis so that the first word was emphasized because it was the most important.
>
> *Sarah, year 10*

The feedback Sarah used so thoughtfully had been provided by her teacher. Ms Tan's own ability to provide such effective feedback was strengthened through the school's participation in professional learning focused on the provision of effective, timely feedback.

Context

Presbyterian Ladies' College, popularly referred to as PLC, is an independent day and boarding school situated in the western suburbs of Perth, Western Australia. It currently caters for approximately 1200 students, with boys and girls enrolled from pre-kindergarten to pre-primary and girls only from years 1–12.

While most students live within a five-kilometer radius of the school, 120 middle and senior school students live in the boarding house. Most boarders are rural West Australians but there are also some international students. A boom in the region's mining economy saw an increase in expatriate families from a range of national, cultural, and linguistic backgrounds. At present, expatriates comprise approximately ten percent of the school population. Being a private school with high fees, most students come from a high to middle socio-economic background. Their parents are predominantly tertiary-educated professionals. They have high expectations for their daughters' academic achievement and for the quality of the pastoral care and co-curricular program the school will provide.

The College teaches the Australian Curriculum whilst also offering the International Baccalaureate program for students in the primary years, the middle years, and at the diploma level. Students perform well in the Western Australian Certificate of Education examinations and the school regularly appears among the top ten schools in the state. However, the school is open entry and does have students with high learning needs. It has an inclusive philosophy and classes are not streamed.

In the past, the school's professional learning foci have been on concept-based learning[1] and on how to integrate the use of technology into the teaching and learning program. Students in years 5–12 have their own laptops and, since 2014, all students in years 1–4 have had their own iPad. Teachers seek to use technology to differentiate the curriculum to the individual.

Beth Blackwood is the principal and Kim Edwards is the deputy principal. Kim led the school's Visible Learning guiding coalition, which included all heads of department and the information and learning technologies (ILT) curriculum manager.

Overview

While PLC has a long record of high academic achievement, the school's belief in encouraging all students to "be the best they can be" means that it is always searching for ways it can do better. When the senior leadership team attended the Visible Learning[plus] introductory workshops early in 2012, they responded to the strength of the messages from research. They were especially taken by the insights into feedback and its role in cultivating assessment-capable learners who are able to regulate their own learning.

These insights were the catalyst for a critical review of the quality of the feedback provided to students and parents in the written reports made at the end of the first semester. As this story will show, the review revealed that both the reporting process and the quality of the feedback provided were causing frustration. The feedback was summative rather than formative; it was not directed to the next steps for learning, and even if it was, it was provided too late to be helpful.

In this school, the search for more effective feedback processes was made through the development of a new digital-learning management system that enables teachers to supply feedback to students and their parents that is highly visible and available at the point of need. At the time of writing, it is too early to make connections between student achievement outcomes and the new reporting and feedback system. However the changes to teacher practice are clear, as is the positive response of parents and students. Critically, students such as Sarah clearly display the characteristics of a visible learner. This is a "way of being" that will stand Sarah and her peers in good stead, not just in terms of short-term improvements in academic achievement, but in a lifetime of learning and growth.

Featured leaders

This story is based primarily on the reflections of the guiding coalition as a whole, but two leaders are quoted directly:

Beth Blackwood has been principal of PLC since 1998. She is committed to the school's role in caring for each student as an individual, and to the mantra that the school's success is only to be measured in the achievements and well-being of its students.

Kim Edwards is responsible for leading the Visible Learning feedback initiative at PLC. Kim has been PLC's deputy principal for over ten years. She has a passion for education and continually seeks ways to improve the teaching and learning program to enhance student achievement. That passion has led her to further her own learning, particularly in relation to the use of technology in the classroom and the implementation of the International Baccalaureate program and a concept-based curriculum. Kim shares her learning with colleagues at PLC and abroad. She has embraced the key messages of Visible Learning, which are closely aligned with her personal philosophy of teaching.

Presbyterian Ladies' College's Visible Learning story

What were the desired outcomes?

While PLC had specific concerns about the degree to which it was meeting the needs of students with high needs at either end of the spectrum, it did have a strong academic record. This was exemplified, for example, in the consistently high results that students achieve in their Australian Tertiary Admission Rank (ATAR). However, as all educators know, the twenty-first century places challenges on us all – challenges that constantly change as the world around us changes. It is not enough to be able to learn successfully at one time and in one particular context. Young people need broader competencies that will enable them to meet new challenges that we may not yet even be able to visualize. This is why the concept of "assessment-capable learners" is so very important. Assessment capability is an essential component of the learning competencies that allow people to survive and thrive in a global world.

In the first half of 2012, the senior leaders at PLC attended the three-day Visible Learning^{plus} introductory series, led by consultant Jayne-Ann Young. The concept of assessment-capability struck a chord. The school recognized that to improve outcomes for all students, not just in the present but on into the future, this was where they needed to focus.

> We wanted to develop assessment-capable learners. Hattie's research highlighted the need for students to become assessment-capable learners, where they can identify where they are, where they want to go and how they are going to get there. Hattie recommends that students must be able to accurately self-assess against the criteria, plan their next learning steps, and monitor their progress. The most important thing we can do to raise achievement is make students assessment capable.
>
> (PLC guiding coalition)

With this in mind, the school leaders decided on the following student outcome as its first priority: "Develop assessment-capable learners who can act on the feedback provided and who can identify where they were, where they want to go, and how they are going to get there." They chose to focus their first impact cycle on students in the middle school, carefully monitoring what happened to decide on whether and how to extend the intervention to other parts of the school.

What knowledge and skills did the teachers and school leaders need to support these outcomes?

The research made it clear that for students to be assessment-capable learners, they needed quality feedback from their teachers. The school's annual report cycle for students in the middle school included Semester 1 reports. This provided an invaluable opportunity to inquire into the quality of the feedback currently being provided. Deputy principal Kim Edwards worked with the heads of department to address the question, "How can we provide better feedback to parents and students, in a timely manner and at the point of need, which is relevant and time-efficient for teachers?" Together, they identified the following issues:

Quality
Many of the comments were a summary of what the student had demonstrated across the previous semester and contained little or no feedback about how to

improve learning. Instead, feedback tended to be oriented towards praise, rather than providing information at the task, process, or self-regulation levels. The following is a typical example:

> Student X approaches her studies with a disciplined and positive attitude. She has demonstrated excellent conceptual understanding and knowledge of the terminology in Economics and has developed a rigorous and methodical approach to the research process. Her work generally shows detailed descriptions and developed explanations that are constantly communicated in well-structured written responses. Student X's work shows satisfactory analysis of concepts and issues. Her positive approach to her learning has helped her produce good results this semester.

Timeliness

Reports were provided at the end of each semester, too late for feedback to inform learning. The end-of-year report had little or no value, as the students were on holidays for two months and the comments were a distant memory when they returned to school the following year.

Summative rather than formative

Informal feedback from parents indicated they did not value the comments but did value the graphs, which showed the distribution of grades across a year group and subject, as well as their daughters' individual grades. Parents reported that their daughters were also more interested in the grades than the comments.

Teacher workload

Teachers spent a great deal of time writing and proofing up to 150 reports at a time. The heads of department noticed that this reduced teachers' focus on teaching and learning and impacted on their well-being, with a higher than usual number of absences due to illness at this time.

Lack of coherence

The fact that parents frequently asked for more feedback on their daughters' progress indicated the need to provide a more coherent picture of student progress. Teachers gave students their rubrics to take home and show their parents. These paper-based assessment rubrics included the teacher comments and, once shown to parents, would be collected and stored by the teacher. As a result, the comments that might have been helpful in developing an understanding of how individuals were progressing in their learning over time were not available to view when required.

The analysis indicated that the following outcomes were most pressing in terms of teacher professional learning:

- changing the way teachers provided feedback to students and parents so that they could develop a comprehensive view of achievements and areas to be addressed; and
- providing more effective feedback that would help grow students as assessment-capable learners.

The introduction of a new learning management system called Seqta[2] was central to the change, as it was deliberately designed to enable timely feedback to parents and students. It combined two portals called Coneqt, one for students and one for teachers. These formed part of a suite of resources that included a software package that teachers could use to do their administrative work. Not only was this integrated system ideally aligned to Hattie's messages about making learning visible, but it was also aligned to the school's previous professional learning about the importance of ensuring new technology in schools is directed to an educational purpose.

The guiding coalition recognized that the new system would require learning for all stakeholders, as the Visible Learning philosophy challenged long-held beliefs and practices about assessment and reporting. The Coneqt system itself required learning in how to use the software. Table 5.1 summarizes the knowledge and skills each group had to learn. Notice the way the learning at each level is aligned towards achieving the priority outcomes identified for students and teachers.

In order to measure and monitor progress, the guiding coalition set in place the following targets:

- 100% of middle years program teachers to be delivering their feedback through the portals;
- increase the number of parents logging in to the parent portal to view their daughters' feedback;
- remove any technical issues parents were experiencing logging in to the system; and
- all students to be competent in their ability to reflect on their learning and set goals to strengthen their outcomes.

Table 5.1 Knowledge and skills of learners

Group	Knowledge	Practices
Students	The students were required to learn a new IT system (Student Coneqt) to access their feedback on all assessment tasks.	The students had to learn how to critically reflect on their learning and outline their next learning steps.
Teachers	The teachers were required to learn: • the elements of quality feedback – task/product feedback, process feedback, and self-regulation feedback; • a new IT system (Coneqt), which included an online (web-based) marks books component; and • to use an online speech-to-text software tool (Dictation Australian Language Pack) as a time-management tool if desired.	The teachers had to learn: • to give less praise and focus on the "next steps" to assist student learning; • to keep feedback simple and specific; • how to write their feedback online rather than on student work, for all stakeholders to view; and • how to speak their feedback (if they wanted to use this software) rather than write it.
Parents	The parents were required to learn a new IT system (Parent Coneqt) to access their daughters' feedback.	The parents had to take greater responsibility for accessing and viewing the feedback provided.
Leaders	The leaders were required to learn: • the same as teachers; and • all aspects of the Teacher Coneqt system so they could manage and lead their departments through the change.	The leaders also had to learn: • how to provide quality feedback so they could manage and lead their department; and • how to manipulate and administer the data on the software system.

What new actions did the teachers and school leaders try?

The guiding coalition chose not to share their review of the reporting system with staff until they had a demonstrable solution in the form of the new learning management system. They worked with the software developers to develop a system that would display the academic results, feedback, and student reflections in a way that would allow parents and students to build a cumulative and coherent view of the learning and the next steps required. The school's action plan is set out in Figure 5.1.

A critical part of the change involved developing a shared understanding of what effective feedback looks like in the context of the PLC community. One means of communicating this was through summarizing the key findings from Hattie's research, outlining the school's requirements, and also providing a range of stems to support the teachers giving feedback. Figure 5.1 is an excerpt from this document.

Action plan: Reporting and ongoing feedback
Goal: To review our reporting process and implement a system of ongoing feedback for learning

Objective	Actions	Date to be achieved	Person/group responsible for achieving this objective	Evidence of achievement or of progress towards achievement of the objective
Review Hattie's research on feedback.	Leadership team to complete the Foundation, Day 1 and 2 Visible Learning[plus] PD Provide Visible Learning Foundation[plus] Day PD to all staff.	Semester 2, 2012	Principal	Visible Learning[plus] PD provided to all staff.
Review current reporting and feedback processes.	Discuss and review the current reporting and feedback process with the heads of department.	Semester 1, 2012	Deputy principal Heads of department	New reporting system developed.
Modify the Learning. Management System (Coneqt) to display the ongoing feedback.	Provide the software developers (SEQTA) of the Coneqt system with mock-ups of both the parent and student views required for the ongoing feedback.	Semester 2, 2012	Deputy principal ILT curriculum manager	Parent and student views developed.
Teacher mark-books to be on Teacher Coneqt.	Provide whole-school and department PD on the mark-book section of Teacher Coneqt.	Semester 1, 2013	Heads of department ILT curriculum manager	All teacher mark-books online by the end of Semester 1, 2013.
Implement a system of ongoing feedback for years 6–10.	Support teachers to move all feedback to Teacher Coneqt.	Semester 2, 2013	Deputy principal Heads of department	All teacher feedback provided through Teacher Coneqt for years 6–10.
Provide quality feedback to parents and students.	Develop staff understanding of the key elements of effective feedback.	Ongoing	Deputy principal Heads of department	Evidence through the mark-books and feedback available to all staff online.

Figure 5.1 Visible Learning action plan (*continued overleaf*)

Objective	Actions	Date to be achieved	Person/group responsible for achieving this objective	Evidence of achievement or of progress towards achievement of the objective
Educate parents on the Coneqt system.	Provide regular parent workshops on the Parent Coneqt system – to be held every three weeks at a range of different times.	Semester 2, 2013	Deputy principal ILT curriculum manager	Increased parent logins to Parent Coneqt. Reduction in the number of parent queries about Coneqt.
	Develop a parent help section on the home page of Parent Coneqt (which does not require password access) to address common questions. This will include a range of movies to support the text.	Semester 1, 2014		
Educate teachers on the Coneqt system.	Provide regular department workshops on the Teacher Coneqt system.	Semester 2, 2013	ILT curriculum manager Deputy principal Heads of department One Degree Coaches	Reduction in the number of teacher queries about Coneqt.
	Provide individual teacher support as required.	Ongoing		
Educate students on the Coneqt system.	Provide an overview of the Student Coneqt system through year meetings and house tutor group.	Semester 2, 2013	ILT curriculum manager One Degree Coaches	Reduction in the number of student queries about Coneqt.
Seek feedback from parents and students on the changes to the reporting and feedback processes.	Conduct survey of parents and students on the changes.	November 2013 and June 2014	Deputy principal	50% or above approval for the changes.
Develop assessment-capable students.	Teachers to require students to complete a reflection through the Student Coneqt system.	Ongoing	Deputy principal Heads of department	All students are completing a reflection either prior to a task or after a task, identifying what they did well and their next learning steps.

Figure 5.1 (*Continued*)

Internal professional development was led by the guiding coalition. This included sharing a range of feedback comments from across the curriculum. Teachers were asked to identify whether the feedback was focused on the task, the process, or self-regulation, and to consider how the feedback might help the student to improve their learning. You can see some examples in Figure 5.2 below.

They also developed a teacher reference tool as a guideline for their feedback, and all groups had multiple opportunities to learn how to use the new learning management system. As well as workshops and one-on-one support where required, this included the creation of video clips explaining how parents and students could access, navigate, and/or control their experience of the portals, and how students could make contributions. These were placed online so that they could be accessed at any time.

The surveys mentioned in the action plan allowed the guiding coalition to address issues as they arose, including modifying the new system. The school also developed some simple and informal ways of monitoring and evaluating the effectiveness of the intervention. For example, each time they held a parent workshop, the leaders asked parents to begin by writing their "burning" questions or concerns on a Post-it. They placed the Post-its on a wall so they could review and address all concerns across the course of the session. As the parents left, the leaders asked the parents to remove their Post-it if their concerns had been addressed.

Technology	Task/Process/ Self-regulation	How does the feedback help the student to improve their learning?
You have done a fantastic and thorough analysis of a range of scrumptious recipes; however, you do need to summarize your findings from each source rather than just stating them.		
… you have captured the essence of Belgium's speciality cuisine and analysed some fantastic recipes. To make any improvement to your level, you would need to summarize findings from a broader range of sources.		
Great to see you were able to change tack with the country. Would have liked to have seen the actual recipes not just the name. Also summarizing the findings of a broad range of sources as stated on the criteria would have improved your grade.		

Figure 5.2 Teacher learning about feedback at PLC

The process of implementing the action plan was not without difficulty. For some teachers, the transition from empty feedback ("sound progress," "good work") to feedback that was more closely aligned to the learning purpose was a significant challenge. Many were inclined to write too much, missing the opportunity the technology provides to offer more effective and timely feedback without increasing teacher workload. Some felt a degree of threat from the highly visible nature of the feedback they provided that could now be viewed by parents, colleagues, and students. Some people, in particular some parents, needed considerable support to learn the new IT system. Some parents – even those who appreciated the ongoing feedback they were getting through the parent portal – found it difficult to give up on the written reports. Kim recalls:

> During the first six months, we experienced an implementation dip (Fullan, 2008).[3] We persevered, provided timely communication, and acknowledged that change created uncertainty for many people. We listened and learnt, ensured we had our facts right before we moved to action, problem-solved when required, and resolved issues and concerns immediately. Small steps towards the bigger goal were considered a great achievement and acknowledged accordingly.

What was the impact of the changed actions?

This intervention involved change for all parts of the middle school community at PLC. The school knows, from its ongoing monitoring and evaluation, that it is getting things right. The data does not yet show the transfer to achievement outcomes, but it does show significant shift in the behaviors of teachers, students, and parents.

The surveys show that students and parents are making a regular practice of accessing the portals and are finding the teachers' feedback useful for understanding student learning progress and the next steps for improvement. This data is extensive, so Table 5.2 provides a brief snapshot with regards to some of the survey questions. Note that the data presented here is of the two extremes, to indicate what can be seen in the school's graphs; that is, significant improvement with regards to all indicators.

An observable change was that in the past, the parent, teacher, and student interviews focused on the teacher providing a summary of student progress and offering a few suggestions for "next steps." With that information now constantly available online, the more recent meetings focused on what the student was going to do to improve their learning and how they were going to get there. This is affirmed in survey data indicating that the majority of parents and students found the interviews attended in early 2014 provided them with information that was not already provided on the portals. Early adopters amongst the parent population have spontaneously thanked the school for the new system. For example:

Table 5.2 Snapshot of survey questions and answers

Student survey	2013		2014	
How often have you accessed the Assessment page on Student Coneqt and viewed the teacher feedback?	Never 1.8%	Frequently 34.9%	Never 1.4%	Frequently 44.8%
Last semester the feedback on Student Coneqt "Was relevant and to the point."	Strongly disagree 3%	Strongly agree 12%	Strongly disagree 2%	Strongly agree 21%
Last semester the feedback on Student Coneqt "Told me what I had to do to improve."	Strongly disagree 6%	Strongly agree 12%	Strongly disagree 3%	Strongly agree 24%
Parent survey	**2013**		**2014**	
How often have you accessed the Assessment page on Parent and Student Coneqt and viewed the teacher feedback?	Never 27%	Frequently 8.8%	Never 5.9%	Frequently 29.2%
Last semester the feedback on Parent Coneqt "Was relevant and to the point."	Strongly disagree 3%	Strongly agree 7%	Strongly disagree 3%	Strongly agree 19%
Last semester the feedback on Parent Coneqt "Told my daughter what she had to do to improve."	Strongly disagree 5%	Strongly agree 7%	Strongly disagree 3%	Strongly agree 24%

> The portal provides a wonderful insight into how my daughter is progressing and what she has to do to improve. I only wanted to meet you and thank you.

The heads of department can use the learning management system to monitor the change in teacher practices and in the student responses. They see a dramatic improvement in the quality of the feedback, as teacher comments have become more relevant and focused, clearly outlining what students have to do to improve. There has also been a significant reduction in praise, though this is an area of struggle for many staff who believe in the importance of always providing positive feedback. There is evidence of teachers responding to the student reflections that tell them how students think they are progressing and what they think their "next steps" are.

Some teachers are experimenting with different ways of providing feedback and results, and different means of engaging students in the reflection process. One approach has been for teachers to withhold feedback until after their students have reflected on a task or learning intention. For example, one group of teachers chose to upload their students' essays to the portal with annotations and feedback but without a grade. They required the students to comment on their strengths and weaknesses and to assess themselves based on the feedback, a process that meant the students started to use the feedback and success criteria as a reflective tool. Some students found this quite daunting but ultimately, rewarding:

> Student X was a classic example of the sort of student who is so driven by the mark/level of achievement that it caused her to baulk at taking risks and often prevented her from even "seeing" the feedback that she was being offered. I had spent a lot of time explaining to students that the feedback was more important than their level/mark and it was the feedback and reflection that would lead to improvement, not their level/mark. I had spent a lot of time (years) explaining this, but this was one instance where I could use technology to shift the process.
>
> The day the feedback was posted (within hours), I received an email from the student explaining she initially hated the idea of having the level/mark withheld, but it had actually liberated her to look at the piece itself, free of the burden of the level/mark. It was clear we had created a context for meaningful reflection. The quality of her reflections improved significantly from that point on.
>
> (Damien Kerrigan)

Students say that they like having the feedback all visible and accessible in one place. It helps with revision and enables them to track how they are progressing and what they need to work on. It also dovetails well with the personalized goal-setting that the school put in place in 2012. This involves one-on-one meetings with tutors to discuss goals and measure success. Alex, a student in year 9, writes:

> I found the format to be particularly beneficial as feedback can be easily accessed and referred to. This digital format is much better in comparison to just a sheet of paper, which could easily be lost and usually ends up being located in the bottom of a folder and never looked at again. Overall, the feedback and the process of reflecting on these comments has allowed me to identify which areas I need to improve in and which concepts I need to reinforce in order to achieve a higher level and further my learning.

Teachers have noticed that many students are hard on themselves when they write their reflections, often stating they know they could have done better by raising their expectations. Students have improved their understanding of why they achieved at a certain level, as well as their ability to identify their next learning steps.

In order to receive a higher level, I need to make sure I use terms such as "reliable" and "fair" correctly, because sometimes my explanations didn't make sense. My scientific reasoning should be more detailed and specific next time as well.

(Marian)

I think I used my language quite well, however to improve I must use more humor and correctly paragraph my work. I need to be careful that I don't change tenses in my writing and that I use more examples other than my own.

(Frances)

Two years on from the start of the intervention, PLC's guiding coalition says:

As we reflect back on our journey and review past report comments and task feedback, it is even more apparent now that this is not the way forward. Popular educational debate focuses on lifting student achievement through national testing. As teachers all know, this does not improve student learning. Hattie's research has demonstrated that the most significant impact on student learning comes through challenging mindsets, setting high expectations, and making learning visible and explicit for all students.

We also learnt that it does not work to tell staff what to do and then expect them to be able to do it. They need time to buy in to the change in philosophy, and understand the research that sits behind it. Expecting they will learn a new IT system quickly does not work. Changing a lifetime of marking practices takes time, effort, and encouragement to ensure the change in practice is ultimately successful.

With this in mind, the team recommends:

- being clear about the objectives you are seeking to achieve;
- planning strategically, consulting widely, and implementing the changes in stages;
- continually reviewing and reflecting; and
- focusing on the solutions rather than the problem.

Continuing the cycle

The guiding coalition at PLC continues to engage with the research and consider how they can apply it to the unique context of their school. They are currently exploring the message about student expectations and self-reported grades:

Hattie (2012) states we need to "provide opportunities for students to be involved in predicting their performance." He argues that "educating students to have high, challenging, appropriate expectations is among the most powerful influences in enhancing student achievement." The key message from Hattie (2012) is that accurate calibration between the predicted performance and the actual performance is more effective than rewarding improved performance.

(Guiding coalition)

The next iteration of the impact cycle will include moving to a system where students predict their scores on assessment tasks prior to completing the task. The leaders also want to move teachers towards a greater focus on formative feedback rather than summative feedback. Given the success of the intervention in the middle school, the trial will also move up to the senior school.

Notes

1   Concept-based learning frames curriculum design around big ideas and principles rather than discrete knowledge and skills. It was developed by Professor Lynn Erickson and has been adopted by the International Baccalaureate program. You can read more at www.lynnerickson.net
2   For further information, see www.seqta.com.au
3   Fullan, M. (2008). *The six secrets of change*. San Francisco: Jossey-Bass.

Part II
Appendix 1

Active reading guide

This is the model of feedback that John Hattie (2009) presented in *Visible Learning: A Synthesis of Over 800 Meta-Analyses in Education*. As you read this story, think about the understandings represented in this model and how you see them being transferred into practice at Monmia Primary School and Presbyterian Ladies' College. There are implications for all members of the school community. See if you can organize your "noticings" in regard to the learning and change for teachers, school leaders, and students.

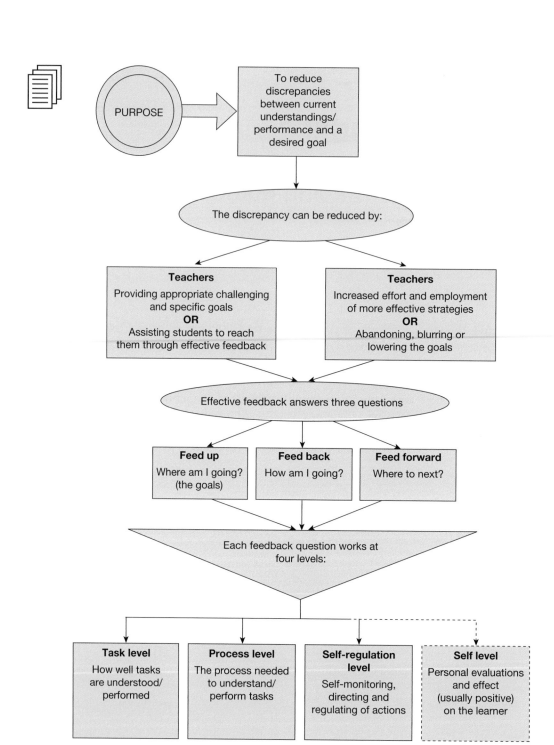

Effective Feedback model (Hattie, 2009, p. 176)

Part II
Appendix 2
Theory to practice

The primary focus of this chapter has been on effective feedback between members of a classroom community, but as Lorraine Bell points out, getting there involves the provision of feedback between teachers, between teachers and school leaders, and between school leaders. The school's professional learning communities and its habits of coaching, observations, walkthroughs, and debriefing conversations provide structured contexts in which professionals can give and receive feedback. Of course, the important thing about feedback is that it is used to plan 'next steps'.

The template below is offered as a self-reflection tool that you can use to record feedback that you have recently been given by a student, colleague, or other member of your learning community, and to think about how you responded to that feedback. Remember that it is okay to reject feedback that is not aligned with your purpose.

Making feedback on practice work

The context was …

My purpose at the time was …

The feedback was provided by …

The feedback was that …

This is an example of task/process/self-regulation/self level feedback:

My response was to …

The reason for my response was …

The outcome of this was …

On reflection, I have learnt that …

Visible Learners

6

Stonefields School

New Zealand

At Stonefields School, I've learnt that taking risks and being confident in myself is really important and I keep working on that. I am also so much more confident to share my ideas in our group. I believe that I have really improved. I have also learnt that it doesn't matter what age you are or how big you are, you can always collaborate with anyone. By putting all our ideas together, we can create a better solution than if we did it on our own. The learning process has been one of the biggest parts of learning here at Stonefields. It guides me through my learning, helping me to be more in charge of my learning, and I will use it when I am at high school and beyond.

Hana, departing year 8 student, 2011

I have learnt a lot at Stonefields School, especially in reading. I have learnt lots about the brain and how we think. I have learnt how to be an independent learner by using the progressions, and self-learning, and learning from others. I like it how teachers encourage us to be self-directed and not just give us time-consuming tasks that I already know how to do. The learning is relevant and challenging for me personally, and is what I need to learn to improve. I have also learnt a lot about writing and the different structures to use when writing for different purposes. I also like the learning process at Stonefields School because it gives me a road for learning and helps me learn how to learn.

Luca, departing year 8 student, 2011

These departing year 8 students were already exhibiting the characteristics of a visible learner after just one year at the school. In this learning story, you will read about the processes Stonefields School has undertaken to develop in students the ability to take such confident control of their own learning processes and progress.

Context

Nestled on the site of an old quarry in central Auckland, New Zealand, Stonefields School is a new school with a new philosophy of learning. The student population reflects both the diversity and the rapid growth of this increasingly multicultural city. The school opened in 2011 with a roll of 48 students in years 1 to 8. Within three years, the roll had climbed to over 300 and was predicted to reach its intended maximum of 560 within a few more years. While the school is situated within a comfortable middle-class suburb, its roll also draws from an area where many people experience socio-economic disadvantage. The ethnic composition of the school is approximately as follows:

- 40% Pākehā (New Zealand European);
- 8% Māori (Indigenous New Zealanders);
- 10% Pasifika: mostly Samoan, with some Niuean and Rarotongan students;
- 25–30% Asian: 10% are Chinese, and there are also significant numbers of Sri Lankan, Indian, Pakistani, and Filipino students.

Given this mix, it is not surprising that 50% of the students speak a second language at home and over 20% qualify for the school's English for Speakers of other Languages (ESOL) roll.

The school is led by an enthusiastic team consisting of principal Sarah Martin and associate principals Chris Bradbeer and Kirsty Panapa. As foundation leaders, they have had the unusual opportunity to participate in the appointment of all new staff, selecting teachers, teacher aides, and support staff who share, support, and indeed helped construct the school's special approach to teaching and learning.

Overview

The opportunity to create a new school was both a challenge and an exciting opportunity for the Stonefields School community. From the beginning, Sarah and her team made decisions that reflected their vision for the future, for example, they:

- chose to create "learning hubs"[1] for students at different schooling levels, promoting collaboration for both teachers and students;
- selected information and communications technology that could be integrated into teaching and learning (rather than its focus), and appointed staff with expertise in its use; and
- chose furnishings and an open-plan layout that gave students multiple options about where and how they would learn.

In all their decisions, the leadership team turned to the research about what works best for students, and to local examples of effective practice. Their aspiration was to prepare students for a world in which a passion for learning is a core survival skill, and to create a team of professionals who would collaborate with each other and with the wider school community to both teach and model this passion.

This learning story describes some of what the school has done to create a community of visible learners. Its primary focus is on Katherine Jackson, a teacher of students in years 0–2.

Featured teacher

Katherine Jackson is an experienced early childhood and new entrant teacher who has taught in both the United Kingdom and New Zealand. She has a passion for developing assessment-capable new entrant learners. Katherine is constantly inquiring into new ideas and strategies to shift students' learning when the tried and true methods of teaching do not meet individual needs. Through innovation and professional inquiry, she actively reflects on her own practice to meet the needs and create shift for all learners.

Stonefields School's Visible Learning story

What were the desired outcomes?

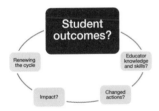

When Stonefields School's foundation staff first gathered in January 2011, the lead team presented them with a vision of a school that would "nurture, inspire, and challenge learners to actively understand, push boundaries, and achieve success in learning for life." The vision was underpinned by four vision principles:

1. Building learning capacity: know, believe, and stretch self as a learner.
2. Collaborating: relate, participate, and value diversity. Make a contribution.
3. Making meaning: use tools, strategies, skills, and knowledge to break codes, understand, and take action.
4. Breaking through: strive to achieve success and happiness in learning and life.

Sarah, Kirsty, and Chris wanted staff to reconceptualize learning – to think about what learning and teaching *could be*, rather than what it had always been. They asked, "What do we want our students to be able to do when they don't know what to do?" In the course of a week, Katherine and her new colleagues co-designed a set of learner qualities that they believed students needed in order to be effective learners. They settled on the following: wonder, reflect, question, think, connect, be self-aware, and be determined (see Figure 6.1).

Figure 6.1 Learner qualities

Staff believed that if they explicitly fostered these qualities, their students would come to understand and take control of the entire learning process and that this would lead to accelerated achievement. Drawing on their shared knowledge, staff agreed that the learning process has three facets:

- making meaning;
- building knowledge; and
- applying understandings.

It was important, then, to not only monitor student achievement outcomes but also to pay close attention to student behavior and, in particular, the ways students talked about their learning. Teachers and leaders wanted to hear students using the language of learning while talking knowledgeably about their own progress. An innovative approach used to monitor progress towards this growth in student agency was to develop a set of indicators that describe progress in relation to each of the learner qualities (Figure 6.2). These show development from "little in place" to "break through," a point at which the disposition becomes completely embedded and intuitive.

Student progress is individually monitored and the results collated in graphs. The school is able to dig deeper into what this means by regularly recording short video clips of 24 target students as they respond to three questions:

"What makes a good learner a good learner?" (Or "What do successful learners do?")

"What do you do when you get stuck in your learning?" (Or "If you have a problem to solve, what is the process you go through?")

"When you want to advance your learning or have a question you want to answer, what steps do you take?"

Building Learning Capacity

	Definition	Little in Place	Developing	Proficient	Break Through
Questions	A way of finding out.	I don't ask many questions.	I can ask "skinny" questions.	I use a wider range of questions, 'skinny' and 'deep' to get information.	I constantly ask questions to seek further information and deepen understandings.
Reflects	Thinks about and looks back on the learning to decide how it went and where to next?	I am not sure what reflection is or means.	I reflect on learning with support or prompts e.g. question starters.	I know reflection is an important part of the learning process. I can talk about when, what and how I reflect.	I understand reflection helps me with my learning. I use it continuously across a range of situations.
Thinks	To reason about, reflect or ponder.	I don't think much during my learning.	With support I can use thinking organizers and strategies to further my learning.	I use various thinking tools and strategies to deepen my thinking and learning.	I naturally select the most appropriate thinking tool and strategy to reach a desired decision, outcome, solution or situation I am faced with.
Connects	Linking knowledge together to create new understandings.	I am unable to make connections or links.	I can sometimes make connections with support or modelling. Sometimes I have an "aha" and I see a link or connection.	I make many links and connections between pieces of knowledge to create new ideas or deeper understandings.	I constantly look for and use knowledge to connect with old and new learning to develop new understandings.
Is Determined	The ability to stick at a challenge task when you feel like giving up. The desire and determination to self improve and succeed.	If things are too tricky I give up.	I can self talk to persevere with tasks that are a little tricky.	I have a number of strategies that help me to be determined when tasks are challenging.	I choose from a range of strategies to overcome obstacles, problem solve and self improve as a learner. I have a determination to learn through tasks I identify and commit to achieving next learning steps.
Is Self Aware	Aware of yourself as an individual, your being, actions, thoughts.	I am not so aware of my actions and thoughts.	I know what my strengths and next steps are.	I am aware of what makes me special. I take action to sharpen my strengths and work towards achieving my next steps.	I am conscious of what makes me tick, my thoughts and the actions I need to take to self improve as a learner.
Wonder	To be amazed at, the desire to know something.	I am not sure what it means to wonder.	I like to wonder and imagine possibilities.	?	I wonder to come up with ideas about what might be (fluency) from many different perspectives (flexibility). I can elaborate these ideas (elaboration) and come up with an original idea (originality).

Figure 6.2 Learner quality rubric

The baseline data from the first year shows that students lacked understanding of the learning process and often took a "distal" view of learning, meaning they were dependent upon others to manage their learning. The following were typical responses to the questions about what makes someone a good learner:

Do what the teacher says.
Be good.
Focus.
I don't know.

The main curriculum focus in the first year was on reading. This was informed by data – only 51% of the students who entered the school in February 2011 were achieving at or above New Zealand's National Standards (NS) in Reading (Ministry of Education, 2009). While the strategic goal was for all students to achieve at or above the NS, the specific targets were more modest, though still ambitious:

- Below: less than 70% reading at or above National Standard.
- At: 70–85% of students reading at or above National Standard.
- Above: 85–95% students reading at or above National Standard.
- Stretch: more than 95% students reading at or above National Standard.

What knowledge and skills did the teachers and school leaders need to support these outcomes?

If students were to acquire the language of learning, as represented by the seven learner qualities, teachers themselves needed to grow their capability to scaffold them. Furthermore, if they were to foster reading literacy, they needed to grow as teachers of reading.

The leaders sought outside external expertise for the professional learning opportunities they needed, finding that the Visible Learning^plus program closely aligned with their aspirations for both staff and students. Cognition's Visible Learning^plus consultants Kate Birch and Jayne-Ann Young took on the role of critical friends in this journey. However, the learning was ongoing as teachers and leaders monitored what they were doing and its impact on students. Where necessary, specific areas were addressed through targeted professional learning from other providers.

Part of this in-school learning was, and is, incidental, as with three teachers working together in each hub, there are constant opportunities for informal observation and feedback. However, it is also deliberate. Teachers in each hub maintain a shared "thinking journal" in which they record their insights about what they want their learners to look like and the effective teaching practices required to achieve this. This is a valued resource for reflection in their regular professional conversations. Katherine explains:

> A lot of my most powerful learning has come from listening in on colleagues and observing them every day. Through this I've picked up how others elicit feedback and feed forward, use progressions, and do their planning. I might love something they've done or not be sure about something. I'm lucky because I can follow up when we reflect together in our hub.

The assessment tool e-asTTle is particularly valued as a means of gathering and analyzing data about teacher impact on literacy and numeracy. The school accessed help from external providers to develop staff understanding about how electronic tools can be used to closely monitor the progress of individuals and groups. Video clips of brief teaching interactions and of the target students' responses to the questioning about their learning processes are also valuable resources for professional discussion. Over time, the school leaders hoped that this attention to student voice would become embedded in teachers' professional practice.

What new actions did the teachers and school leaders try?

Stonefields School has undertaken a variety of actions to create its visible learners. They include the prominent use of explicit cues – including visual cues – that make expectations visible, and also the construction of learning partnerships between school and home.

Using visual cues to focus reflection and feedback

The visitor to Stonefields School is immediately struck by the visual cues that help students focus on their reason for being at school and how to achieve. The four vision principles are each represented in the school grounds by a large rock and, in the foyer, by a set of much-loved puppets (see Figure 6.3) that assistant principal Chris Bradbeer wields to great effect. They, and a set of icons for the learner qualities, are displayed on the walls and repeated in stickers and certificates. Each learner quality is associated with a particular gesture that is used each time it is referred to, a strategy that is particularly supportive for younger students and those with special education needs as well as for students for whom English is a second or additional language. When prompting students to reflect on their learning, teachers encourage students to identify the specific learner qualities they utilized and provide feedback with the appropriate certificate or sticker. Perhaps most critically, the rubrics in which progress towards development of the learner qualities are described are written in "child speak," and students and teachers jointly decide where to place a student in relation to each quality.

Figure 6.3 A Stonefields learner with Rocky

Santiago: Writing.

Rocky: You've done lots of writing, haven't you?

Santiago: Yes!

Rocky: What have you been writing?

Santiago: [Reads] I am thinking. I am happy.

Rocky: I'm happy, too. What fantastic writing! What learning qualities did you have to use?

Santiago: Determined.

Rocky: Being determined. Did it take a long time to do this writing? I'm so proud of you, Santiago, and I bet Mrs Jackson is proud of you, too. And let's have a look back and see how much your writing has changed. Look at that! And look at that one! You have been so building your capacity in writing. I'm going to give you a special sticker. Is that ok?

Santiago: [Wreathed in smiles, Santiago nods his assent.]

Learning is not always easy. The school has adopted James Nottingham's metaphor of "the pit" to communicate to students the concept of the zone of proximal development: the place where they feel stuck and need to consciously reflect on the learning process and the necessary relevant qualities to get out again (see Figure 6.4).

Like the learner qualities and principles, progress towards achievement in key learning areas is also made highly visible. For example, in Katherine's hub, the reading progressions are represented by a set of colored beehives on which the criteria for achievement are written in language the students can understand. Each student is represented by a bee, which is moved as the student progresses through the levels. In this way, students can see where they are in terms of the big picture, as well as the "next steps" to get to where they want to go (see Figure 6.5).

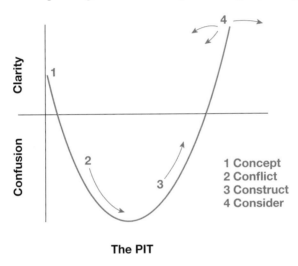

The PIT

1 Concept
2 Conflict
3 Construct
4 Consider

Figure 6.4 The learning pit

Figure 6.5 Reading bees

In both writing and numeracy, the progressions are also recorded in students' books, and specific times are set aside for students to reflect on how they are doing. The expectation is that:

> [Feedback] will be specific and will assist the students towards next learning steps and closing the gap in their learning. Feedback will occur as students are doing the learning and will involve the learner.
>
> (Stonefields School feedback codes)

Katherine sets aside the Thursday writing session to go through the previous week's writing with her students. Usually this is undertaken in groups and pairs of students with similar needs. She uses specific questions to prompt reflection and to promote feedback and feed forward:

> It's really important to have time built into the program for the children and teachers together to reflect and observe. So for example, I use the Thursday writing session for us to reflect on the writing from throughout the week, and we go back to the progressions and say, "Have we done a picture plan today? Was it relevant to what you then attempted to write about? Let's highlight the ones we've attained and what our next steps are." Or "If you haven't drawn a picture plan that relates to your writing, what do you need to do next time to connect your picture plan to your writing?" So again, there's that reflection, and I personally feel it's really critical to build it into your teaching timetable. The time is planned, and it's sacrosanct.

Students are also actively encouraged to scaffold each other, using the language of learning that they see and hear all around them. For example, each week one of the older children in Katherine's hub brings a book that they can read to their peers. Teachers scaffold the students to use their new learning to provide feedback to the person reading the story. Katherine explains:

> They use what they know from the guided reading sessions to give feedback to the person reading the story to the group. The language comes from the success criteria that are set out for the progressions. The feedback might be "I like the way you used expression" or "I like the way you paced your reading." Then we'll ask for some feed forward, providing modeling and prompts as a reminder that this is about how we can improve. Some children have been so immersed in the learning language, they use it automatically. They might say, "Next time you need to use a louder voice," or "Turn the book around so we can see the pictures."

Each student in Katherine's hub also has their own learning steps booklet recording their individual learning steps. This serves as a constant reminder that each person is on a unique learning pathway. Teachers make their own learning pathways visible to their students. For example, Katherine shares with them the challenges she finds in getting to grips with information and communications technologies.

Katherine also uses visual means of supporting learning for students who are English language learners. She buddies them with a peer who can help with translation, but then uses the whiteboard to communicate directly through pictures and images.

Information and communications technologies are valued learning tools at this school and another way in which learning is made visible. The progressions are available online on the school's Google site so that students and parents can access them and interpret them at any time. Each learning hub has a blog where students and teachers share their learning with each other, with the wider school community, and with people in schools around the world:

> We find that blogs are a great tool for showing progress. They capture our achievements as a hub. We've found this better than Knowledge Net, as we can talk to each other. People are looking in from around the world and all the parents can access it. We use the blogs for celebrations and to set out our next learning steps.
>
> (Sarah Martin)

Sharing responsibility with parents

As a teacher of new entrant students, Katherine plays a key role in building the school's relationships with parents and families. In New Zealand, students can enrol for school on their fifth birthday, so the transition process is ongoing. At Stonefields, this challenge is exacerbated by the high numbers of families deciding to join this new school.

Stonefields seeks to build partnerships with parents and families that are focused on learning. The intention is that responsibility for fostering learning is shared and that students experience smooth transitions between their learning at and away from school. To this end parents, like their children, are supported to acquire the language of learning and to understand the expected progressions for writing, reading, and numeracy.

For most families, transition to Stonefields School begins with an invitation to meet the staff in the term before their child starts. At this induction session they are told what to expect – how the school operates and its approach to learning. Each family then attends a "Portfolio Connect" where they meet the child's "guardian teacher" – the teacher who will be primarily responsible for their welfare during their first year at the school. This session provides the guardian with the opportunity to learn from the child and their family. Insights can be gained about, for example, the child's thinking about learning or their passions at their early childhood learning center or at home. That information is then used for planning appropriate learning programs. Students then go to school for three visits where they have the opportunity to get involved in their "guardian groups," perhaps going to a physical education class or the library. Parents are expected to attend on the first visit but can make their own choice on other days. The child is matched up with a "buddy," chosen on the basis of the Portfolio Connect conversation.

When a new entrant starts school, they are given a booklet for use at home and at school. The following is an extract from the introductory letter:

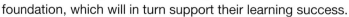

Dear Parents/Caregivers,

Welcome to your child's "Foundation Stones to Learning" booklet.

As your child begins their formal schooling there is a lot of essential knowledge that they need to learn to become successful in both Literacy and Numeracy. The purpose of this booklet is to ensure your child has the essential alphabet, word and number knowledge to build a strong foundation, which will in turn support their learning success.

Building Learning Capacity
Know, believe and stretch self as a learner

This learning is part of Building Learning Capacity, one of our vision principles. The essential knowledge learning is detailed below:

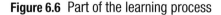

Figure 6.6 Part of the learning process

After the initial five weeks, teachers review progress with parents and work with them to set their child's next learning steps, including reference to the learner qualities. They are shown how they can go to the school's website to view the progressions and to see their relationship to the focus of the week and its specific learning intentions, success criteria, and learning activities. They learn how they can access their children's records and are introduced to some of the support materials to which the website links. Recently a parent portal has been developed for the school website, providing comprehensive information and resources for parents and families.

Scaffolding for parents continues throughout their child's time at the school through workshops and one-on-one support, with a strong focus on the seven learner qualities and, more generally, on the language of school and learning.

What was the impact of the changed actions on the desired student outcomes?

You will recall that the Stonefields School vision is to "nurture, inspire, and challenge learners to actively understand, push boundaries, and achieve success in learning for life." Specific long-term desired outcomes are that students:

- can use and understand the language of learning;
- can use progressions to identify where they are in their learning and where they need to go next; and
- know what to do when they don't know what to do.

The specific focus has been on reading, and so the school has looked for evidence of students experiencing accelerated reading progress.

Teaching staff see parents and families as a key resource for learning, and so they also look for evidence that this partnership is growing and that it is impacting positively on students.

Using and understanding the language of learning

Katherine finds that initially, her five-year-old students tend to simply parrot the language of learning, though they do know and accurately use the gestures for the learner qualities. Over time, their understanding grows. This is corroborated by the continued collection and analysis of student voice, which provides data to monitor shifts happening in students' dispositions (learner qualities), capacity to make meaning (using the Learning Process), changes in conceptual understandings, and ability to collaborate.

For example, the collated data on learner qualities demonstrates a gradual improvement in students' ability to talk about their learning in relation to the learner qualities. When asked to reflect on the specific learner qualities that helped them to get 'out of the pit' in a particular instance, they are increasingly able to identify the relevant qualities and explain how they helped. In formal learning sessions, students are learning to use appropriate language to provide each other with feedback and feed forward.

The following interaction took place after Riley, a junior student, had read a favorite book to her hub:

Student 1: Speak louder.
Teacher: [Modeling appropriate feedback] Next time, I think you can speak louder.
Student 2: Next time, you can speak with more expression.

Teacher: Anyone got some other feedback?

Student 3: I liked the way you showed us all the pictures and you showed them slowly so we could see them.

Teacher: Good feedback. One new feed forward.

Student 4: Maybe next time you could hold the book a bit higher so that people at the back can see the pictures?

Katherine has observed that students are also using the language of learning, including the specialized language of literacy learning, in quiet, one-on-one exchanges. She recalls overhearing a year 2 student providing feedback to a friend who had just read her a story: "I like the way you gave expression when you read sentences with an exclamation mark."

Using learning progressions

The overt sharing of the learning progressions and of individual student progress has had a number of effects. An effect it has not had, to the surprise of some, is that students do not compare themselves to each other. Rather, they compete with themselves, setting high, challenging goals that they are determined to achieve. Another important consequence is that the progressions support both teachers and students to explicitly connect their feedback and feed forward to the criteria for success. In Katherine's words:

> The beehives are absolutely critical. The children know that in each hexagon there is a progression and they know exactly what they're working on. I have a little boy who has just moved to the green hive. So they're actually completely visible physically and he moved his little bee across to the green hive and we talked about what the next learning steps were. And I said, "You don't just stop, do you?" And he said, "No, I'm going to get to the next hive along." So it's absolutely critical because they can see all the color bands that are represented by the beehives, and you ask them where they want to be, and they want to be at the top within three weeks [laughs] so there's that self-motivation and self-belief. … They always intrinsically believe they can get a huge amount further than where you think they're going to get or their parents think they might get. So they're not limited by the Standards[2] or anything like that. If you say, you're going to be at the end of Green at the end of year 1, well, you don't want everyone to be at the end of Green by the end of year 1, we want them to be exceeding that and the children naturally drive that. … The children know what they're learning because they know where they want to get to, but it's so reinforced because we've got a really good school–parent partnership and because we talk about feedback all the time. "Let's reflect on where we're at. This is what we did in this learning this week. Actually, we haven't quite got the inferencing questions. And to really get to Blue, we need to be able to start to answer inferencing questions." And

this is it. We use that vocabulary, because that's the vocabulary we're using in the classroom.

Knowing what to do when they don't know what to do

The metaphor of the pit and the growth in student understandings about the learning process and the learner qualities have proved more than cognitive tools. They also build students' emotional resilience. Students are not afraid of being stuck; in fact, they welcome it. This is demonstrated by the following transcript of a video clip[3] that Courtenay, a student in Learning Hub 3, made about "getting out of the learning pit":

> Courtenay: Hullo, I'm Courtenay and today I'm going to be talking to you about the pit.
> Voice off camera: Hmm. What's the pit?
> Courtenay: What is the pit, I hear you ask? Well, the pit is a part of our learning when we get stuck in our learning and we just don't know what the answer is. We use the seven learner qualities and the learning processes to help us reach different steps to get out of the pit. Finally, we can break through and say that we've got it. Then we move on to a different pit. Yay! Coming in and out of pits is fun and that's the way we learn here at Stonefields.

Accelerated reading progress

Katherine finds that it can be difficult to get true baseline data for the significant percentage of her students who come with English as a second or additional language or who have grown up in homes that do not use the academic language of the school and so do not tend to achieve as expected against New Zealand's National Standards for Reading, Writing, and Mathematics. Because of this, progress in the first six months can seem slow. However, after the first one or two years, the data shows shifts that show students making improvements at well above the expected rate of progress.

A clearer picture emerges when we focus on the 49 year 1–8 students who entered the school on day 1. Figure 6.7 demonstrates the rapid and significant improvement in these students' overall reading achievement, with a near doubling in the numbers at or above New Zealand's National Standards in Reading in the two years from February 2011 to December 2012. As earlier noted, the school's 'stretch target' is for over 95% of students to read at or above the appropriate National Standards, so this ambitious goal was achieved for this group.

Home–school partnership

Parental engagement is evident in the response to an invitation to the parents of students whose reading was below target to observe a guided reading session. Forty-one out of a possible 42 parents attended the session. Katherine shared that a reason for the high attendance rate was the enthusiasm of parents attending the first of the two available times, who found it valuable and encouraged others to attend. "You get the buy-in and the word spreads."

Reading Cohort A %	Well below	Below	At	Above	Well above	Total at/ above	Total above
February 2011	2.0	46.9	34.7	16.3	0.0	51.0	16.3
June 2011	2.0	20.4	42.9	32.7	2.0	77.6	34.7
December 2011	2.0	10.2	26.5	59.2	2.0	87.7	61.2
June 2012	2.2	2.2	30.4	52.2	13.0	95.7	65.2
December 2012	2.3	2.3	34.1	43.2	18.2	95.5	61.4

Figure 6.7 Cohort A – reading data in relation to the National Standards

Katherine finds that parents' ability to access the planning documentation on the school's website means that they can reinforce the learning from school.

Parents' appreciation of the quality of their children's educational experience is evidenced in the "good news" section of the school's website. One parent enthused:

> I just wanted to say a quick thank you to you and your team for my daughter's progress this year already. I think the key thing is how motivated and excited she is to learn and achieve. I think that this had started from the year 1 stage, but she is always excited to tell us how the day went and what she did. Clearly a sign that the teachers are doing a fantastic job. She really admires and looks up to her teachers and they have been so supportive during the natural behavioral developments that seven year olds go through. So just a quick thank you to say how much we appreciate what everyone is doing there.

Continuing the cycle

It is clear from school documentation and from listening to Katherine and her colleagues that this is a school in which learning and adaptation are constant. This is true at both the micro level, in moment-by-moment interactions with students, and also at the hub and school-wide level. An example was the decision by teachers in the junior hub to reorganize their timetable for 2013, recognizing that this group of students had a greater need for support in phonics and writing than in numeracy. At the same time, the teachers observed that this strategy was not enough for some students, who needed extra intervention.

The school also continues to explore how digital technology can work as a tool to support pedagogy. The learning progressions are now digital and the website[4] goes through ongoing refinements that open teaching and learning to scrutiny by the Stonefields community and by interested educators from around the world.

Katherine recommends focusing on one area of learning at a time – remembering, of course, to maintain coherence through keeping students constantly attuned to the qualities and processes that support all learning. She advises:

> Choose one curriculum area that you want to focus on, such as reading, writing, or mathematics. Use progressions. Write them in "child speak" and put them on the wall. Talk about them constantly to learners and to parents. It will gradually filter out. Those kids will say they want to be at W, X or Y and Z at the end of term.

Most of all, she says, "Be brave! Try new things!"

Notes

1 Each hub is an open modern learning space that accommodates the equivalent of three classes of learners and three teachers.

2 This is a reference to New Zealand's National Standards in reading, writing, and mathematics.

3 Courtenay's clip is available at http://learninghub3.blogspot.co.nz/2011/11/getting-out-of-pit.html For more student perspectives on the pit, see www.youtube.com/watch?v=RC1rNb6eLbg

4 The school welcomes visitors to its website at www.stonefields.school.nz

7

Gustav Vasaskolan

Sweden

The reading tree helps us keep track of our reading progress so our teachers know how to help us.

Student

We have our own dots that we use. When we reach the next level in our reading progress, we move our dots to the next branch.

Student

Both the students cited above are eight years old and in the second grade at Gustav Vasaskolan. Their comments relate to a "reading tree" that they use to plot their own progress. The students' comments indicate a sense of ownership of this process, along with an understanding that it provides useful information for their teachers to plan "next steps."

Context

Gustav Vasaskolan is located in Stockholm, Sweden. It is over 125 years old and is set in a very attractive part of the city where most residents are relatively well-off. Today, Gustav Vasaskolan has about 450 students divided into 18 classes. It is usual in Sweden for students to stay with the same teacher for two to three years.

Students at Gustav Vasaskolan range in age from six to ten years, so in many countries the school would be considered an elementary or primary school. The school is organized into four units. Each unit has a pedagogical leader who is part of the school leadership team, alongside the principal, Lena Arkéus and assistant principal, Karin Petersson. Like all schools catering to this age group in Sweden, the school employs "*pedagogs*" (day-care workers, also called "*fritidspedagogs*") who are specially trained to work with students during their leisure time before, after, and sometimes during school. Gustav Vasaskolan is well-respected by its local community and is an attractive destination for teachers. With its long history, the school prides itself on being a place people want to belong to.

In 2011, the Swedish government brought in sweeping reforms, responding to data from international studies such as PISA[1] and TIMSS[2] indicating that Swedish children were not performing well in contrast to students from other similar countries. The reforms included the introduction of a new national curriculum that allows greater flexibility for school planning while at the same time setting up a much stricter system of accountability. These reforms set the expectation that schools must be much more focused on student outcomes, an expectation that is backed by the introduction of a national assessment system for students in years 3, 6, and 9 and a new qualifications system for students in the upper secondary school. A more finely-tuned grading system adds rigor to assessment.

The new regime demands that teachers select instructional strategies that will scaffold their students to achieve the valued outcomes of the national curriculum as measured in the assessment system. School leaders are responsible for leading the change, including providing the necessary professional learning, revisiting the way their schools are organized, and managing of resources.

Overview

While the national reforms can be seen as a top-down approach to schooling improvement, teachers and leaders at Gustav Vasaskolan embraced the changes. They valued the opportunities offered by the new curriculum and the new focus on student outcomes. However, the reforms entailed an important shift in thinking for their school and the leaders understood that, for the changes to be successful, staff needed new knowledge and ideas on how to work with the students. Initially, Gustav Vasaskolan responded to the reforms by engaging in teacher professional learning in areas such as formative evaluation, mathematics pedagogy, and differentiated instruction. The school's leaders could see signs of progress but felt a more systematic approach was needed if they, their teachers, and ultimately their students were to maximize their potential. When Lena and Karin attended a breakfast workshop led by Visible Learning[plus] consultant Bitte Sundin, they immediately recognized a whole-school approach to improvement that appeared to meet their needs.

A feature of Visible Learning at Gustav Vasaskolan is the inclusion of *pedagogs* in the intervention. Teachers lead student learning during the school day, but *pedagogs* work with students throughout the day so it is vital that their thinking is aligned and they use common language and teaching strategies. Lena and Karin share leadership of the intervention with five teachers and *pedagogs* who each take responsibility for leading the learning of one group of teachers and *pedagogs*.

At the time of writing, Gustav Vasaskolan is not ready to characterize itself as a Visible Learning school. They are early in their journey and they lack the baseline data necessary to track improvement in students' academic outcomes. Nevertheless, this story shows that, given a context where teachers and leaders are already open to learning and can see its purpose, quick gains are possible. Interactions within classrooms and between colleagues are now far more learning-focused, and systems and routines are being set up to allow progress to be understood and monitored. Students at Gustav Vasaskolan are already beginning to exhibit some of the important characteristics of visible learners.

Featured leaders and teachers

The Visible Learning intervention at Gustav Vasaskolan was initiated by Lena Arkéus and Karin Petersson.

Lena Arkéus has been the principal for seven years. Lena has long experience in teaching young children. She became a *pedagog* in 1980 and has been a school leader since 1995.

Karin Petersson, the assistant principal, has been a school leader for the past eight years. Previously, she taught children from the preschool level to grade 2.

Gustav Vasaskolan's Visible Learning story

What were the desired student outcomes?

In 2011, the Swedish Riksdag implemented sweeping reforms aimed at improving students' educational outcomes and raising the status of the teaching profession. The new regime challenged schools to interrogate the impact of instruction on student outcomes. For the first time, there was an assessment regime for measuring student progress at the primary level. The revised curriculum set out core content while still allowing schools room to design curricula tailored to the students in their context.

The reforms were a significant challenge for schools throughout Sweden, and Gustav Vasaskolan was no exception. Never before had the state set expectations for young learners, and teachers and schools had not been expected to measure, monitor, and report upon progress towards those expectations. Consequently, there was little concept of assessment as a force for learning and teachers were not in the habit of engaging in feedback practices closely connected to student progression. Fortunately, while the practices were new, the aspirations were not.

Teachers at Gustav Vasaskolan were keen to embrace outcomes-focused teaching. The problem was deciding where to start. A breakfast workshop led by Visible Learning^plus consultant Bitte Sundin, and attended by principal Lena Arkéus and assistant principal Karin Petersson, appeared to provide the answers.

Often in education you work with a specific subject, or take a course, or go to a seminar but somewhere along the way, you forget it or stop using the ideas. But this was something we felt could be a part of everything we do, since it's not only about practical tasks – things you can measure – but also about new mindframes and a new way of meeting the needs of our students.

(Lena Arkéus)

After consulting with colleagues, Lena and Karin invited Bitte to collaborate with the school in implementing Visible Learning. One of the first steps was to gather evidence about whether, and to what extent, students were displaying the characteristics of visible learners. After conducting student interviews and focus groups, the school discovered that students tended to take a passive approach to their learning, leaving control and direction to their teachers.

Lena and Karin brought the evidence together for staff to consider and discuss. Together, they agreed that they wanted all students to become visible learners who saw themselves as their own teachers. They wanted to establish a school climate where dialogue, as opposed to monologue, was commonplace, and where students, teachers, and leaders gave each other effective feedback.

What knowledge and skills did the teachers and school leaders need to support these outcomes?

Teachers and the leadership team at Gustav Vasaskolan shared a strong commitment to realigning the school towards student learning. In order to do this, the teachers themselves knew they needed a new set of knowledge and skills. Bitte Sundin's presentation at the breakfast meeting resonated with Lena and Karin because it offered a whole-school approach to the challenge of orienting the school towards student learning outcomes.

The whole school should be a part of the work and development, because initiatives work better when it is from the ground up. All staff, not only the leaders, needed to be a part of the new initiative. We realize that this supportive and cooperative culture is not easy to establish and takes years of hard work. However, the staff at our school believed in the changes being addressed in Sweden and they wanted to be ahead of them.

Nearly a year ago, during autumn break, we started with our first two days of Visible Learning. Two days, because we wanted to include our entire staff, both the teachers and our day-care staff, since their work is integrated into everything we do. After those two days, we started to analyze ourselves. We followed up on this with another meeting in January.

(Lena Arkéus)

An immediate professional learning need was to learn to gather, collate, and interrogate data, using both qualitative and quantitative evidence to drive an improvement process that would lead to better outcomes for students. Up until 2013, Gustav Vasaskolan had relied upon anecdotal data. Data collection practices varied and staff lacked the practice and processes needed to interrogate data and use it as evidence to inform their own learning and that of their students. Professional development opportunities focused on formative evaluation revealed to teachers that they needed increased knowledge on how to see, and prove, evidence of learning. They wanted to address the following questions:

- Why do we collect the student data we collect?
- How do we use that data after it is collected to guide student learning?
- What do we do with the information?
- How do we share it with students?
- How do we share it with parents?
- How do we share it with each other?

The Visible Learning framework provided the tools and practices staff needed to answer those questions, while also raising the three critical ones:

- Where are we going?
- How are we going?
- What are our next steps?

Sweden's new assessment regime provided a description of progression that Gustav Vasaskolan could use to get an understanding of expected progression with regard to the outcomes it addresses. In particular, it sets out some broad markers for addressing the first two of those critical questions. The question about 'next steps' demanded that teachers and leaders deepen their understanding of the instructional strategies that would best enable students to achieve the intended outcomes. John Hattie's research provides the professional knowledge about the strategies that are known to work and Visible Learning provided a means for the school to explore the application of those strategies in their own context.

Essentially, from the very beginning, there were three main areas of learning for the educators at Gustav Vasaskolan:

1 learning about the mindframes needed to impact positively on student outcomes;
2 learning about evidence-based practice; and
3 learning about the instructional strategies that work to achieve the outcomes you want for students.

Gustav Vasaskolan staff were structured into four teaching teams, each working with a particular group of students. While the leadership team took overall responsibility for the initial inquiry, all staff participated in data collection and contributed to the analysis. All staff were involved in completing the Visible Learning^plus Matrix, participating in the creation of student focus groups and the implementation of classroom surveys. Walkthroughs and observations were introduced early on, allowing opportunities for the teams of teachers to engage in professional dialogue around the instructional strategies they were learning about, but it was the process of collaborating to complete the Matrix that built upon and sustained teacher enthusiasm. Teachers chose to work within one of five groups, each focused upon one of the themes from the Matrix. Each team collected data with regard to their own theme. They tried new ways of working, and then reported on what they had learnt to the whole staff. The leadership team drew the collaborative learning together as the basis for developing the school's action plan (Figure 7.1).

Through these conversations, every member of staff participated in establishing a shared statement to encapsulate their vision for their future work with Visible Learning. That vision is set out in Table 7.1 (with an English translation in the right-hand column).

Figure 7.1 A team of teachers and *pedagogs* present on their Matrix

Table 7.1 Gustav Vasaskolan's Visible Learning vision

Swedish	English
På Gustav Vasaskolan har vi tydliga mål för eleverna för att få dem att se sin kunskap. Den didaktiska medvetenheten gör att vi jobbar med metakognition som idé och vi tydliggör för eleverna vad som förväntas av dem. Var är vi-vart är vi på väg är de viktiga frågorna.	At Gustav Vasaskolan, we have clear goals for students to make them look at their own knowledge. We use didactic awareness, which means teaching students to think about the way they learn. Using metacognition, we are clear to students what is expected of them. Where we are and where we are on the road are the important issues.
Vi synliggör lärandet och utvärderar hur det går. Självbedömning används givetvis i varje ämne. Eleverna har egna verktyg för att bedöma sig själv och för att kunna se vad nästa steg är.	We visualize learning and evaluate how it goes. Self-assessment is of course used in each subject. Students have their own tools to assess themselves and to be able to see what the next step is.
Ett redskap för självbedömning som används är matriser. Dokumentation är viktigt och vi gör det tillsammans med eleverna. Kvalitet på arbeten diskuteras med eleverna, så även progression.	The self-assessment tools used are arrays.[3] Documentation is important and we do the arrays with the students. The quality of work is discussed with the students, and we focus on progression.
Visa nästa steg-feed forward-är viktigt och att alla får individuella målsättningar.	Showing the next step forward is important and ensuring that everyone has individual goals.
Dokumentationen är synlig och vi har synligt lärande på väggarna, ex som uppsatta mål, och matriser. De vuxna är tydliga vägvisare.	Documentation is visible and we have visible learning on the walls. For example, the set goals and the matrices.
Vi tror på att varje barn kan och vill och vi har höga förväntningar på alla elever. De kan och vill anta utmaningar.	We believe that every child can and wants to learn and we have high expectations for all students. They are able and willing to accept challenges.
Därför skapar vi också utmanande undervisning där eleverna är aktiva i sitt eget lärande. I de pedagogiska planeringarna är eleverna också delaktiga, och vi synliggör den proximala utvecklingszonen genom förståeliga bedömningsmatriser.	Therefore, we also create challenging education where students are active in their own learning. Students participate in educational planning and we make the zone of proximal development visible through setting out understandable rubrics.
Kunskapskraven är tydliga, vi är lyhörda och synliggör elevernas lärande på olika sätt. Vi använder prov före och efter ett område för att se varje barns framsteg. Matriser, utvärderingar, enkäter, reflektioner och kamratbedömningar är viktigt.	The knowledge requirements are clear, we are responsive and make student learning visible in different ways. We use the sample before and after a section to see each child's progress. Matrices, evaluations, surveys, reflections, and peer assessments are important.
Personalen arbetar tillsammans och gör gemensamma planeringar. Detta syns i ett övergripande planeringsschema som finns tillgängligt för alla. Vår tid används effektivt, bland annat genom rastscheman och tid i parallellen.	The staff work together and make joint plans. This is seen in the overall planning scheme that is available to everyone. Our time is used efficiently, including through the break schedules and time in parallel.

Swedish	English
Vi lär av varandra och delar med oss av metoder och exempel. På personalmöten delger vi varandra sådant vi lärt oss, och vi utvärderar, analyserar och överlämnar.	We learn from each other and share our methods and examples. At staff meetings, we provide to each other the things we learnt and we evaluate, analyze, and submit our evidence of impact.
Vi observerar elever och ger feedback till pedagogerna. Vi har kommit överens om att ge feedback till varandra och reflektera över vad man sett. Hur observationerna ska gå till är bestämt i förväg, och vi har ett färdigt schema som gör det möjligt för pedagogerna att genomföra observationer hos varandra.	We observe students and give feedback to the teachers. We have agreed to provide feedback to each other and reflect on what we have seen. How observations should go is decided in advance, and we have a complete schedule that will enable educators to conduct observations of each other.
Undervisningen förbättras hela tiden, och vi sätter data i relation till bra inlärningsstrategier. Vi utgår från insamlad data för vidare planering.	Teaching is improving all the time and we pull out the data in relation to good learning strategies. We start from the collected data for further planning.

Gustav Vasaskolan identified five themes for their future learning and change. The themes are based upon the school's vision. They are:

1   the visible learner;
2   feedback;
3   challenging learning;
4   learning organization; and
5   collecting and using data to inform teaching.

The leadership team incorporated all these themes into the school's action plan.

What new actions did the teachers and school leaders try?

Bitte observed that although Lena and Karin took a gentle approach, the staff responded immediately and enthusiastically. They read all they could find on Visible Learning, including John Hattie's books, *Visible Learning* and *Visible Learning for Teachers* (which has been translated into Swedish), and any additional material they could find on the Internet. James Nottingham's website, Challenging Learning[4] proved helpful and Stonefields School's (see the Stonefields School story on pages 125–141) website and YouTube clips provided a valuable model of what a Visible Learning school looks like.

> I got many inspiring examples of how to make learning visible in the classroom
> and it made me very eager to change my teaching. I could not wait to try it in
> my classroom!
>
> (Classroom teacher, anonymous response)

Visible Learning was the central focus of all shared staff time, either in the teaching teams or as a whole staff. The teachers were excited that John Hattie's focus was on learning and not just on teaching and keen to learn all they could about the learning strategies that had the highest effect sizes. They were especially interested to learn what they could about reciprocal teaching, productive teacher–student relationships, and strategies for developing metacognitive skills.

The teachers were immersing themselves in this learning about effective instructional strategies at the same time as they were collecting the evidence necessary to complete the Visible Learning^{plus} Matrix. Student voice is central to the data that is collected and there were many discussions about what this was telling them. Teachers began to look for opportunities to attend to student voice in the classroom.

Given the focus on student outcomes, an early part of the program was the introduction of learning intentions and success criteria and the expectation that feedback should be targeted to the intended learning. None of this was usual practice in Swedish schools. The implementation of walkthroughs and observations provided an opportunity for teachers and school leaders at Gustav Vasaskolan to share their learning about how to make the expected learning explicit to their students. In feedback conversations and at staff meetings, teachers talked about what effective practice looked like, and how to improve.

Effective feedback requires an understanding not only of the broad outcomes set out in the national curriculum but also of the smaller steps it takes to achieve them. The teachers collaborated to develop matrices and rubrics that provided the criteria for achieving the outcomes they wanted students to achieve in specific parts of the curriculum. They developed worked examples to show their students exactly what they expected. Figure 7.2 is an example of these tools, and Figure 7.4 shows them in use.

Some teachers made "reading trees" (Figure 7.3). Students were given sticky dots, and when they made progress and went to the next reading level, they moved their dots to the next branch to show progression. This was a fantastic visual for students and also for parents, who were able to see the progress their children had made and where they were in relation to other students in the classroom.

Figure 7.4 shows a model of a futuristic playground that was created by students in the first grade. The quality of the work is a consequence of the high expectations the students set themselves in the success criteria they created to evaluate the work.

Matrix – the three most common religions			
• Visualise what the student can and should be able to do • Visualise the learning experience for both students and teachers • Tools for evaluating • Tools for self-assessment • Clarify what students should learn	I can name three religions	I can tell you about some similarities between the three religions	I can tell you about some similarities and differences between the three religions
	I can name the different places (buildings) nearby where people can practice religion	I can pair three sites with the right religion	I can tell you about some similarities and differences between the various places where people practice religion
	I can name a few events from the three religions	I can pair the events with the correct religion	I can tell you about some similarities and differences between events within the three religions
	I can name a few symbols from the three religions	I can pair the symbols with the correct religion	I can tell you about some similarities and differences between the three religions' symbols

Figure 7.2 A Matrix for religious education

Figure 7.3 A reading tree

Figure 7.4 First graders' technical project – playground of the future

TECHNICAL PROJECT SUCCESS CRITERIA

Criteria: Construction

☐ I can make a simple design with the support of a pedagogue.
☐ I can make a simple design along with some classmates.

Cooperation (self-assessment)

☐ I participate in the group's work but I find it difficult to compromise.
☐ I participate in the group's work and I am able to compromise.
☐ I take responsibility for the group's work and I am able to compromise.

Documentation
☐ I make simple sketches of the design with the support of a pedagogue.
☐ I make simple sketches where the [individual] design elements are visible [or "apparent"].

Figure 7.5 First graders' technical project – success criteria

What was the impact of the changed actions on the desired student outcomes?

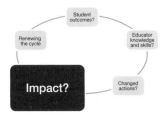

While the Visible Learning program is still new at Gustav Vasaskolan, Karin Petersson reports a significant change in teachers' talk and orientation:

This work makes teachers very active and interested in what they are doing in their lessons. The talk between staff has deepened – we always talk about teaching and learning now.

Teachers are demonstrating the mindframe of a change agent. In an evaluation, one teacher said:

The work with Visible Learning made me very aware of how important my own leadership in the classroom is, and how important it is to find out what the students really learn.

Visible Learning invites teachers to experiment with new ways of teaching. Kerstin Colldén is an experienced music teacher who had spent many years trying to teach students how to move their hands and feet at the same time. This ability to coordinate movement is necessary for playing instruments such as drums, but is quite difficult for young children to achieve. In the past, Kerstin had facilitated this through direct instruction, but had been disappointed at the slow rate of progress. After learning about how she could use checklists of criteria to make the learning more explicit, she found that all her current students learnt the required movement:

Visible Learning shifted my focus from holding the knowledge to sharing it with students in a way that they all can become assessment-capable learners. This is the best teacher professional development I've ever had during all my years in teaching.

(Kerstin Colldén)

Lena saw the biggest change in student progress when it came to conferences with parents. In the past, the intention had been for the conferences to be led by students. However, in practice they had tended to be adult-centered, with parents and teachers doing much of the talk. This is unsurprising, as students had not had the language for talking about their learning. After implementing Visible Learning, Lena says:

We gave the students more space and let them describe their own progress and understanding. Students now have the words for this, and so the quality of the conferences has improved.

It has been exciting for both leaders and teachers at Gustav Vasaskolan to see that their students are already reaping the benefits after just a few months of implementation of Visible Learning. Many students have already gone from sitting in class waiting for their next assignment to becoming assessment-capable learners who are engaged in thinking about their "next steps." Visible Learning has shifted the thinking of the school community and changed their focus from teaching to learning. Lena says:

> In Sweden, we have a democratic philosophy, which means we work by getting consensus from the group. This takes time, but it makes change possible. Real change in teachers' minds takes consensus, and we are making that happen.
>
> Becoming a Visible Learning school may be something that is several years into the future for us. We may never even end up there. We don't know at the moment. But we have started a process, which is something I find very exciting. And I don't think you can speed up the process. You just have to let it run its course; otherwise, it won't work. Because it is very much about adopting new mindframes and understanding how to meet our students' needs, and these are things that just don't change quickly.

Continuing the cycle

The whole staff has been a part of the work and the learning, which has helped unify them, as well as inspire them to keep moving forward. They share ownership of the action plan they all contributed to and know that their current focus needs to remain on success criteria, effective feedback, making learning more visible, and talking about learning with their students.

The crucial next step for Gustav Vasaskolan is to begin calculating effect size to measure progress. This is not something they could do before, because most classes did not have grades for students. They had not used many standardized tests or a pre-test/post-test model because this was not a requirement in the past. Sweden's new exams provide a valuable opportunity to get standardized achievement data they can use to guide and further improve teaching and learning.

Notes

1   Program for International Student Assessment: www.oecd.org/pisa
2   Trends in International Mathematics and Science Study: http://nces.ed.gov/timss/
3   This is a reference to the use of matrices and rubrics.
4   www.challenginglearning.com

8

Hodge Hill Primary School

UK

Imagine if students at your school told you this:

> I'm scared to put my hand up in case I'm wrong.
> Sitting at the back is better, because no one notices your mistakes, because you can, like, hide.
> People who are good at learning get everything right.
> We feel sad and unhappy if we make mistakes, because we get our work wrong.

These are the words of young people who are not visible learners. Worse, it seems that these young people find learning a risky venture. In this story, you will learn how teachers and school leaders at Hodge Hill Primary School transformed the way their students thought and talked about their learning. Today, students are visible learners – each is the personal hero of a learning journey over which they have increasing control.

Context

Hodge Hill Primary School is a large school in the city of Birmingham in the United Kingdom. Over 90% of the school's students are Asian, with the majority being Pakistani. A significant percentage of students are learning English as a second or additional language and many are from low-income homes. The school has a rapidly expanding roll, rising from 540 students in 2011 to 720 in 2014. A major building program has been required to accommodate this expansion.

The students range in age from the four-year-olds in the reception class to the eleven-year-olds in year 6. In order to ensure students feel safe and secure and are given the individual attention they deserve, they are organized into four 'phases', each with its own team of teachers and leaders: one at reception level and one each at years 1–2, 3–4, and 5–6. Each phase is led and managed by a phase leader, with the support of an assistant head teacher. The four phase leaders are part of the senior staff and meet weekly with the senior leadership team and the school business manager.

Head teacher Laura Kearney works alongside a deputy head teacher and three assistant head teachers. In such a large school, members of the senior leadership team do not have classes of their own. Instead, each leader supports colleagues with planning, team teaching, coaching, and mentoring while also holding a specific area of responsibility.

Overview

September 2011 was a significant time at Hodge Hill Primary School. An inspection by the Office for Standards in Education, Children's Services, and Skills (Ofsted) noted significant weaknesses in the quality of teaching and levels of student engagement. As happens every year at Hodge Hill, the start of a new school year brought a surge in new enrolments. And in the same month, Laura Kearney took up the position of head teacher.

Internal monitoring by the guiding coalition, led by Laura, affirmed the picture presented in the Ofsted report:

> Pupil progress and levels of attainment were low at the end of Key Stage 1[1] and, although there were some signs of improvement, this was not consistent or rapid enough by the end of Key Stage 2.
>
> (Hodge Hill guiding coalition)

Over the following 18 months, Laura led the work necessary to strengthen the leadership team and improve teaching. The next Ofsted[2] report, in March 2013, acknowledged the strength of the leadership team and the positive school climate, but stated that teaching was "not yet consistently good" and that the improvements in progress were only recently evident. It also acknowledged the existence of a school improvement plan that "is based on accurate self-evaluation of the strengths and weaknesses of the school by the senior leadership team based on rigorous monitoring." That monitoring revealed the passivity of students as learners and the predominance of teaching practices that reinforced that passivity.

The stage was set for improvement, but the school needed a robust vehicle that could stand up to the disruption caused by the burgeoning student numbers and the ever-expanding teaching staff that this necessitated. Visible Learning has proven to be that vehicle. In only one year of implementation, there has been a remarkable shift in the relationships between teachers and students, leading to a situation where students have significantly more control over their learning and are rapidly acquiring the characteristics of a visible learner. Recent data analysis indicates that this has contributed to an impressive rise in student achievement.

Featured leader

Head teacher **Laura Kearney** joined the school in 2011. Laura has a broad range of experience in primary schools with much of that at senior leadership level. She believes that a school should be an enjoyable, exciting, and safe place where students feel confident to take risks when learning new things. She is passionate about ensuring that students are equipped with the language, skills, and understanding that will empower them to be leaders of their own learning.

Hodge Hill Primary School's Visible Learning story

What were the desired student outcomes?

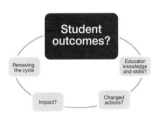

When Laura was appointed as Hodge Hill's head teacher in September 2011, she found a situation where both teaching practice and student achievement were variable. Some good monitoring practices were already in place and she worked with a re-formed leadership team to use what was needed to build teacher capability, particularly in mathematics teaching. However, the Ofsted inspection in March 2013 confirmed the team's assessment that more was needed, particularly in the areas of teacher evaluative capability and student ownership of the learning process. Laura explains:

> Lesson observations evidenced that too often learners were passive; not fully engaged in the learning process. They saw learning as something done to them rather than them having some control over it.
>
> Learning objectives were often vague, resulting in success criteria that were not helpful. Often pupils did not connect with the success criteria and the teachers themselves did not really understand their purpose. The teachers knew they should be using success criteria but weren't sure how they should be used and the expected impact. Even though the criteria were explained at the beginning of the lesson, they were then not used at all during the lesson. As a result, the students didn't know where they were in their learning at any given time and relied heavily on the teacher to tell them.
>
> Pupils were very reliant on teachers for feedback. Feedback was predominantly aimed at the task level, with some at the process level, but it was rarely at the self-regulation level. This reflected the teachers' lack of understanding about the use of success criteria.
>
> Generally, pupils viewed mistakes as failure and their learning stamina was low. Their focus was on getting the right answer and they would regularly rub away errors, thus losing all the evidence of good learning that takes place as a new concept is mastered.

The search was on for a whole-school approach to professional learning that would put students at the center of learning. When Laura and deputy head teacher Julie Guzder attended a Visible Learning^{plus} Foundation Day with John Hattie and Deb Masters, they recognized an approach that could support them to achieve their aspirations:

> What we heard resonated with us strongly; particularly the strands of the Visible Learner and Know Thy Impact. These tied together, in a rational way, how we wanted to equip our pupils as more effective learners and how we wanted to support our teachers to become more evaluative practitioners.

Laura, Julie, and Jenni Porter, the school's Visible Learning coordinator, drew on evidence they already had and new evidence gained through application of the Visible Learning^{plus} tools to get a deeper understanding of the degree to which students displayed the characteristics of a visible learner. Some of this learning is synthesized in Figure 8.1.

These findings, along with those about the needs of teachers and school leaders, were shared with staff and the school's governors. The video recordings made a particularly strong impact on staff, who were surprised at the students' responses. Seeing and hearing their students' voices was something new that challenged teachers' perceptions of their impact on students.

The school used the collated information to clarify its valued outcomes for students: the knowledge students needed to become visible learners, along with the practices that needed to become routine:

> Pupils need knowledge of:
> - what an effective learner is;
> - the vocabulary associated with learning;
> - the purpose of learning objectives and success criteria;
> - peer and self-assessment using success criteria;
> - the purpose of feedback and how to use it to improve their learning;
> - their role in contributing to the improvement of our school; and
> - the power of error in improving learning!
>
> Pupils need to make the following practices routine:
> - apply an agreed learning vocabulary to their daily work in order to engage with and make choices in their learning;
> - actively engage with the success criteria and apply this to what they are learning;
> - use the success criteria to judge what progress they have made and what they need to do next;
> - use the success criteria to help their peers do this also;
> - use the feedback from the teacher/peers to improve their work;
> - use the learning vocabulary to feed back to their teacher on their progress; and
> - be unafraid to make mistakes and use them as a vehicle for improvement.
>
> (Hodge Hill Primary School, valued outcomes for students)

On the basis of its evidence of need, the school decided that the aspect of students as visible learners that it should prioritize first was that of student assessment capability.

- **Good Learner video** – We videoed two pupils in every class responding to the same question - what makes a good learner? Pupils were not given any prompting or preparation prior to the video so that we could get a real snapshot of our pupils' perceptions:
  - Around ⅓ of pupils referenced behavior such as good lining up, eating your dinner, don't talk, etc.
  - Around ⅕ talked about doing good work and being rewarded / getting it right / don't make mistakes.
  - Around ⅕ emphasised listening to and looking at the teacher.
  - Less than ⅕ talked about relevant characteristics such as making decisions, listening to others, explaining your work.

- **Pupil focus groups** – In order to get greater depth in our understanding of pupil views, we also conducted focus groups in every year group, asking a range of questions around being a good learner:
  - Although we had done a lot of work around use of Learning Objectives and Success Criteria, pupils did not connect these to being a good learner.
  - Pupils clearly lacked a learning vocabulary – there was a lack of a common language of learning across the school.
  - Pupils saw learning as teacher directed – they did not take ownership.
  - We did not have a culture where error was welcomed – too much focus on product rather than process (also evident in teacher views).

- **Learning Walkthrough** – A Learning Walkthrough was conducted across the school and we spoke to 70 children about their learning:
  - Pupils were able to describe what they were doing rather than learning (21% of pupils could describe what they were learning / 73% described what they were doing (task)).
  - The majority were unable to explain how they would know when they had learned a concept (9% described what they would know by the end of the lesson / 30% said the teacher would tell them / 34% couldn't respond).
  - Pupils recalled feedback linked to grades/marking policy (10% could recall specific feedback they had been given that made a difference to their learning / 18% couldn't respond).
  - Over half could not explain their next steps (9% could talk about their next steps / 54% couldn't respond).
  - Most understood why they were learning a particular concept (41% linked it to the learning journey and progress; 26% couldn't respond).

Figure 8.1 Students as visible learners, 2013

What knowledge and skills did the teachers and school leaders need to support these outcomes?

Supported by Visible Learning[plus] consultant Craig Parkinson, the leadership team used the Visible Learning[plus] Matrix to develop their understanding of the knowledge and skills that teachers, school leaders (including the governors), families, and the community needed in order to support students to develop as visible learners. In this example, you can see the learning needs that were identified for teachers:

Teachers need knowledge of:

- what an effective learner is and ways to promote these characteristics;
- devising effective learning objectives and success criteria and how to use them effectively;
- ways to actively engage pupils in the learning objectives/success criteria;
- what work looks like at each National Curriculum level (accuracy of assessment);
- how to plan based upon where pupils are now and where they need to get to, mapping out clear progressions (their expected learning journey);
- different levels of feedback and how they can use this to best effect;
- ways to engage pupils in self- and peer-assessment;
- characteristics of the assessment-capable learner and how to recognize these;
- how to interpret and respond to pupil voice to improve the effectiveness of their teaching; and
- how to create a safe environment where pupils can make mistakes and learn from them.

Teachers need to make the following practices routine:

- consistently model, promote, and use the agreed learning vocabulary;
- ensure learning objectives are very specific and success criteria support pupils in achieving them;
- use the success criteria throughout the lesson, supporting pupils in using them to evaluate their progress and identify their next step, and model this process continuously;
- engage in continuing professional development (CPD) and collaborative work with colleagues to make sound assessment judgments – take responsibility for ensuring a good subject knowledge;
- use strategies to accurately capture pupil starting points and then plan the steps on the learning journey (starting point to destination – use the learning objectives and success criteria);

- develop own marking and feedback for greatest impact on learning – engage in CPD and implement strategies as agreed;
- regularly ask the pupils about their learning: "What worked / didn't work?" "What could you do differently that would help them learn better?"
- celebrate error – support pupils in understanding the positive aspect of error and model how they can learn from the mistakes; and
- focus on deep learning rather than surface. Emphasize the process rather than the product to promote deep conceptual understanding. (Teachers need to have secure subject knowledge to do this confidently.)

(Hodge Hill Primary School, valued outcomes for teachers)

The identified learning needs of the other stakeholder groups were similarly addressed at achieving the desired outcomes for students and were connected with those for teachers. For example, there were goals that:

- leaders would "Use knowledge of the assessment-capable learner to support teachers in developing this through modeling and coaching in the classroom"; and
- families would know "How they can support their child in being a good learner."

What new actions did the teachers and school leaders try?

The in-depth evaluation was the basis for mapping out an improvement journey in which the school would "use research and effect sizes to guide our improvement strategies so that we use more of the strategies that make the most difference" (Laura Kearney). The leadership team developed a set of planning documents that:

- set out detailed measurable targets for improvement (for example, "By March 2014, during walkthroughs, it will be evident that all classes are routinely using learning objectives and success criteria and pupils will fully understand what these mean");
- included development plans for four "focused priorities" related to assessment-capability, literacy and mathematics achievement, and leadership; and
- set out a timeline that clearly outlined what was to happen in the school's Visible Learning journey, and when.

Initially, there were to be seven whole-school focus areas:

1   The creation of a culture where *mistakes and misconceptions* are something to be celebrated as an important part of learning.
2   The creation of a *learner profile* setting out the skills and dispositions of a good learner.

3   Strengthening the use of *learning objectives and success criteria* as critical tools for understanding and monitoring students' learning journeys and enabling students to self-assess.

4   Supporting *accurate assessment* so that teachers can provide appropriate scaffolding and feedback.

5   Shifting *leaders' focus onto how learners are learning* rather than how teachers are teaching.

6   Providing *effective feedback*, with an initial focus on that from teacher to student.

7   Building the concept of *teachers as evaluators* who use information about the impact of their teaching on learning to take control of their own professional learning.

An eighth focus area was added later, that of *making teacher learning visible*. This was an outcome of the work on *teachers as evaluators,* which demonstrated the need to revise the school's approach to professional development and find ways to share examples of effective teaching practice focused on student learning.

The learning and change has been undertaken at different levels. For example, at a whole-school level, it has involved the development of a learner profile, and in the phases, it has led to the development of imagery (such as a Formula One race track) to convey the concept of a learning journey. The use of this imagery makes the language of Visible Learning a very potent presence throughout the school.

Figure 8.2 shows an example of a learning wall. It includes prompts about where students are in their learning journey and the dispositions that make for an assessment-capable learner. It reminds students of the questions they need to be asking of themselves as they regulate their own learning.

Figure 8.2 Good learners at Hodge Hill Primary School

The leadership team devised a coaching program in which teachers worked in triads, each led by a leader from middle management. Each triad was expected to develop an inquiry question related to the school priority of enabling students to become assessment-capable. The teachers then had to review the academic research related to their inquiry question and use this to refine their inquiry further. Each teacher taught a baseline lesson, reviewed what happened with their two colleagues, and then planned another lesson in which they sought to apply the feedback they received, as well as their learning from their inquiry. They then evaluated the impact of the change in practice and identified whether and how they would embed it in their ongoing practice.

What was the impact of the changed actions on the desired student outcomes?

The year 6 triad focused on the use of success criteria. Together with their students, these teachers developed a color-coding strategy that students could use to indicate where they had been successful in their work in relation to the success criteria. The teachers found that this engaged the students in self-assessment, an activity that helped them understand where their starting point was, how well they were doing, and what they needed to do next. In particular, the lowest-ability students have grown significantly in confidence and can, for the first time, talk deeply about their learning. The two images below (Figure 8.3) provide an example of this strategy in use.

The value of an approach to professional learning that is guided by inquiry into the impact of teaching on student learning is that failures and setbacks are seen as an opportunity for learning rather than a source of embarrassment. The following story provides powerful evidence of students as visible learners who recognized that, in this instance, the source of the error was their teacher, and who were comfortable in providing her with valuable feedback that helped her to improve … an episode that then had a ripple effect around the school!

> We did some training on learning objectives and success criteria, but then further monitoring found that pupils were still not connecting with them. Jenni, our Visible Learning coordinator, then conducted a focus group in her class and asked her pupils about their learning objectives and success criteria. She was astonished by their feedback: she had thought they fully understood them but they told her they didn't and offered insights into how it could be improved. She adjusted her approach and really strengthened the work on this in her classroom.
>
> Jenni shared this with the whole staff, modeling how to use pupil voice effectively and how to be an effective evaluator. This gave staff the confidence to go and talk to their own pupils about their effectiveness.

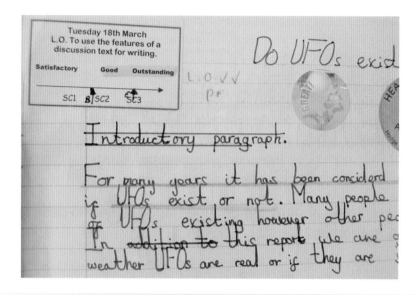

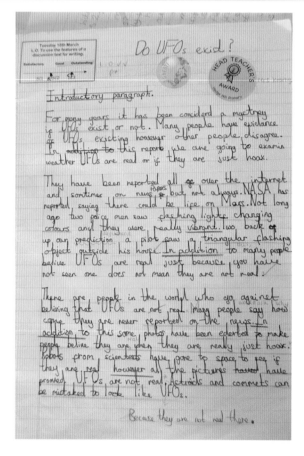

Figure 8.3 Student self-assessment at Hodge Hill Primary School

Laura actively promoted this approach, [while] reassuring teachers that they did not have to share the outcomes of their pupil focus groups with anyone. It was not a formal monitoring exercise; rather, it was a strategy teachers could implement to get information they could use to improve learning for their pupils. A number of teachers are now informally using this approach on a regular basis.

(Guiding coalition)

When the leaders repeated the monitoring exercise implemented at the start of the school's Visible Learning journey, this is what they heard:

year 3 student: "A good learner is when you can remember your work and use the learning journey to know where you're going."

year 4 student: "A good learner is when you can look back on your work and be reflective using the success criteria."

year 5 student: "A good learner is someone who collaborates and reflects on his work."

year 6 student: "A good learner works when you ask questions about your learning and you're assessment-capable and mark where you are on the learning journey."

Figure 8.4 shows the comparison in responses between the first video of students talking about what makes a good learner (made in May 2013) and the second video (made in June 2014).

The data from the videotaped interviews was correlated with further data from student focus groups and "learning walks" that involved the guiding coalition visiting all classrooms and interviewing students about their understandings of the learning. The data on each of these sources was collated and used to evaluate the impact of professional learning on teacher practice and student outcomes. This rich data is what supports the following explanation of the data in Figure 8.4.

Good work: The student thinks good learning is about doing good work and getting it right.

Previously, the students talked about a good learner doing "good work" but struggled to explain what this meant. In the most recent video discussions, no pupils referred to doing "good work." In the focus groups, students said they believe that the good learners are not the people who get the highest marks, but the people who make the most progress. They talked positively about the power of error, expressing the belief that their learning is more secure when they have made mistakes and learnt from them. A minority of older students say that they still don't like making mistakes but they're not afraid of them and understand their importance to learning.

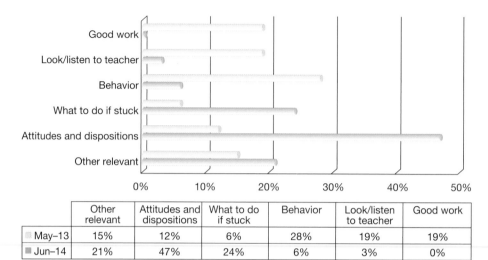

What makes a good learner?
Video comparison May 2013 and June 2014

	Other relevant	Attitudes and dispositions	What to do if stuck	Behavior	Look/listen to teacher	Good work
May–13	15%	12%	6%	28%	19%	19%
Jun–14	21%	47%	24%	6%	3%	0%

Figure 8.4 Students as visible learners, 2014

Look/listen to the teacher: The student thinks good learning is about listening to and looking at the teacher.

In May 2013, students thought that a good learner will sit up straight, looking at the teacher and listening to what they are saying. By June 2014, only three percent of pupils referred to good behavior as a characteristic of a good learner.

Behavior: The student thinks good learning is about good behavior.

In 2013, over a quarter of students associated good learning with good, well-mannered behavior. A year later, this had dropped to 6%.

What to do if stuck: The students do not know what strategies to use when they don't know what to do.

Previously, pupils relied heavily on the teacher to help if they were stuck and could discuss few other strategies. Now students talk about being resourceful, independent, and risk-takers, and of the importance of persevering when they don't know what to do. They refer to their peers as a source of learning and explain that they are not reliant on the teacher as they can use "working walls" and the learning objectives and success criteria.

Attitudes and dispositions: The student can explain the attitudes and dispositions of a good learner.

In June 2014, 47% of students were able to describe these characteristics, as opposed to 12% the previous year. Drawing from the school's learner profile, now called the Hodge Hill Learner Code, they talked to the leaders about being reflective, persevering, learning from your mistakes, being a collaborator, challenging themselves, being an investigator, and thinking through problems.

Othe relevant: The student can identify other practices of a good learner.

In 2014, students suggested that good learners also share their ideas, describe their work, read non-fiction to find out about real things, make decisions, listen to others, give good explanations, use resources, do homework, work as a team, use the knowledge in their brain, use the working walls, and talk to their partners.

Student progress and attainment now demonstrates a clear trend of improvement in all subjects, for all groups of students. More students have now made "better than expected" progress at the end of Key Stage 2 than in previous years, with greater numbers of students achieving at the higher levels at the end of the Early Years Foundation Stage and KS1. Much of this is attributed to the improved awareness, by teachers and pupils, of progression within the learning journey and the learning behaviors that drive this.

This is the "headline data" for the end of Key Stages 1 and 2 from 2013 to 2014:

End of Key Stage 1
- Reading at Level 2B+ has improved by 10%; at Level 3 by 20%.
- Writing at Level 2B+ has improved by 12%; at Level 3 by 8%.
- Maths at Level 2B+ has improved by 19%; at Level 3 by 12%.

End of Key Stage 2
- Reading at Level 4+ has improved by 12%; at Level 5 by 10%; 6% improvement in the numbers of those making expected progress.
- Writing at Level 4+ has improved by 7%; at Level 5 by 3%; 5% improvement in the numbers of those making expected progress. (The school didn't have as much work to do in writing as in other subjects.)
- Maths at Level 4+ has improved by 19%; no change at Level 5. 11% improvement in the numbers of those making expected progress.
- Reading, writing, and maths combined: Level 4+ improved by 13%.

Laura reports:

> The picture of improving achievement is reflected in our other year groups, also. We still have much work to do but we know that our students are now much better equipped to challenge themselves to reach the higher levels.

Laura offers the following advice to other schools:

> Visible Learning is not a fixed strategy that you take out of a box, pick up, and put down in your school. You need to use the framework to spend time reflecting upon what it means in your school ... and that may be different in every school.

> Establish your baseline by dedicating plenty of time to finding out what your pupils, staff, and parents think, know, and understand. This will be the start of your learning journey and the process of evaluation will help you to crystallize your aspirations.

> Give the whole staff a good understanding of why Visible Learning is the best approach for your school – share your evolving findings widely so that they understand the rationale.

> Capitalize on the other opportunities that arise as a result of the work that you do to make learning more visible, but stay true to your aspirations.

> Create a culture of openness, trust, and confidence amongst staff and pupils.

Continuing the cycle

At the time of writing, Hodge Hill Primary School was still in the early stages of its Visible Learning journey and has a lot to do before meeting its long-term targets. The whole-school data that the leaders collect and collate to understand the outcomes of the professional learning for staff and students is the basis for identifying specific next steps for a new cycle of learning. At the time of writing, these include:

- exploring each characteristic of the assessment-capable learner in greater depth so that there are shared understandings and each student is well supported in mastering these in order to become an effective learner;
- introducing a software system that allows teachers to video their own lessons so they can then review them on their own or with a colleague to help improve learning;
- further developing strategies to develop teachers as evaluators and change agents;

- embedding strategies for student self- and peer-assessment; and
- supporting teachers to be more consistent in their provision of self-regulation feedback.

Notes

1   Education in the UK and a number of other countries is organized into broad age bands, known as Key Stages. Key Stage 1 encompasses the first part of primary education (children aged from about 4–7 years) and Key Stage 2 encompasses the later stage (children aged from about 7–11 years).

2   Ofsted is the English Office for Standards in Education, Children's Services and Skills. They inspect and regulate services that care for children and young people, and services providing education and skills for learners of all ages.

9

Åsgård Skole

Norway

Well, I have checked the criteria. I start with a capital letter, I have neat handwriting, there's space between the words, and I have a punctuation mark at the end. I have met the criteria and if this is not correct, there's something wrong with the criteria!

Second grade student

In August 2013, the typical student at Åsgård Skole would not have been able to explain the purpose of their learning or how they were progressing. Less than a year later, this seven-year-old boy clearly understands what he is supposed to be showing in his writing and how he can use success criteria to tell whether he is on track. Importantly, he knows that sometimes criteria can be wrong. Nothing is sacrosanct and an effective learner is a learner who can challenge the "rules of the game."

Context

Åsgård Skole is a primary school serving 330 students aged from six to 12 years old. There are 40–50 students at each year level, and each level is taught by three teachers who work as a team. The school is set in the small municipality of Ås, which is outside Oslo, Norway. Ås is situated in a high socio-economic area, with one of the highest average levels of education in Norway.

The Norwegian University of Life Sciences (NMBU) is located in Ås and attracts students and teachers from all over the world. If professors or students at NMBU bring their children to Norway, Åsgård Skole is the school the children will attend. The municipality also has immigrants and refugees who work in various industries around the town and in Oslo, so the school has a mix of Norwegian students, immigrants, and students staying for just a few years. Typically, about 25–30% of the students come from another country and around

25–30 nationalities are represented. Most of those countries are within Europe, Asia, and Africa.

Schools in Norway do not have school boards like schools in the United States and other countries. Parent representatives participate in discussions about the students' working environment rather than their learning. On the other hand, the leader of the Skole Fritids Ordning (SFO) or after-school club[1] does take an important part in these discussions.

Overview

Åsgård Skole was regarded as a high-achieving school for many years, but when the school leaders began to dig deeper into their student achievement data, they found that they were not maximizing student growth. In late 2011, the leaders attended a conference where Deb Masters and James Nottingham presented the key ideas about Visible Learning. This inspired the leaders to learn more and the next year, they took the opportunity to attend a second Visible Learning conference where Professor John Hattie spoke. Following that conference, all schools in the municipality decided to embrace Visible Learning. In August 2013, all local teachers and leaders participated in a Visible Learning[plus] Foundation Day where they were introduced to the central precepts.

Åsgård's guiding coalition consisted of the head teacher, deputy head teacher, two team leaders, and the leader of the SFO (after-school club). This story of impact describes the first year of the school's Visible Learning journey. In that time, the guiding coalition focused on the use of learning intentions, success criteria, effective feedback, and effect sizes as a means to improve students' achievement outcomes and help them become assessment-capable learners.

Featured teachers and leaders

Laila Bakken is the head teacher and **Marianne Skogvoll** is the school's deputy head teacher. Both were members of the guiding coalition, a reflection of the importance they placed on the Visible Learning[plus] program.

Ingvild Johnsen and **Else-Marit Lillås** teach the seven-year-old students in year 2. They took an informal role in leading learning as they tried out the ideas with their second grade students and then talked with their colleagues about their experiences and the impact on their students.

Åsgård Skole's Visible Learning story

What were the desired student outcomes?

After making the decision to participate in the Visible Learning[plus] program, Åsgård Skole's leaders formed a guiding coalition that combined formal and teacher leadership. They had many issues they wanted to address. One of the areas of concern was the school's performance on the Norwegian national tests. The guiding coalition was puzzled that their students only achieved average scores. Given that most are from affluent backgrounds, they felt that the students should be achieving at a higher than average level. Additionally, there were big variations in the scores students achieved from one year to another. Why were students who did well one year not doing so well the next?

While the results from the national tests were shared with the whole staff at staff meetings, Åsgård Skole did not have a good system to ensure this process led to meaningful learning or change. Teachers were not taking the time to unpack the results to understand what they meant, to address questions about lower-than-expected or inconsistent achievement outcomes, or to use the results of such inquiry to establish common goals for student outcomes.

Another concern was about the lack of consistency in teacher practice. This concern arose from parent feedback. Parents said that when their children transitioned from one year to the next, they often found big differences in the nature and quality of the information they were given about student progress. Some teachers were very specific and used student data to map out the journey ahead, while others seemed quite vague and appeared to proceed on the assumption that all would be well in the end. Allied to this, there was no clear picture of expected progress. What one teacher saw as good work might be assessed very differently by another teacher. This lack of clarity was very confusing to both students and parents. When parents asked teachers to explain these inconsistencies, the teachers did not seem able to provide an answer.

The Visible Learning[plus] tools and a national survey provided a means to go deeper into the issues. Every year, students in Norwegian schools complete a national survey where they answer questions about their learning, their learning environment, friends, and other information regarding their educational pathways. An examination of the patterns in the data for Åsgård Skole revealed that students had consistently said they did not get much feedback from their teachers. This was puzzling, because teachers believed they gave feedback "all the time" and because feedback, including student peer- and self-assessment, had been a school-wide focus for several years. When the guiding coalition started talking to students and seeing the world through their eyes, they realized that students:

- thought of feedback only as written comments in their books;
- thought effective feedback was something the teacher could give them, and only the teacher; and
- understood praise to be an effective form of feedback.

Observations revealed that students only provided feedback to each other in the form of praise, such as "good" and "well done." While the teachers had discussed what Effective Feedback should look like with each other, it was apparent that these understandings had not been shared with the students or modeled in their practice.

When the guiding coalition assembled a student focus group to ask about their understandings of teaching and learning, it became clear that students had no shared language of learning or of the characteristics of a successful learner. When asked, "What is a good learner?" students typically answered, "Someone who does as he's told and listens to the teacher." Students explained that they often misunderstood what their teachers wanted from them and that often the reason for this was that their teacher hadn't explained the learning intentions. When asked, "How do you know what you are learning?" they typically said, "Sometimes the teacher writes the learning intentions on the blackboard." When prodded a bit more, the students answered that "They [the teacher] did it more in the start of the school year." One student even said, "Sometimes it looks like the teacher doesn't really know either!" This was another puzzle because ostensibly, learning intentions had also been a feature of Åsgård Skole's pedagogy for the previous three years.

The process of calculating effect sizes affirmed the guiding coalition's concern that students were not progressing as well as they should be. School leaders and staff were especially struck by the discovery that students who were considered bright and clever typically had a lower rate of progress than the rest.

Åsgård Skole's guiding coalition concluded that they wanted students to become assessment-capable.

> We wanted all our students to aspire to assess their own learning and have the knowledge, skills, attitudes, and language they needed to do this. We knew that one way for students to become assessment-capable was to make sure teachers were using clear learning intentions and success criteria. It was time we made learning visible for our students.
>
> (Åsgård Skole guiding coalition)

What knowledge and skills did the teachers and school leaders need to support these outcomes?

Åsgård Skole's leaders left the Visible Learning Conference with ideas of what they wanted to change, but it wasn't until they began meeting as a team with the staff and collecting evidence from students and parents that they recognized how many areas they wanted to change and the implications for professional learning. The challenge was daunting, but the team was determined to make the changes necessary to achieve better outcomes for their students and the wider school community.

The student interviews and focus groups had revealed significant gaps between students' perceptions and those of their teachers. Teachers were making assumptions about students' understanding of the learning and feedback that were not borne out in the evidence. They needed to:

- make sure they were clear about the learning intentions and success criteria so that students could understand the learning purpose and participate more actively;
- align their lesson planning with those learning intentions;
- provide feedback at the three levels of task, process, and self-regulation;
- listen to student voice and encourage classroom dialogue;
- release control of learning and accept the need for change; and
- understand their impact on the student outcomes.

Else Marit, a member of the guiding coalition, says that a critical part of the learning was about how to better track student progress, to know where they were at and for her to know what to do next:

> I need to *know* where the students are in their learning, so that I can plan the next steps. They can't afford to rely only on my gut feeling.

Where assessment capability was the priority for students, for teachers it was the Visible Learning strand of Inspired and Passionate Teachers. But how was the school going to achieve these goals? The leaders knew they had to refine the school's priorities further if they were to avoid initiative fatigue. They decided upon the following:

Know thy impact: Teachers did not always understand their impact on student learning. Although some students were high-achieving, many were not showing a year's worth of growth or more in a year's time. This was directly related to the instructional strategies being used in the classroom. Teachers needed to know thy impact.

Effective feedback: Teachers and students had the mistaken belief that praise was effective feedback. After a great deal of professional dialogue, the guiding coalition knew that teachers needed to learn how to provide feedback that was oriented to the task and to the process, as well as feedback that would promote self-regulation.

Instructional strategies: Classroom environments were characterized by a great deal of monologue and very little dialogue. This diminished student engagement and achievement. Teachers needed to explore John Hattie's research about the instructional strategies that have a positive effect on student learning and seek to implement them in their classrooms.

Learning intentions and success criteria: Learning intentions and success criteria had been part of pedagogy at Åsgård Skole for several years and were used by almost all of the teachers, but the leaders realized that they were not being used well. They were written into the students' weekly plans, but teachers were not using them as a tool to engage the students in their learning. Teachers needed to know how to use these strategies effectively and consistently and to ensure students understood what they were. They also needed to communicate them to parents, addressing parental concern about the lack of clarity regarding student learning goals. The leaders also identified a gap resulting in learning intentions, and thus planning, tending to focus on the acquisition of knowledge rather than on the broader competencies young people need to function successfully within a rapidly changing global environment.

Evidence collection: Teachers needed to understand what evidence they should collect (for example, samples of student work and pre-tests and post-tests) to show where students were in the learning process and where they needed to go next.

Reading: Not all students were making appropriate progress in the area of reading. The guiding coalition purchased a tool for tracking reading progress. The teachers needed to learn to implement the tool and use it to consider next steps for learning.

What new actions did the teachers and school leaders try?

The guiding coalition developed a strategic plan for implementation over the next two years, shown in Figure 9.1. It sets out learning intentions and success criteria for each of the elements of Visible Learning that the leaders wanted teachers to adopt.

The strategic plan incorporated multiple opportunities for teachers to learn about the research and theories that sat behind the new strategies they were learning about. All staff took part in weekly meetings where they worked on their focus areas and shared stories of success from their classrooms. Every second week, teachers worked on creating learning

Topic: Good academic development for all learners				
Aspirations – vision	**Targets 2013**	**Actions**	**Timing and responsibilities**	**Monitoring**
Teaching at the school is targeted, a range of different methods is used, and it is adapted to the learner's individual needs. The learners take ownership of their own learning; they know what the goal is and how to get there. They can assess their own and others' work in a good way.	All instruction in Norwegian, mathematics, and English has learning intentions and success criteria so that all learners know where they are going and how to get there.	Learning intentions and success criteria are in use in all lessons, starting February 2013. (Part of long-term plan)	Staff meetings to build knowledge, share ideas, and learn from each other. On the agenda every second week. Leadership team makes a schedule for all staff meetings.	Student survey on learning in May (grades 5–7) Mapping test in reading in September and April (all year levels) National tests (grade 5) Learner–teacher conversations (teachers have one hour per week) Walkthroughs
	Assessment: the learners can assess their own work in a good way.	All learning and teaching has learning intentions and success criteria so that learners can assess themselves. All year levels try out different ways of self-assessing, starting February 2013.	Staff meetings to build knowledge, share ideas, and learn from each other. On the agenda every second week. Also on the agenda of team meetings.	
Students receive academic challenges that stimulate their desire to learn, persistence, and curiosity. They have capacity for creative and critical thinking; they work well together and have good basic skills. Teaching at the school is targeted, a range of different methods is used, and it is adapted to the learner's individual needs. It arouses engagement. We inspire the learners!	The school has a joint plan for progress in reading and writing. All year levels use the plan. Put into use in August 2013.	A work group starts in February 2013. The reading supervisors are central to this work. Review with all staff in August. Reading supervisors help each year level implement the plan.	Work group has the plan finished, June 2013. Leadership follow up their work. Staff meeting, August	Student survey on learning in May (grades 5–7) Mapping test in reading in September and April (all year levels) National tests (grade 5) Learner–teacher conversations (teachers have one hour per week) Walkthroughs
	The school has a joint plan for mapping and monitoring reading and writing. Put into use, August 2013.	Revise the current plan – completed in June. Review with all staff	Reading supervisors and leadership. Staff meeting, August	
	Teaching at the school is targeted; a range of different methods is used.	Sharing is on the agenda of every staff meeting (15 minutes per week). Staff share from their own teaching practice.	Leadership makes a schedule for all meetings, and staff put themselves on the list.	

Figure 9.1 Strategic plan

intentions and setting success criteria that were aligned to those intentions. During these meetings, they often worked in pairs or in groups so they could draw from each other's expertise. An early discovery was that often, what they had called "learning intentions" were actually success criteria.

The work involved review of the curriculum being offered in classrooms. The question was not only the clarity of the learning intentions, but also their quality. Deputy head teacher Marianne Skogvoll says:

> We wanted to design learning around meaningful learning intentions that incorporate attitudes and skills, as well as knowledge. This is so important in the modern world. Most of the time, we plan to grow students' knowledge and quite often, we support them to develop certain skills, but our full mandate is to teach attitudes and values, as well. Our teachers worked in pairs or small groups designing lessons in which we were very intentional about learning in terms of skills, attitudes, and values, as well as about the knowledge that was to be transmitted. This work was also intended to support teachers to provide effective feedback that was consciously directed at scaffolding students in their performance of the task or process or their ability to self-regulate.

The guiding coalition used the teachers' ideas about the skills and attitudes students need to create a learning wall.

> The learning wall sets out the different ways of thinking and includes the skills the students need. The learning wall hangs on the wall as a visual reminder that there are different skills students need to learn. The teachers and learners choose one or more of the skills to focus on. For example, if they were practising the skill "comparing and contrasting," the teachers would take "comparing and contrasting" down from the learning wall and explain what it means.

> (Laila Bakken)

Marianne Skogvoll made a learning wall for each classroom, and Else-Marit Lillås and Ingvild Johnsen, both of whom work with year 2 students, used it when they worked with their class. They found that by purposely displaying the skill on the learning wall and then taking it down to talk to during their conversations with students, they could better clarify the purpose of the learning. The learning wall also helped foster the development of a common language of learning, amongst staff as well as students. When they first looked at the learning wall, the teachers realized that they differed in their understandings of the words. Over several whole staff meetings they worked together to find out what each word meant to them as a collective.

The teachers also developed the metaphor of the "learning road" (Figure 9.2), using it to help students visualize their learning as a journey.

Figure 9.2 Else-Marit Lillås and Ingvild Johnsen next to the learning road

> The road is where you place the learning intention at the end, as the destination. The criteria are placed along the way. Each criterion is like a roadblock the learners have to pass, so in some learning walls there are pictures of traffic lights and other "blockers" along the way, and the criteria are placed along these.
>
> (Laila Bakken)

Reading was a particular focus and the guiding coalition wanted to use a new reading tool[2] that would show the progress students were making over time. The school decided to start by piloting the reading progress tool at just one grade level. Else-Marit Lillås and Ingvild Johnsen were first to try the tool with their second grade students in 2013. They then shared their experiences and trained other staff members so they would know how to use it when it was implemented across the school in May 2014. Else-Marit Lillås also taught other staff members how to calculate effect sizes on the newly adopted screening tests. These tests are to be conducted twice a year.

What was the impact of the changed actions on the desired student outcomes?

Although they gave themselves a period of two years to complete the turnaround, the school saw major changes within the first year. The focus on learning intentions and success criteria soon bore fruit, as the leaders observed evidence of students being able to articulate their learning process to their teachers. Classrooms are becoming communities of learners where students are able to clearly articulate the learning intentions and success criteria and identify "where to next." Marianne Skogvoll says, "Students were able to talk about learning, not just about what they were doing, and this change came very quickly."

Classroom observations revealed that teachers were able to differentiate between task- and process-oriented feedback and that they were using exemplars to explain these differences to their students. This lifted the quality of the feedback students were giving to each other and themselves. Teachers noticed that students were providing each other with less praise while actually helping their peers understand where to go next.

Marianne Skogvoll recalls:

> The second graders were learning to write full sentences, and the teachers had made criteria and put them up on the learning road. One little boy came to Ingvild [the teacher] and said he had finished the task, he had checked the criteria, and it was all good. Ingvild read his sentences and saw they were all just nonsense. She asked the boy to go check the criteria again. So he did. He came back and said, "Well, I have checked the criteria. I start with a capital letter, I have neat handwriting, there's space between the words, and I have a punctuation mark at the end. I have met the criteria and if this is not correct there's something wrong with the criteria!" Ingvild realized he was right – they had forgotten that a sentence must make sense! She gathered her class, told them what had happened, and they started making criteria together. This was a real eye-opener for the teacher and she said, "This is seeing the learning through the eyes of the students. I didn't realize!"

This is an example of a student developing assessment capability. It is also an example of a teacher who loves the challenges you get being a teacher, and also being a learner herself. In Ingvilds's words, "Learning new things and getting my beliefs challenged is what really motivates me."

At the time of writing, it was too early to see any change on the national tests because the students had not yet done them. However, Marianne says the data being generated through using the Visible Learning^plus tools (Figure 9.3) on their reading data provides ongoing evidence of progress:

> The test scores were first calculated into effect sizes and then Excel made this lovely diagram! You could also see the progress for each student without calculating the effect sizes but when you do, it becomes much clearer who has made the most progress and who has not. We tend to forget that those who are already doing quite well also need to be challenged. The use of effect sizes makes the progress quite clear, and then the teacher needs to dig into the results. It's also a nice model because it makes our focus visible. We often focus on the two upper parts of the quadrant, thinking that's where we want our students to be, when in fact it's the right part of the quadrant we need to aim for.

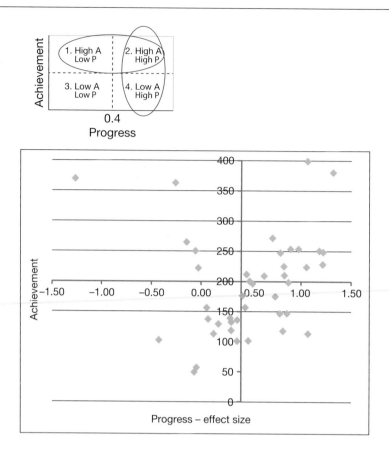

Figure 9.3 Progress and achievement data, year 5 reading

In addition to students and teachers, parents began to understand learning intentions and success criteria and could contribute to the discussion with their children. During parent conferences, some parents with multiple children in the school remarked that they could now see that different teachers were using the same language and that this consistency was a marked change from the past.

Marianne and Laila believe that a critical reason for the speed of the improvement is the time and support that staff have been given to understand and to adapt to the changes the school has sought to make. That time means that teachers don't just learn isolated strategies for application in particular circumstances, but the deeper theories that mean they know when to use those strategies, how, and why.

The time for the teachers to work together trying out the theories and examples provided at the staff meeting was so beneficial for everyone involved. Time is something that teachers feel they do not always have, so to provide time to work on the new actions to support student outcomes was highly important, and something teachers appreciated. It helped insecure teachers get started and turned some other teachers into teacher leaders, because they had more knowledge in the newly adopted areas.

(Laila Bakken)

Teachers need time to work together when you want to change practice. It means leaders have to focus on what they want to achieve, and they might need to put other things aside. It's also important to give good reasons for the change (theory and research). The leaders need to know their stuff to be able to lead the process. And always think about the mindframes (both for teachers and leaders). They are very powerful.

(Marianne Skogvoll)

Continuing the cycle

While Åsgård Skole has many inspired and passionate teachers on its staff, some are yet to make the change. The school is confident that the excitement that is being generated will ensure that this happens:

First of all, we need to get all teachers to be as inspired and passionate as the profiled teachers. That means continuing to focus on learning intentions and success criteria. We need to continue to share good practices with one another. It's not embedded in the whole school yet, but much has been achieved in just eight months. … It's quite impressive to see how quickly things can change when you do the right things!

(Guiding coalition)

The school's leaders intend to continue to use staff meetings to work together on the specific focus areas, exploring the evidence from research and its transfer to practice, keeping the focus on learning. A next step will be to show exemplars from different classrooms. The school also intends to connect the work on learning intentions, success criteria, and feedback to other strategies used within the Visible Learning[plus] program, such as peer observation and micro teaching.

Notes

1 A high proportion of Norwegian students attend these clubs, where they can play, do homework, or join in with other activities such as a choir, chess, football, or drama group.
2 This was a tool that the school purchased. It incorporates two tools: one for the teacher to use and one for the student.

Part III
Appendix 1
Active reading guide

Having read Part III, you may like to use the following template to record what you noticed about the Visible Learning characteristics displayed by students at Stonefields School, Gustav Vasaskolan, Hodge Hill Primary School, and Åsgård Skole. You can also record your thoughts about what the teachers and school leaders did to prompt these behaviors.

A Visible Learner is a student who…*	Examples observed in the learning story	Inferences about how this was achieved
can be their own teacher		
can articulate what they are learning and why		
can talk about how they are learning – the strategies they are using to learn		
can articulate their next learning steps		
can use self-regulation strategies		
is assessment-capable (understands the assessment tools being used and what their results mean) and can self-assess		
seeks, is resilient to, and aspires to challenge		
can set mastery goals		
asks questions		
sees errors as opportunities and is comfortable saying that they don't know and/or need help		
positively supports their peers' learning		
knows what to do when they don't know what to do		
actively seeks feedback		
has metacognitive skills and can talk about these (systematic planning, memory, abstract thinking, critical thinking, problem solving, etc.)		

Note
* This list is from *Visible Learning*^plus: *Evidence into Action: Workbook One*, page 13.

Part III
Appendix 2

Theory to practice

In these chapters, you have learnt about what Visible Learning looks like for the students, and you've learnt something about the process taken to achieve it. The point is not so much about the specific strategies or practices, but about the multiple ways in which learning is made visible for and by the whole school community. You could use this template to note some ideas you would like to try and to record and reflect upon what happened. Ideally, you will use this in collaboration with colleagues with whom you can share your learning, making it visible.

A Visible Learner is a student who…	Practices or strategies you intend to try	What actually happened? What was the impact of the change? Why do you think this was?
can be their own teacher		
can articulate what they are learning and why		
can talk about how they are learning – the strategies they are using to learn		
can articulate their next learning steps		
can use self-regulation strategies		
is assessment-capable (understands the assessment tools being used and what their results mean and can self-assess)		
seeks, is resilient to, and aspires to challenge		
can set mastery goals		
asks questions		
sees errors as opportunities and is comfortable saying that they don't know and/or need help		
positively supports their peers' learning		
knows what to do when they don't know what to do		
actively seeks feedback		
has metacognitive skills and can talk about these (systematic planning, memory, abstract thinking, critical thinking, problem solving, etc.)		

Inspired and Passionate Teachers

10

Clevedon School

New Zealand

Just a few short years ago, Clevedon School was in crisis, with an external review revealing significant concerns about the quality of teaching, school leadership, and school–community relationships. Today the school is firmly embarked on its Visible Learning journey. Both teachers and leaders strive to achieve excellence in their daily work. They have constructive learning relationships, plan collaboratively, and use well-designed systems and processes to track the effectiveness of their teaching.

> At our team meetings, our team leader encourages us to discuss what has been working well in each of our classes. We share assessment results and lessons that have been effective. I enjoy sharing any strategies that have helped my students to become visible learners, such as using exemplars and rubrics or how I am sharing assessment data with students and how they are setting goals from this. I feel comfortable sharing this with my team, as I know that they all see themselves as learners and it's going to help all of our students to become more successful learners.
>
> *Rachael Baker, teacher*

This story describes how a school emerged from a time of trouble to recreate itself as a learning community that shares a passion for ensuring success for all.

Context

Clevedon School is situated in a semi-rural area 40 minutes' drive south east of Auckland city. It is a "full" primary school, meaning that its 380 students span years 1–8. The majority are Pākehā (Caucasian New Zealanders), 15% are Māori (Indigenous New Zealanders), and just 2% are Pasifika. Most are from fairly affluent backgrounds. Students are organized into classes of 25–30, some combining year levels. There are three e-learning classes, to which students bring their own iPads.

Principal Julie Schumacher shares leadership duties with her deputy, Edeh Nobari, and four team leaders who work with teams of teachers working with students spanning particular year levels.

Overview

In 2010, an evaluation by New Zealand's Education Review Office (ERO) validated the complaints parents had been making to the Ministry of Education about the quality of the education their children were receiving at Clevedon School. Consequently, the Ministry appointed a limited statutory manager[1] to work with the schools' leaders to address the concerns that had been identified. These included the quality of teaching, the failure to gather assessment information and use it to improve learning, the failure to develop or implement a process of self-review and improvement, and the loss of community confidence. The issues were manifest in a falling school roll and a staff turnover rate of 90% over three years.

The school made progress, resulting in the withdrawal of the statutory manager by March 2011. At the beginning of that year, Julie Schumacher was appointed principal, bringing with her a wealth of expertise in professional development. She was a Visible Learning[plus] consultant for several years, running workshops and making presentations in New Zealand, Australia, and throughout Asia. In 2012, Edeh Nobari became deputy principal, bringing with her international experience in educational consultancy. Working with the team leaders, Edeh and Julie sought to reignite the passion of their staff, reminding them of their moral purpose as educators and creating the learning-focused context they needed to achieve that purpose. This story provides an insight into the school's journey, finishing with the impact it had on the professional growth of novice teacher Rachael Baker.

Featured teacher

After travelling and working in the advertising industry at home and abroad, **Rachael Baker** returned to New Zealand and entered teacher training. Her first appointment was in 2011, at Clevedon School. As a new and enthusiastic teacher, Rachael was wide open to new learning and challenge. Julie values the fact that Rachael always demands the very best of herself: "She wants to know that she is making a difference and she wants the tools, systems, and processes that will allow her to do this." Rachael helped set up and teach in one of Clevedon School's first e-learning classes and is also the school's e-learning leader.

Clevedon School's Visible Learning story

What were the desired outcomes?

Clevedon's school community had high expectations of student achievement back in 2010–2011, but the indications were that these expectations were not being met. We can only provide indications of the picture at that time rather than concrete baseline data because the school did not have processes in place that would allow quantitative data to be systematically gathered, shared, analyzed, and tracked. None of the data was electronic and there was no writing data. Furthermore, most teachers and leaders did not understand the value of qualitative data, especially the rich information to be gained from attending to student voice. The poor quality of the data and its organization meant the school could not establish and monitor progress towards meaningful student outcomes. These issues were highlighted in the evaluation report by New Zealand's Education Review Office, which also highlighted the lack of trust across the school community.

As a newly appointed principal, Julie Schumacher launched a full review that would enable the school to prioritize the areas for improvement. Talking to students and observing classroom interactions, it was clear that students lacked the dispositions of effective learners. They didn't know what a good learner was or how to become a good learner themselves. They were not able to discuss their learning, where they were at, or what their "next steps" were. On this basis, Julie and her staff agreed to prioritize the following student outcome:

> That students are assessment-capable and understand and can articulate:
> Where am I going? What are my goals?
> How am I going? What progress is being made towards the goal?
> Where to next? What activities need to be undertaken next to enable better progress?

What knowledge and skills did the teachers and school leaders need to support these outcomes?

Working collaboratively, first in their teams and then all together, the staff created a document outlining what an assessment-capable learner at Clevedon School looks like. By describing this in terms of different levels, they gave specificity to the outcomes they were seeking. However, the lack of baseline data meant that teachers and leaders did not have the information they needed to understand their impact on student outcomes and use that insight to improve teaching and learning. This practical barrier was accompanied by an attitudinal one. Teachers were unused to receiving feedback on their teaching and, given the lack of trust that the Education Review Office[2] had observed, they were not open to learning from it. These issues, alongside the unsettled nature of the school that had included several leadership changes, meant they had lost their sense of direction.

> We needed to develop the inspiration and passion across the school. We knew we had to focus on the mindframes of teachers. They needed to believe in themselves as change agents.
>
> (Julie Schumacher)

Because of the school's situation, it had to use the Education Review Office's tools to conduct its self-review. Through that process the school decided upon the following valued outcomes for teachers:

To have teachers who:

- are passionate and inspirational, believing in their ability to make a difference for students;
- provide a consistently high quality of teaching that gives students ownership of their learning and incorporates effective feedback;
- implement "teaching as inquiry"[3] as everyday practice and know the impact they are having on student progress and achievement;
- use assessment and effect sizes to inform teaching and learning;
- are skilled in gathering, analyzing, and sharing data, including feedback from students;
- track student progress against agreed learning progressions;
- are collaborative and supportive, working together to maximize their impact on student learning; and
- have a culture of reciprocal feedback that supports whole-school improvement.

Due to the loss of relational trust across the entire school community the next valued outcome was: "to lift the community's confidence in the school." This loss of relational trust extended across the parent community. In New Zealand, school governance is in the hands of an elected Board of Trustees made up primarily of parents, alongside the principal and a staff representative. While Julie, as principal, took primary responsibility for building relational trust amongst staff and students, it was the Board of Trustees who took primary responsibility for the outcome of lifting the community's confidence in the school.

Achieving these valued outcomes required whole-school change for improvement. This is evident in the valued outcomes the school established for its whole community:

To have a school:

- that has strong systems and processes across the school to enable the above [outcomes for students, teachers, and community] to take place; and
- has a recruitment process focused on "passion," enthusiasm, and a willingness to learn.

The evidence is clear that effective school leadership is critical to improvement, and so Clevedon School's final valued outcome was "to have school leaders who know that their primary role is to lead learning and help other teachers to grow." Edeh Nobari explains:

> This means leaders who are able to use and analyze data to measure impact and ascertain areas of need, who can support teachers in their learning and development, and who can lead teams to set goals and raise student achievement and progress.

What new actions did the teachers and school leaders try?

Given her familiarity with the concept of Visible Learning from her work alongside John Hattie, Julie knew what the research said about how to improve teaching and learning. However, her first task in 2011 was to work on establishing relational trust, a process that took place alongside the whole-school review. In the following years, the school took a phased approach, as follows:

- Year 2: professional learning for teachers to enhance teacher practice;
- Year 3: know thy impact (measuring effect sizes, understanding progress, analyzing data, and so on); and
- Year 4: using student voice and embedding and reinforcing all learning.

Some of the new actions that the school has taken as it has moved through these phases are described below. The purpose is not to give the full picture, but to provide a window into four years of complex redevelopment.

Building leadership capacity

Julie recruited the entire leadership team into the leadership of Visible Learning, a decision that meant she could model to them the leadership practices she wanted them to put into place with their teams. She was careful to model the concept that effective leaders of learning are learners themselves, who are open to the challenging feedback that facilitates growth. For example, she reformatted meeting agendas to focus on learning and prompted open discussion around problems and issues by using questions and prompts such as, "I wonder …," "I have noticed …," "What do you think …?" "What evidence do we have …?"

Julie also needed to help grow the professional knowledge the team leaders needed to be leaders of learning. She selected professional readings on effective school leadership that the team read and discussed, considering how they could implement the research findings with their teams and across the school. The Ministry of Education's recently published synthesis of the evidence on school leadership and student outcomes (Robinson et al., 2009) was a key and trustworthy source.

The need to appoint a new deputy principal provided Julie and her Board of Trustees with the opportunity to seek out Edeh Nobari, whose expertise was consistent with the school's Visible Learning vision. Julie and the board agreed that Edeh's primary focus would be on teaching and learning through the provision of one-on-one coaching and mentoring for team leaders, and targeted professional development for individual teachers.

Establishing relational trust

The process of building trust and improving communication required Julie to be open herself. She made it a policy that all classroom doors and her own office door would be kept open to colleagues and parents alike. She seeks to communicate and consult with all stakeholders, for example, through regular parent consultation meetings and newsletters. Staff meetings, be they at the team or whole-school level, include regularly scheduled time to share practice and data, review impact, and provide each other with feedback. Staff interactions are guided by protocols that keep the focus on respectful collaborative learning.

Relationships between students and between teachers and students are addressed, in part, through participation in New Zealand's Positive Behavior for Learning initiative, a school-wide program that Clevedon School uses to make expected behaviors visible.

Staff are expected to build genuine learning relationships with parents as well as students through a variety of media, including homework books, email, and three-way conferences where parents, teachers, and students set and monitor progress towards the students' learning goals.

The Board of Trustees supports this work wherever it can. For example, the board uses its monthly reports to parents as an opportunity to celebrate the achievements of staff and students.

Transparency is critical to building relational trust. Julie says, "We make a point of always sharing the background to what we are doing – where we're at, why we're doing it this way, and where to next."

Creating a shared vision

The process of revisiting the school's vision and values was valuable in itself as a means of building relationships between teachers, leaders, and the wider school community, as it provided a meaningful context for people to get to know each other and share beliefs and aspirations. At the same time, it was an essential component of the leadership team's strategy for re-energizing teachers and giving them a sense of purpose. The PRIDE values (Figure 10.1) are constantly reinforced in all communications. They are acknowledged in the PRIDE awards given to students at school assemblies and featured prominently in the school newsletter.[4]

The core values for staff are linked to the PRIDE values. They are reviewed and modified every year through a consultation process that includes all staff.

Staff professional learning

A culture of professional learning is nurtured through both internal and external professional development, including facilitation from the school's Visible Learning[plus] consultant, Kate Birch. Much of that learning has centered on John Hattie's Visible Learning research, but John's research is the condensation of messages from researchers worldwide and the school is very open to exploring this and going deeper. Teachers at all levels of the school are expected to engage with professional literature so that any decisions or discussions around practice are driven by research into what works.

Much of the learning takes place in the year-level teams where teachers carry out joint inquiry into how the research applies to their practice. In one example,

Our Vision
To develop Clevedon Students who are life-long learners with the knowledge, skills, attitudes and values to meet the challenges of their future.

Our Mission
Clevedon kids living and learning with PRIDE (Passion, Respect, Integrity, Diversity, Empathy)

Passion   Respect   Integrity   Diversity   Empathy

Passion/Kai-Ngākau	Respect/Whakaute	Integrity/Pono	Diversity/ Mannakitanga	Empathy/Aroha
We strive for personal excellence.	We care for ourselves, others and the environment.	We are truthful, sincere and trustworthy.	We welcome, include and celebrate.	We are kind, considerate and helpful.
Whāla ai e tātou te iti kahuangi.	Manaaki ai tātou i a tātou anō me te taiao.	He tngata pono, he tangata tika, he tangata aroha tatou.	Ka whakatau, ka whakakotahi, ka whakanui tātou.	He iwi manawa popore, he iwi awhina, he iwi manaaki tangata tātou.

Figure 10.1 Vision, mission, and values

teachers experimented with pulling out a small group of students who were not achieving their expected level in writing. While only one teacher worked directly with the students, the whole team was involved in planning the teaching strategies and monitoring their impact. This was extraordinary. Monitoring with e-asTTle indicated effect sizes achieved for individual students of 0.05, 0.71, 0.96, 1.10, 1.18, and 1.41. The teachers shared what they had learnt with the whole staff, building the school's collective knowledge about effective literacy practice and teaching as inquiry.

Observations and walkthroughs provide teachers with regular feedback on how well they are transferring the research to their practice and their next steps for learning. Professional learning is now integrated with appraisal, with teachers expected to provide evidence of their progress towards set goals and to reflect regularly on new learning. While these goals are tailored to each teacher, they have three main foci:

- raising student achievement and improving progress;
- developing assessment-capable learners; and
- using student voice to inform programs.

Establishing systems, processes, and school-wide expectations

A significant focus of the intervention was for the school to establish shared understandings about the expected progressions of learning and to establish a systematic approach to the collection, recording, and reporting of data.

Given the school's lack of information about student achievement in writing, considerable early attention was placed on establishing Clevedon School's expectations for progress in writing from children who had been at school for a certain number of weeks (10, 20, 30, and 40 weeks) and then yearly through to the end of year 8. This collaborative and literature-driven activity culminated in the school developing a set of writing progressions documents, along with rubrics and exemplars in "student-speak." Figure 10.2 is a photograph of a wall of exemplars that the school used to set up its writing expectations.

To make all this work, teachers needed support to understand assessment tools such as e-asTTle, to engage in learning conversations around the data, and to calculate effect sizes for their classes – and to use these to evaluate their impact on student learning. The new tools and processes were not just for the use of adults, but also for students. This is why the staff developed the "student-speak rubrics," basing them on the e-asTTle writing rubric.

The school has been keen to adopt technology as a tool for learning, finding Google documents a valuable means of collecting, sharing, and tracking a range of information, including achievement data and student feedback.

Figure 10.2 Developing writing progressions

What was the impact of the changed actions on the desired student outcomes?

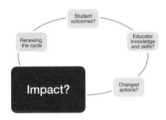

The impact at the whole-school level

In terms of the impact on student outcomes, the overall picture is positive. Visitors to the school are in no doubt that students are assessment-capable visible learners, and the data on academic achievement shows that progress is usually made at a greater than expected progress. The data does throw up puzzles, though. For example, in 2013, the e-asTTle writing data indicated an effect size for students in year 3 of only 0.26 but the STAR[5] (NZCER, 2001) reading data had an effect size of 0.78. Julie Schumacher reflects:

> Some year groups are making greater than average progress and some are not. The data is the catalyst for the conversations, for teachers to embrace the mindframes of being an evaluator, of seeing assessment as feedback to themselves about their impact, as change agents …. The journey has begun and it's what we do about the data that will make the difference.

The focus of this story is on inspired and passionate teachers and here we will focus on one: Rachael Baker. In the rest of this section, we will learn from Rachael about some of the ways this whole-school improvement journey has impacted on her and her students.

Rachael took up her appointment at Clevedon School in 2011, the same year Julie began as principal. Given conditions at the school at the time, there was a risk that this enthusiastic young teacher could have become swiftly disillusioned and burnt out. Instead, she is still there and still excited about going to work each day.

Figure 10.3 Rachael Baker and students

In this section, Rachael shares her reflections to describe how she exhibited the characteristics of an inspired and passionate teacher throughout the school's implementation of Visible Learning.

Participating in professional learning

> Regular professional development opportunities helped me to reflect on my practice and inform its development. Going to different courses and doing different professional readings really helped to shape my philosophy and pedagogy. When I went to John Hattie's Festival of Education[6] session about Inspired and Passionate Teachers, he talked about knowing your impact, using assessment data to inform planning, collecting student voice to help gauge the impact of your teaching, and collaborating with other teachers. Suddenly the learning we had been doing about all of these things started to make sense and come together in my head.

Building relational trust: knowing where to go when the going gets tough

> I enjoy sharing resources and strategies that have worked in my teaching with other teachers. At our team meetings, all syndicates have time set aside for sharing and I have also been asked to discuss my planning at staff meetings. An open-door policy and a willingness by all to help me meant that I could ask questions of anyone. For example, Julie was happy to come and help me explain how to read e-asTTle pathways. I can also speak to other teachers who might have recently taught a similar concept and ask them what worked and borrow resources. The teachers in our school are all really happy sharing; this collaborative way of working makes us all more efficient.

Observing the practice of other teachers and having regular observations of my own teaching helped me to reflect on what was working and what I could improve on. Knowing that the feedback I received was based on a school-wide goal helped me to take it on board without feeling it was a criticism of my personal practice.

There have been hard times. During my third year, I had learnt a lot and was eagerly putting it all into practice. I had also taken on many extra roles within the school, helping out on various teams. However, this meant that I lost focus on what was most important. I no longer had a good handle on where my students were at. Having a meeting with our deputy principal brought things back into perspective. We went over all of my data and grouped students based on their biggest gaps. We wrote detailed group plans that really broke down what I was going to teach that group of students and how I was going to track their progress and the effectiveness of my teaching. These group plans took me a long time to write this first time, but now that I am evaluating my impact on a regular basis through formative assessment and collecting student voice, it is easier for me to plan according to needs.

Learning about and implementing systems, processes, and expectations

During years 1 and 2, we thoroughly went over all assessment tools, like e-asTTle, and discussed as a staff how to administer the assessment, how to analyze results, and how to use this data to inform our planning and teaching.

In year 1, we discussed the Visible Learning research and effect sizes and I have now learnt how to work out my own effect sizes. Seeing this data is incredibly motivating and helps me to reflect on my practice. From my data last year, I was able to identify a group of students who were high achievers but making low progress. This year I have set targets for these students, planned the interventions I will implement, and I am tracking their progress to ensure that they become high achievers making high progress.

To help my students understand where they are going and how they are going, I have set up documents for them with the expected level of achievement against each assessment tool for each term. Students then input their assessment data so they can see whether they are meeting expected levels and understand their "where to next."

I keep a thorough record of all assessment results and use our learning management system to help me track how my students are going. I analyze this data and use it to inform my next lot of long-term and group plans. As part of my analysis, I also ask my students to identify what they need to work on and anything they are particularly interested in improving.

We have school-wide systems for planning and as I have become used to these, it is taking less time to complete them. We have all been encouraged to share our planning on Google Docs. This allows me to collaborate with other teachers and use their ideas to help my students.

When I reflect about what has changed for me as a teacher, I think a key thing is that I have become more efficient in what I do. I have systems in place to make the collection and analysis of data quicker. My systems for tracking students mean that I have a really good handle on where my students are at and what their "next steps" are. Writing reports is so much easier now with all my systems in place, including anecdotal notes for all learning. I feel like I have a really good understanding of where my students are at and what their next steps are before writing reports.

I feel like I now know what is important and what is worth spending time on. I feel like I'm making a difference for my students.

Making learning visible

To help make learning visible in my classroom, I set up modeling books that I use every time I meet with a group. The group learning intention and success criteria are clearly displayed in here. I write the key information from the lesson in the book and students write on sticky notes when responding. Students go and get their group modeling books when they want to check work against the success criteria and remember what was discussed or what a follow-on task was. I also include a tracking sheet in the book with the students' names and columns for ticking off when they have achieved a learning intention or when I want to write anecdotal notes about progress. Students like to see me ticking them off on these sheets and often bring me evidence as proof they can be ticked off.

We're an e-learning class so the students also create digital records of their work and reflections. For example, they create video recordings where they think aloud about how they are solving the problem. I often use these videos when teaching other students.

I have had to teach my students what it means to learn and how to be a good learner. I think this is a conversation we don't have enough with our students. At the start of the year and as needed, we have discussed how to ask good questions, how to listen well, how to take notes, manage their time, what to do when you don't know what to do, picking sensible peers to work with, and how to discuss what you have learnt with others.

Developing effective feedback

To set up successful peer feedback in the class, I first modeled how to provide feedback against the success criteria. I provided my students with a sheet of sentence starters to stick into their books and also have this displayed on the class wall.

When writing feedback for my students, I always ensure that it refers back to the learning intention and lets them know which success criteria they have achieved. I do most marking outside of class hours so when beginning a lesson, I give students the first five minutes to read the feedback I have written, discuss it with a buddy, and decide how they are going to address it.

We use Google Docs regularly in class and they are a great collaboration tool. Students are able to write in the document together and see each other's work. Writing is particularly successful when I have paired students of mixed abilities and asked them to write a piece of writing collaboratively. I use the comments feature within Google Docs when writing feedback. Students use it for writing self-assessment reflections and giving peer feedback.

Collecting and using student voice

Rachael systematically collects student voice for a range of purposes. The templates are stored on Google Docs so they are easily accessed, updated, and shared. Figures 10.4, 10.5, and 10.6 are examples of how Rachel gathers and collates information about student progress within their writing groups. Student voice is highlighted, sitting alongside achievement data and Rachael's observations. In combination, the data provide a rich and moving picture of student progress. Figure 10.4 includes the data collected for one student in the first third of a school year.

After Rachael has gathered this information for each student, she considers what it means for the group's next steps. Figure 10.5 provides an example of this. Note the direct reference to student voice.

This analysis is then the basis for planning. Figure 10.6 is the template used for this.

Rachael uses student voice to inform her own learning, as well as that of her students. She notes:

> I have become really reflective about my practice. I want to know whether I have made a difference and whether my teaching has been effective. I enjoy speaking to students about how they think a lesson has gone and taking their thoughts on board. This means that they feel like they own the learning, which makes them more focused.
>
> Every term, I collect student voice about the three key questions: Where am I going? How am I going? Where to next? If the students are not able to verbalize what they are learning, I know that I need to make my learning intentions clearer. If they don't know how they're going, I know I need to make the success criteria clearer and give more accurate feedback.
>
> Recently, I gathered student voice specifically about how I could help the students more in reading. This was a real eye-opener for me to see what my students valued from me and what they wanted more of. For example, I learnt that they really valued group teaching time and wanted more of it.

WRITING GROUP ANALYSIS

Group name:	Teacher:		Room:	Term:	Weeks:

Student names	In-class date **Black – Term 1** **Blue – Term 1, Week 9** **Purple – Term 2, Week 5**	asTTle	asTTle aRs Score	Student voice about learning **Blue – Term 2** **Purple – Term 3**
Connor	Simple plan, needs to expand ideas in planning and writing, needs to improve spelling, needs to improve vocab, misses full stops, organized work well Planning is beginning to have more detail, **Sentences, punctuation, organization** asTTle – good at structure and organisation, work on vocab, sentence, punctuation, and spelling Needs to consistently use punctuation, could improve spelling by learning some spelling rules, is learning to improve sentences. In some texts uses a range of vocab learnt from reading books **punctuation, spelling**			"I don't know. Punctuation. I'm not really good at that. And language features." "Maybe some the things I have been lowest in asTTle. I could look in my portfolio – punctuation, spelling, and vocab."

Figure 10.4 Writing group analysis (snippet)

Focusing on the Learning
Teacher analysis of children's needs in writing
What is the data telling me about what my children can do now, and need to learn?

Sentences R3 to R4/5
Overall, this group needs to learn how to use a range of sentence types and lengths to make their writing interesting. They often have repetitive sentence beginnings, so they need to learn different ways to structure a sentence to help with this. Look at adding detail to a sentence, e.g., adding in *who, what, when, where,* and *how*. Student voice has also suggested that the group would like to work on sentences and organization.

Organisation R4 to R5/6
They also need to work on using paragraphs consistently and knowing when to move onto a new paragraph in each genre. They also need to understand how to structure an actual paragraph with a topic sentence – Point, Explanation, Example – seeing the link to ideas and how these P.E.E. points need to be thought about and come from their planning stage. Also, how to link paragraphs.

Figure 10.5 Writing group analysis (snippet)

Common Learning Needs What is important and therefore worth spending time on, given where my students are at? **Teaching Objectives**	Common Learning Needs **Teaching Strategies and Activities to Support Learning** What strategies are most likely to help my students to learn this?	Planning **Learning Intention** (WALT)	Planning **Success Criteria** (I can)

Figure 10.6 Planning template

Developing assessment capability

My students set goals every term for each subject; one of these is a learning intention from their group and one is a personal goal. I have modeled how to set SMART goals and students have to fill in a template with dates for achievement, steps to reach their goals, and space for them to reflect on their progress. Once a goal has been achieved, students need to record where the evidence can be found for proof of achieving their goals.

I always ensure that I provide my students with leveled exemplars so that they can clearly see where they are going and can check their own work against it to know how they are going. This takes the pressure off me to be the one who holds all the knowledge and power and helps students to really own their learning. In turn, I'm finding that this is improving their progress, as they are more mindful and deliberate in what they do in order to move up on the rubrics.

Developing rubrics for reading and writing as a whole school gave me an insight into the learning progressions for students and a good understanding of the levels. I then began to use the student-speak rubrics in class for writing. I gave them each a copy to stick into their books and then unpacked them with students in group sessions. I modeled how to use the rubrics to self- and peer-assess a piece a work by highlighting evidence of work at a particular level. This helped the students to identify where they were going, how they were going, and where to next. My students are beginning to be able to self-grade a piece of their work and use the rubric to identify areas for improvement.

My students are now eager to show me evidence of how they have achieved a learning intention. They come to me with their work so that I can tick them off on their tracking sheets. They enjoy reading my anecdotal notes in the front of their modeling book about how they are going and what their next steps are.

When they complete an assessment, my students are asking for their results. They want to know what they have achieved compared to last time and how far they have shifted. I'm now working on having my students self-assess their work for formative assessments like e-asTTle writing before I mark their work so they can see what level they might have achieved.

My students are now able to clearly articulate what they are learning, where they should be, and their next steps to fill the gap. This is evident to me both from my own conversations with them, the student voice I collect, and the student voice my team leader and our deputy principal collect as part of our regular monitoring of teaching and learning programs. The students feel they have had a stake in deciding what they will learn next and this has helped them to take ownership of their learning. They know where to go to find their success criteria and are beginning to check their work against this before coming to me. They know that they can be their own teacher and self-assess their work without waiting for feedback from me.

My students are very comfortable with sharing their assessment results with the class and discussing their learning. They value feedback from their peers, as I have taught them how to give constructive feedback against the success criteria. They understand that people have different strengths and we all have different goals that we are working on. They trust that their peers aren't going to laugh at them or their work and know that they can learn from students who have a strength in an area they don't. Those who do 'get it' are confident in teaching those who need more help.

I enjoy seeing how reflective my students have become. They write little notes in their books when they have found a lesson too easy or need more teaching about something.

Next steps for Rachael's class

When I began at Clevedon School, the parent-teacher conferences were just that – they involved the parent and teacher discussing the student's learning with the student present, but providing minimal input. We have now moved to having three-way conferences that are led by the student and all parties have an equal input. With further teacher modeling and practice, I would like to move this to student-led conferences. I will need to ensure that my students are really clear on where they are going, how they are going, and their "next steps" in order for these to be successful.

Julie's perspective

Rachael's growth and confidence is very much a reflection on Julie and the leadership she and her colleagues in the leadership team have provided. Julie says, "It takes time to develop inspired and passionate teachers, but it's like a whirlpool – once it begins, it just grows and grows." She offers the following advice to others:

1   Understand the research well before you begin.
2   Find out where you are at before you begin.
3   Create a well-documented action plan that has a sensible and logical order to it.
4   Be prepared to change the action plan (monitor, evaluate, and re-evaluate).
5   Look for your inspired and passionate teachers and give them the freedom to take risks.
6   Accept that they will make mistakes – just as the students do: in fact, encourage the errors!
7   Provide all the support possible for them to get it right.
8   Know your moral purpose and when the going gets tough, go back to it and stick with it!
9   Do it – it is exciting!!

Continuing the cycle

Looking to the future, Julie says:

We want to continue on our journey. We are now ready for some timely external review and assistance to evaluate where we are as a school and what our next steps are. We want a revised action plan that acknowledges where we are at and what our next steps are in the Visible Learning journey. We want Rachael and others in our school to become mentor teachers to one another and assist them to develop Visible Learning in their classrooms. We want this to be deliberate, planned, and focused, not just hit-and-miss. We want teachers who are willing to take the risk to go with our teachers to DIE[7] for on this exciting journey.

Notes

1   Where the Minister or Secretary of Education perceives that there is a risk to the operation of an individual school, or to the welfare or educational performance of its students, they may apply an intervention which requires the school's board to engage specified specialist help.

2   The Education Review Office (ERO) is the New Zealand government department that evaluates and reports on the education and care of students in schools and early childhood services.

3   The notion of "teaching as inquiry" is embedded in the New Zealand curriculum. The concept is essentially the same as the impact cycle, as it is about teachers improving teaching and learning through inquiring into the impact of teaching on students. You can read more at http://assessment.tki.org.nz/Assessment-in-the-classroom/Teaching-as-inquiry/Teaching-as-inquiry-useful-readings-and-links

4   Notice that the school's values of respect and diversity are manifest in the provision of te reo Māori versions of the values.

5   STAR stands for Supplementary Tests of Achievement in Reading. It is a standardized assessment tool developed by the New Zealand Council for Educational Research.

6   A celebration of education held in three New Zealand cities in April 2014. See www.festivalofeducation.org.nz

7   Julie is referring to John Hattie's use of the acronym DIE to stress the importance of diagnosis, intervention, and evaluation.

11

Moberly School District

USA

The glory of this work is that Building Principals started visiting the beginning teachers' classrooms and were seeing the learning targets and goals being posted. They observed many of the teachers referring to the targets throughout the lessons. As the beginning teachers started experiencing the increased student engagement, they would share their excitement with their colleagues, which generated an interest in learning more.

Tara Link, new teacher coordinator, Moberly School District

Quite often, pre-service programs do not adequately prepare new teachers for the challenges of the classroom. This is the remarkable story of how the learning of beginning teachers generated an enthusiasm for Visible Learning in their more experienced peers.

Context

Moberly School District[1] is located in a semi-rural area 40 miles north of Columbia, Missouri. The town of Moberly has a population of 13,700 and the total K–12 school population is approximately 2,500 students. Moberly's population includes a large percentage of single-parent homes, blue-collar workers, and families living at or near poverty levels. This is exemplified by the fact that 62% of students are entitled to a free or reduced-rate breakfast and/or lunch, a percentage that is high compared to many other schools around the country.

The district comprises seven schools (often referred to as "buildings"), each with its own principal. It is led by one superintendent and two assistant superintendents. Moberly's educational leaders consider their district to be educationally progressive. They point to the high number of professional development opportunities for staff and the many support systems in place to help meet the needs of students and their families.

The professional development opportunities begin upon teachers' first entry to the profession. The district employs a new teacher coordinator who runs an induction program for beginning teachers across all the district's schools to support them to make those first steps into their new careers. The program is called SHINE, which stands for "Supporting, Helping, and Inspiring New Educators." It serves beginning teachers throughout the Moberly School District, regardless of the grade level of their students or the subject they teach. The learning opportunities and support SHINE provides include mentoring by more experienced teachers.

Overview

New teacher coordinator Tara Link wanted to give beginning teachers in Moberly School District a deeper foundation of knowledge and skills than is typical of teachers who have just come out of pre-service teaching programs. The first years are a challenging time for most new teachers, so she needed an approach that would focus on what really worked and had the capacity to reduce rather than raise teacher workload and stress. Tara knew a great deal about Visible Learning, and liked the emphasis on student learning and the instructional strategies that have the highest impact on student learning.

Over the course of a year, Tara provided professional development intended to help Moberly's new teachers understand the instructional strategies they could use to shift students from surface to deep thinking. Much of that learning was about the effective use of learning intentions and feedback. She monitored the transfer of learning to practice through evidence-based walkthroughs, increasingly conducted alongside school leaders. In the process, she not only inspired the new teachers but also created a wave of excitement among mid-career and veteran teachers. As understanding of the Visible Learning research and its impact in the new teachers' classrooms grew, the district leaders made a decision to roll out the program to all teachers. They applied for a state grant and set up a guiding coalition to lead the systemic implementation of Visible Learning across the district.

Featured teacher

Tara Link has been an educational professional with the Moberly School District for 19 years. She began her career as a sixth grade science teacher, later teaching reading and study skills in a middle-school setting. For the following four years, she was a K–2 Title I interventionist, leading professional learning at a primary school. Tara was appointed new teacher coordinator six years ago. Her goal is to help teachers bridge the gap between educational research and its application in the classroom.

Moberly School District's Visible Learning story

What were the desired outcomes?

Tara Link's position as the coordinator of new teachers meant she was often present in teachers' classrooms. It concerned Tara that many of the students she observed seemed disengaged from their learning. When she asked them what they were learning, most responded by describing the learning activity, rather than the learning goal or their progress towards that goal. This was not surprising, as Tara noticed little evidence of teachers setting and explaining the learning intentions.

When Tara and her colleagues on the Moberly School District Professional Development Committee read John Hattie's *Visible Learning for Teachers* (2012b), they recognized an opportunity to address this issue. Tara then attended a Visible Learning[plus] workshop facilitated by Ainsley Rose, a Visible Learning[plus] consultant, which confirmed this impression. With the support of Moberly's district leaders, Tara contacted Ainsley, seeking guidance on how they might use the Visible Learning approach to move the new teacher program forward.

Tara, Ainsley, and the district leaders launched a deepened inquiry into what was happening for students in the Moberly School District. After gathering and reviewing their evidence, Tara, Ainsley, and the district leaders agreed that students needed better support to:

- think critically for themselves and make good decisions in response to the vast amounts of information from various mediums confronting them each day; and
- understand the targets for their learning, how they were progressing in relation to those targets, and how to improve their learning through self-reflection.

Based on their inquiry into and their understandings about the research on effective instruction, Moberly School District's leaders decided that their priority outcome was for students to become assessment-capable. While the program would begin in the classrooms of beginning teachers, the district leaders hoped that in time, this would serve as a pilot for teachers across the district.

What knowledge and skills did the teachers and school leaders need to support these outcomes?

SHINE provides Moberly's beginning teachers with the classroom support and professional development they need to support student learning. While classroom management is an initial focus, Tara and the other district leaders believe that quality instruction and teacher practice are the best forms of classroom management, and key to student learning. The program takes two years and is a co-operative effort: Tara, the district's school principals, and the mentor teachers all collaborate to provide the best possible support for the new teachers.

In any form of collaborative professional learning, it is essential to identify exactly what it is that you want all teachers to be able to know and do. This targeting to need is especially important for beginning teachers who may already be feeling quite overwhelmed. They don't have the time or mental energy to spend on untested theories or ideas.

> There are some critical elements of instruction that impact on student learning that all teachers, no matter what age group or subject they teach, should incorporate into their practice. As a professional educator, a teacher should be a student of his or her students, knowing what they need and responding accordingly. If we are to maximize the learning opportunities for students, their teachers need to be provided with a basic foundation of understanding. They then also need the opportunity to experiment with integrating their learning into their practice and they need to be given resources and tools to help them learn from their students.
>
> (Tara Link)

The books *Visible Learning* (Hattie, 2009) and *Visible Learning for Teachers* (Hattie, 2012) helped the school district to decide where to start by identifying and illuminating the elements of teacher practice that have the greatest impact on student learning.

The big picture goal at Moberly was for students to become assessment-capable learners, and so the goal for teachers was that they would help provide the pathway for students to achieve this outcome. John Hattie's research shows that assessment capability is contingent on teachers' provision of effective feedback and that this, in turn, requires teachers to establish and implement clear learning intentions, success criteria, and learning progressions. Student assessment and student self-reflection are forms of feedback that can be used to drive linked learning for students and teachers.

Tara and her colleagues in SHINE needed to check whether their theories about teacher needs were borne out by the evidence. Their critical question was "What do my students/beginning teachers need to know?" They addressed the question by asking the new teachers to consider all of the things they did that the research showed had only a small or even negative influence on student outcomes. The results of this inquiry affirmed the leaders' theories about where to start. Essentially, the leaders recognized that this meant that they and their colleagues needed to shift from providing students with information to guiding their thinking. It was important for teachers to stop doing the thinking and working for their students.

While the teachers' professional learning was predicated on the needs for students, there was also another level of need. School leaders had to become intentional about providing feedback regarding the use of learning targets and talking with students about what they were learning during classroom visits.

What new actions did the teachers and school leaders try?

Tara Link and her team read everything they could find about learning intentions, explicit teaching, and feedback. Ainsley Rose assisted with information, guidance, and feedback. During a whole-day professional development workshop with beginning teachers, Tara provided learning activities and readings to help them understand why learning intentions and success criteria are so important and how they could implement them in their classrooms.

The leaders established an open-ended timeline for implementation, understanding that this is a learning process for both students and teachers. They started small and built upon success as it occurred. Nevertheless, they made it clear from the start that they expected to see learning intentions and success criteria incorporated into everyday practice.

> When John Hattie says that "Learning is hard work", that statement goes for teachers as well as students. Adults like to sometimes believe the hard work is done after they do it once, but the teaching profession is about lifelong learning and the work is never done. This was continually conveyed to teachers.
>
> (Tara Link)

The workshop was followed by classroom visits that gave Tara and the school leaders the opportunity to provide teachers with feedback and engage in discussions regarding the successes and challenges of implementation. They used the learning intentions and success criteria to focus the feedback conversations on the areas they and the teachers wanted to change and to help keep their eyes on the impact of the teaching on the students.

The observations and discussions soon indicated a pressing need to adopt a common language for referring to learning intentions. The team wanted to select words that would be user-friendly for the students. After much reading and discussion, the team adopted the terminology of "learning targets" for the daily information, skills, or processes a student should learn during a lesson, and "learning goals" for the larger goals that the learning targets would lead towards.

This is how one of the new teachers explained learning targets to his students:

> I tell my students that learning targets are just like a grocery list. If you go to the grocery store with a list of things to get, you are focused and can check off items on the list as you go. You also feel like you accomplish your goal when you leave the store. You are saving time and money. On the flip side, if you go to the store without a list, you will most likely leave with anything and everything, and you will easily lose focus – especially around the holidays.
>
> (Kim Welch, third grade teacher, Gratz Brown Elementary School)

Tara and her team provided numerous Visible Learning workshops throughout the district at the K–8 level. In addition to working with beginning teachers in the Moberly district, Tara began talking about Visible Learning to new and experienced teachers throughout the state of Missouri. These workshops incorporated experiential activities that helped teachers see the value of learning targets and goals from a student perspective. Tara checked the immediate impact on teachers by conducting surveys and inviting written comments.

It can be easy to get caught up in the mechanics of implementing a new idea or practice and forget to check the impact on student learning, and teachers had a hard time shifting their focus from their teaching to student learning. Teachers often asked Tara and her team, "Am I doing this right?" Typically, they responded, "Watch, listen, and talk to your students. They will let you know by their actions, thoughts, and performance." The leaders modeled this by spending time with the students when visiting classrooms and asking the students about the learning taking place.

Across the district, teachers were reading as much as possible on Visible Learning. Key readings included *Visible Learning for Teachers* by John Hattie (2012), the article "Know Thy Impact" by John Hattie (2012), and *Learning Targets* by Connie Moss and Susan Brookhart (2012). This reading, coupled with feedback from teachers and classroom observations of the interactions between students and teachers, determined Moberly's next steps as the initiative developed.

The leadership team wanted teachers to do this reading because they wanted them to think beyond ad hoc strategies to the principles and theories that explain why a particular strategy is the right one to choose for a particular group of students and for a particular purpose.

> For the intervention to be successful, teachers needed to understand the ideas and then get follow-up support and the time and space to "muddle" with the implementation to discover what could work for them and their students and to discuss their challenges and successes. They needed to plan, test, and check for impact.
>
> (Tara Link)

Tara wanted to ensure that the professional development would be sustained through the provision of appropriate resourcing, including time and support for teacher dialogue. Initially, it was her role to follow up on the learning from the workshops, but she wanted to make sure everyone understood the new strategies and could support their implementation. This meant ensuring that school and district leaders (administrators) understood them as well.

> There needs to be a bridge between the knowledge that teachers and administrators have. As administrators shift away from being transformative leaders to being instructional leaders, it is important that administrators understand Visible Learning and know what to look for when they enter into classrooms on a daily basis. No longer silos, these different levels in a school need to work together.
>
> (Tara Link)

What was the impact of the changed actions on the desired student outcomes?

Their weekly observations showed Tara and her team that most teachers were presenting written learning targets and success criteria to their students and explaining what they were learning and why. As implementation proceeded, both the teachers and their students became increasingly proficient at using the targets and criteria to clarify learning and provide feedback. Students who had normally been passive were now actively engaged in their own learning. Their language shifted away from "What I am doing" to "What I am learning." Interviews with students revealed a growing ability to talk articulately about their progress towards the targets. The teacher who used the grocery list analogy observed:

> I have noticed that students are more focused during instruction than they were last year. I think the learning targets give them a goal to work for, which is essential in learning anything.
>
> (Beginning teacher, Example 1)

You know that Visible Learning is working when the students start teaching the teachers:

> I was in a first-grade classroom and the students were seated on the carpet in front of the teacher. The teacher proceeded to begin a lesson with students that included a game for which students were to stand or sit down, depending on the type of word provided. The purpose of the game was for students to focus on word endings.
>
> About halfway through, a little boy raised his hand, stopping the momentum of the game. The teacher called on him. Looking at the board on which the learning targets were written, he told her, "Our learning target for today is

blends and that is not what we are doing." This was magic. The student held the teacher accountable for the target and that is what he was expecting to learn about.

(Tara Link)

Visible Learning is about what works for all students. One beginning teacher commented on how her students with special education needs were starting to find educational success and to embrace the challenge of new learning:

I find with my students with special education needs, the concepts don't look so overwhelming and it helps to focus on what is really important for that lesson.

(Beginning teacher, Example 2)

The shift was not without resistance. As educators, we are used to encouraging vulnerability in our students, but can find it hard to let go of control and admit that we don't always have the right answers. A lot of the learning has involved challenging thinking, especially about the position of the teacher within the classroom. The quotes below, from two beginning teachers, show how small successes in the face of such vulnerability can build understanding and commitment:

I will admit that I was skeptical about the effectiveness of learning targets when the concept was first presented to me. I had a difficult time understanding how this was different from the objectives that I already used to teach my students. In my head, I knew what I wanted my students to do during the lesson and the objective was typed in my lesson plans each day. However, the more exposure I had to learning targets, the more I realized this was a very different approach to instruction than just knowing the objective you were hoping to cover that day.

(Beginning teacher, Example 3)

At the beginning of this school year, I began using learning targets. I began being intentional about not only what my students were going to be doing during the lesson, but what they were expected to learn during the lesson. My instruction has completely changed since implementing learning targets. My students have taken control of their learning. They know exactly what they are supposed to know by the end of the lesson. If I forget to tell them their learning target, they ask! It is amazing to see the transformation that has taken place with my students. The quality of their work has improved and overall, their tests scores are higher than my previous classes. I have become a believer in learning targets and know that it is well worth the extra effort to write them on the board.

(Beginning teacher, Example 4)

A seventh-grade communication arts teacher embraced the challenge and new learning. She chose her most challenging class to try out learning targets. By the end of the year, both student and teacher attitudes improved, along with the students' overall investment in their learning. The students achieved grades in the state assessments that were comparable to those achieved by students in the classes of more experienced teachers. The program began to have an impact on the mentor teachers, who could see the impact the learning targets, goals, and feedback were having on students in their mentees' classes. Several began to learn along with and from their mentees of their own volition. This created a buzz around the school district. Teachers talked during lunch and on other informal occasions, and some visited classrooms that were using Visible Learning strategies. They told their leaders that they wanted to adopt the same strategies in their classrooms. Visible Learning was something they wanted to do, too.

The district's leaders responded by making Visible Learning part of the continuing professional learning for all teachers across the Moberly School District. This learning takes place collaboratively in teachers' grade or subject area teams. It is supported by the use of a new evaluation form created by the district's leaders. The new form incorporates prompts for observers to look for expected practices such as the implementation of learning targets and observe their impact on students. It is intended to be more than a checklist. Instead, its purpose is to help guide formal and informal professional learning conversations between teachers, school leaders, and district leaders.

The Visible Learning program that began with a specific group of teachers spread across a district is now spreading through all levels and has even had an influence in other districts. It's still early days for Moberly District, but this is a significant impact. Looking back on the district's journey so far, Tara Link advises:

> Compliance by itself doesn't work. There must be a true understanding of why it is important to create assessment-capable learners. In addition, being too rigid in expectations for how learning targets/goals, feedback, and student self-assessment looks can be damaging. This puts too much emphasis on the tasks and not on the purpose. Teachers have to know that they need to find out what works best for their students' learning and respond accordingly. There are some guidelines and key understandings that have to be the guiding force in the decision made, but providing too narrow a sandbox within which to work can undermine the purpose, which is student learning.
>
> Give yourself [the leaders and teachers] permission and time to try out new learning and really become a student of the students. Provide the opportunity for reflection and collegial conversations and take the time to understand the critical importance behind the Visible Learning work. It takes leaders willing to pose questions that require critical thinking of teachers, and leaders who are willing to dig in with the teachers to try things on and determine what works and what doesn't work – but more importantly, to know why it is or isn't working. It doesn't happen overnight, but quality work never does.

When teachers keep the focus on student learning, they will never go wrong. Culture is everything. Just as feedback to students thrives and is most effective in the presence of mistakes, it is imperative that mistakes are valued and embraced as teachers work to effectively implement learning intentions, feedback, and student self-reflection.

Continuing the cycle

Moberly's next steps, with the help of Ainsley Rose, will be to focus on student self-reflection as a form of feedback for the student and as feedback for teachers. They will seek ways to support students to align their self-reflections with the learning targets and success criteria. The district also needs to find ways to better systematize the collection and analysis of data.

Note

1   In the US, a school district may look different depending on which state you visit. In some states, it may constitute all the schools within a county while in others, a school district may constitute all the schools from one town or a set of neighboring towns.

12

Wolford Elementary School

USA

Wolford Elementary School has worked hard to shift the thinking of staff and students. Through the collective effort of the school's leaders, teachers, and its Visible Learning[plus] consultant, Ainsley Rose, Wolford teachers are redefining what it means to be an inspired and passionate teacher.

> I like to let my students play a major role in their own learning. For example, in writing, each student helps develop their own specific goals of what areas they need to address, using a rubric and checklist. I meet with the students to go over their goals, approve their goals, and get their justification as to why they picked each one.
>
> *Jennifer Ingram, first grade teacher*

> Students with special needs, especially those with behavioral challenges, tend to get a strong sense of satisfaction from being in charge of their own learning and behavior. They love to "own" their successes. When I conference with the students prior to MAP[1] testing and set a score to "beat," those kids will work so hard, and for many, the reward is just actually beating the score, not tangible reinforcement, as I had expected.
>
> *Amy Thomas, special education team leader*

At Wolford Elementary School, school is not centered on the adult in the classroom, but on the students. Whatever the individual characteristics of a student, what matters is their learning and how they can progress. Imagine if this were how all teachers approached teaching and learning.

Context

Wolford Elementary School is part of the McKinney Independent School District in McKinney, Texas. The school has 600 students, from kindergarten through to fifth grade. The school is located in a high socio-economic area, but its demographics have been shifting in recent years and it now has many single-parent households and many households in which the mother works outside the home. In the 2005–2006 school year, the school had less than 2% economically disadvantaged students. In 2013–2014, 13% of students were economically disadvantaged.

Eight percent of the school's student population is African-American, 12% Hispanic, 5% Asian, and 84% Caucasian.[2] For 2% of students, English is a second or additional language. Twelve percent are classified as having special education needs, and Wolford has two units for students on the autism spectrum.

In its first year, Wolford's Visible Learning leadership team consisted of Carol Turquette, the assistant principal; Fran Gratt, the principal; and teachers Christal Matthews, Dorina Rocas, Lynette Higgins, Cindy Megelich, and Wyn Brawner. They were joined by others in the second year of implementation, bringing in new expertise and perspectives.

Overview

Achievement results at Wolford Elementary School indicated that teachers were doing a good job, yet each year, teachers walked away feeling like they could do better and go deeper. Responding to this observation, the school's leadership team took time to think about and discuss student engagement and teacher practices. They came to the conclusion that students were not actively engaged in their own learning and that teachers needed support to find better ways to engage students.

The search for solutions took assistant principal Carol Turquette to a Visible Learning[plus] training session held in her area. Carol felt that the approach being described was exactly what her school needed. Supported by consultant Ainsley Rose from the Corwin USA Visible Learning[plus] team, Carol and the rest of the school's leadership team worked with teachers to do the professional learning necessary to increase student engagement. As teachers experimented with applying their learning to the way they worked in classrooms, they became increasingly committed to the principles of Visible Learning. Today, both students and teachers at Wolford continue to grow the enthusiasm for learning that is characteristic of a visible learner.

Featured leader

Carol Turquette is the assistant principal of Wolford Elementary. She has been an educator for well over 30 years, working with students in grades K–12. As well as having been a general education teacher, Carol is a special educator with specialties in dyslexia and in teaching English as a second language. She has been a mentor coordinator as well as an administrator. Carol enjoys providing professional development on a variety of topics.

Wolford Elementary School's Visible Learning story

What were the desired outcomes?

Staff at Wolford Elementary School were concerned that while students typically did well in comparison to those at similar schools, they did not seem to be fully engaged in their learning. They were also aware that changing demographics meant that the student population was becoming more diverse, with a greater range of both strengths and needs.

Carol Turquette has strong beliefs about teaching and learning:

> My greatest concern is that we as educators are proactive in seeking out the knowledge and skills necessary to enable every one of our students to be successful learners. I believe that when one child fails to learn, it may have a small impact on a school but it represents 100% failure for that child and is unacceptable. I can never give up in my quest to bring the ability to learn and to demonstrate success to every child. I am horrified at the thought that our school would be behind the curve and that our students would suffer if our demographics continue to change and we aren't prepared for teaching the children who enter our community.

When Carol attended a Visible Learning[plus] workshop in 2013, she recognized the intervention as the answer the school had been looking for. She and principal Fran Gratt established a team that brought leaders and teachers together to lead the school's own Visible Learning intervention.

In a Visible Learning intervention, the initial inquiry into the specifics of students' needs should always be to prioritize the student voice. At Wolford, this included a process where the Visible Learning leadership team videoed students answering the questions "What makes a good learner a good learner?" and "What makes learning fun?" A sample of student responses to the first of those questions is given in Table 12.1. As you can see, the majority of students connected good learning to good behavior rather than to the strategies and characteristics that the research shows lead to success.

Table 12.1 Sample of student responses to "What makes a good learner?"

Grade	Responses
Second grade	"When you work hard and listen to the person teaching you and try your best."
Third grade	"Always focusing and paying attention to what the teacher is trying to tell you." "When like you kinda pay attention in class, follow directions, and don't goof off all that much."
Fourth grade	"When you listen to the teacher, you learn a lot more stuff and have better grades."
Fifth grade	"Well, it takes respect and great listening." "Well, what makes a good learner is education and listening to your teachers and do your work most of the time and try your best at everything you do. That will help you to get a better education and learn a lot more than other people so that you can pass more tests and get better grades." "A good learner always pays attention."

The inquiry confirmed the theory that students at Wolford needed to better understand both the value of active participation in their own learning and the skills and strategies that make this possible. They needed to learn, for example:

- how to grow in autonomy and independence as learners;
- how to set their own learning goals and assess their own learning in relation to those goals;
- how to engage in collaborative learning with their peers;
- the difference between "good behavior" and learning behaviors;
- how to connect new information with known information; and
- how to engage in deep thinking.

The staff agreed that their primary goal was for students to walk away with a better understanding of what learning was about, and they needed to become inspired and passionate teachers to help students get there. This integration of student and teacher need is evident in the following set of inquiry questions that the school drew up to guide, inform, and monitor its journey:

- *Meaningful student engagement*: Does the student persist in the face of difficulty? Do they understand the "Qualities of a Good Learner"? Does the student take reasonable risks in responding, extending, questioning, and/or producing products? Is the student actively and authentically engaged in the learning?
- *Success in learning*: Do students consistently demonstrate success in learning through multiple measures? Are these measures aligned with the learning

objective? Can the students explain their thinking, project, assignment, or task? Do classroom discussion, feedback, and student language demonstrate an alignment with the learning objective? Is there evidence of annotated exemplars or rubrics for student use?

- *Critical thinking and problem solving*: Do students demonstrate success in problem-solving activities? Do students utilize, initiate, or devise their own strategies for critical thinking and/or problem solving? Are students consistently engaged in critical thinking and/or problem-solving activities?
- *Alignment*: Is the lesson objective in alignment with the TEKS[3] and written as an "I can" or "I will" statement? Can students tell the teacher what the objective is?
- *Self-directed*: Are students consistently successful in extending the learning? Can they question appropriately (directed to teacher or peers)? Do students collectively share ideas?
- *Instruction*: Does the student view errors as important steps in the learning process? Does the teacher listen to students? Do students have opportunities to instruct others?

What knowledge and skills did the teachers and school leaders need to support these outcomes?

In the next phase of the impact cycle, the leadership team used the Visible Learning[plus] Matrix as a tool to deepen their understanding of the knowledge and skills they and their colleagues needed to better support students while reframing themselves as the Inspired and Passionate Teachers described by John Hattie. As a consequence of this inquiry, the team identified the professional learning needs in Table 12.2.

The team set out a Visible Learning action plan with an intentionally fluid timeline which means it can evolve as teachers and leaders examine and reflect on their practice. The action plan is accompanied by planning documents that make the actions and the theories behind them visible to the whole staff.

What new actions did the teachers and school leaders try?

The areas of learning identified in Table 12.2 are integrated and require supportive processes and structures. The leadership team decided that much of the learning would take place through reorienting their grade level teams to student learning and introducing protocols to foster greater collaboration amongst teachers. Within their teams, teachers would have opportunities to co-design challenging and engaging lessons utilizing high-yield instructional practices, and would have a safe place in which to talk and share their learning. In line with the

Table 12.2 Professional learning needs at Wolford Elementary School

Foci	Aspects
Classroom interactions	Ensuring that practices with higher effect sizes become standard in every classroom. Making learning visible. Teacher and student feedback. Teacher–student relationships. What to do when students don't achieve the intended outcomes. Understanding learning progression and that students learn at different rates.
Professional collaboration	Team planning that focuses on student learning. Inspired and passionate teachers need to feel safe in sharing their data with team members during planning sessions in order to determine strengths and weaknesses within teams. Collaboration between teachers on instruction and student learning needs to increase, allowing teachers to evaluate their own teaching practices and make adjustments to meet the needs of their students, regardless of special needs, economic status, ethnicity, behavior, native language, etc. Team planning needs to be focused on the work, with lessons clearly aligned to the student expectations in the curriculum.
Evidence gathering	Know thy impact: Addressing the effect teachers have upon their students. The need to analyze student data for strengths and weaknesses in student learning and in their own instruction. Using data from multiple sources. Utilizing multiple measures of data (district benchmarks, state assessments, DRA, MAP, iStation, TEMI, etc.) to analyze student and teacher performance.
How am I going?	Teachers need to reflect on their own practice and their strengths and weaknesses in planning and instruction. Teachers need to know how to offer focused and specific feedback to students and parents to allow them to understand where students are in their learning, where they are going, and how to get there.
Building community	"Walls" need to come down within grade levels, allowing students to be shared based upon teacher strengths in order to maximize learning outcomes. Parents need to understand the shift from teaching to learning to enable them to support their child's learning from the home.

idea of "intentional evolution,"[4] the team is currently refining the protocols for professional learning conversations. Instead of having them individually decided on within grade levels, it is now seeking greater standardization so that expectations are better shared and understood across the school.

At the start of the 2012 school year, Carol led Visible Learning workshops for the whole staff. She focused particularly on the role of teachers as evaluators who constantly evaluate their impact on their students. She reinforced the message that assessment is feedback to the teacher that tells them how they are doing with their students. Teachers explored the concept of effect sizes and the instructional strategies that the Visible Learning research has shown to be most effective.

Further professional development sessions focused on the learning strategies that would complement and support the teachers' goals and provided them with extended opportunities to engage in planning and review. Teachers examined the difference between "expert" and "experienced" teachers and the importance of explicit teaching that is focused on clear learning intentions and criteria for success. They developed a shared understanding of the qualities of an effective learner and of the "learning pit"[5] and began to design and construct rubrics and annotated exemplars (Figures 12.1, 12.1, and 12.3).

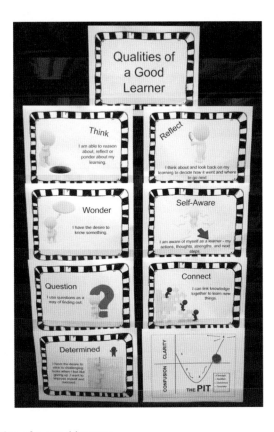

Figure 12.1 Qualities of a good learner

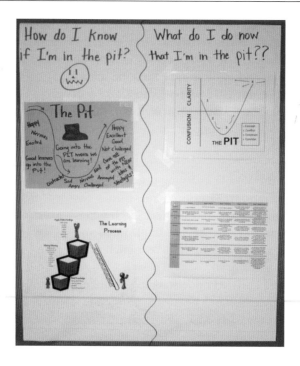

Figure 12.2 Example of the pit being used in a special education resource room

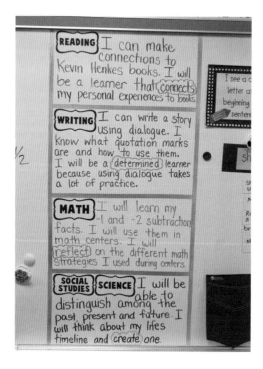

Figure 12.3 Example of including learner qualities with daily learning intentions

The Visible Learning leadership team sought to keep the intervention in the forefront of teachers' thinking through maintaining a regular supply of information. For example, they sent weekly electronic newsletters to all staff, and Carol established a school blog. When time allowed, the leaders attended and participated in the team meetings. Carol also sought to include parents, explaining where Visible Learning came from and why Wolford was using it. In a newsletter, she wrote:[6]

> Our family of teachers at Wolford continue in their own learning journeys, allowing them to lead our students to even greater achievements. We are focusing on the work of John Hattie, Professor of Education and Director of the Melbourne Education Research Institute at the University of Melbourne, Australia. Hattie produces some of the most influential work in educational research today.

As the teachers implemented the changed practices and tried out the lesson plans they had developed with their teams, they also opened their classrooms to frequent walkthroughs and observation by the leadership team. The district requires the school to use a standardized walkthrough form, but the leaders use the inquiry questions (see pages 220–221) they had developed with the whole staff to guide their observations. They found that this meant they could offer constructive feedback that did not come across as criticism.

In all interactions, the leadership team communicated the message that this intervention is about everybody's learning, including their own. By doing this, they hoped to make teachers feel safe to open up their practice. At the same time, they wanted teachers to understand that they were expected to take ownership of the Visible Learning strategies and implement them in their classrooms. Visible Learning was not to be an optional extra.

This intervention was not without barriers. The Wolford team had to work within the constraints of the State of Texas and Federal Government. Wolford, along with all schools in Texas, has curricular requirements and state-mandated assessments. Teachers do not have a lot of autonomy in what they teach or their daily time requirements. But that did not stop them. Through inquiry and conversation, the leaders fostered an understanding that teachers control their level of collaboration. They control the "how" of their instruction, the effects they have on their students, and the focus on student learning.

What was the impact of the changed actions on the desired student outcomes?

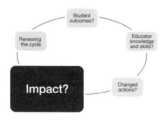

The single biggest change at Wolford Elementary School is that their language and behavior now focuses on learning, as opposed to teaching. Carol Turquette says:

I think in the past, we viewed learning as a by-product of teaching. Don't get me wrong, we have always valued student learning, but prior to Visible Learning, our teaching was the focus. We put so much time and energy into ourselves and what we were teaching. We looked at student attention and student activity as the single most important thing in our classrooms by which we could measure learning, as it happened in real time. But we all knew, deep down, that our kids were often, possibly frequently, disengaged, and didn't have a clue as to what was going on. They certainly didn't understand themselves as learners. Of course paying attention and behaving appropriately are important, but now my teachers talk about "learning." I expect it will continue to impact us greatly as we grow and learn.

The leaders observe that teachers now take ownership of daily operations, not only on their grade level, but also of the school as a whole. They come to the school's leaders with suggestions and solutions to issues, instead of complaints. Professional conversations abound, centering on the effect teachers are having on their students. The tenor of these conversations reveals that teachers view themselves as active facilitators of learning, as opposed to instructors.

During walkthroughs and classroom observations, the leaders notice higher levels of student engagement in the learning. In one fourth-grade classroom, an observer heard a student say, "Please Teacher, please Teacher, can we have five more minutes? I really want to solve this problem!"

Students are able to discuss their own learning: where they are, where they need to go, and how they will get there. They can work independently and in small groups while the teacher is engaged in small group instruction. They are focused on the learning, with conversations centering on learning instead of their social lives.

There are signs that students are developing an understanding of what is expected of them and using this to reach higher goals. For example, the first-grade teachers developed annotated exemplars for their writing rubric, which they then modeled to their students (see Figure 12.4). Later, students were observed using these exemplars as they composed their own writing.

A measure of improvement is student use of the learner qualities and the analogy of 'the pit'. When one of the kindergarten teachers was struggling with a program on her Smart Board, one of her students piped up and said, "It's because you're in the pit, Ms Grant!" A first grade student was overheard telling his teacher, "I was

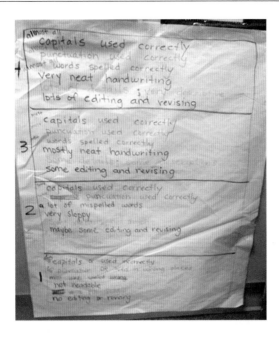

Figure 12.4 A writing rubric developed by Michele McGilvray and her second-grade students

deep down below the pit" while a second grader, when asked about an antonym for a word other students were raising their hand to answer, said, "Wait, my wheels are turning, let me think" and then shared his response. When thinking of his strategy for approaching a mathematics problem, this boy said, "Man, I'm really in the pits for this one."

Teachers are trying out instructional strategies like classroom discussion, reciprocal teaching, concept mapping, and worked examples. They regularly scan the room and, upon noticing a flagging of concentration or focus, offer energizers to boost oxygen levels to the brain and return students to states of engagement. Students also let the teachers know when they need a brain break. This ability to understand their own need to self-regulate has also had a positive impact on learning, as students are able to gauge when they are losing focus on their work and use appropriate techniques to adjust.

One of the new initiatives has been to invite older peers into classrooms to offer academic support to younger students on an as-needed basis. The leaders notice that the relationships this fosters are helping to create a warmer, more caring environment at the classroom level and across the school.

Teachers are becoming practised at evaluating their own practice and the impact they have on their students. They implement new practices and make changes to what they are doing based upon student need. They monitor themselves and their peers through data reviews and professional collaboration. The school has set up systems and processes to support this ongoing inquiry, for example:

- The leaders do frequent walkthroughs in classrooms, offering feedback and support to staff.
- Leaders and teachers monitor multiple sources of data. Data discussions are held with grade-level teams and individuals.
- Individual student needs are discussed in Response to Intervention (RTI) meetings, with solution strategies being discussed and offered to the teacher for implementation in the classroom.
- Grade-level team leaders report weekly to administration regarding progress and outcomes from their planning sessions.

An example of inquiry into impact is the kindergarten team at Wolford. Upon examining the data in 2010, the team noted that about 22% of their students left kindergarten at the end of the year reading on a Diagnostic Reading Assessment (DRA) level 10 or higher. Although the district standard was set for kindergarten students to end the year reading at levels 4 to 6, the Wolford standard was set to have all students leave kindergarten reading on a level 10 or higher. The team felt that with focused instruction, and with making learning visible, their students would be successful with more challenge. By the end of the 2012 school year, 62% of students reached that standard. The teachers examined the effect they had on their students and determined that their procedures and schedule needed further refining to meet their goal.

> Our teachers had determined that they were wasting a lot of time on managing behavior. With a little fine-tuning, they are now able to support their learners with some of the gentlest learning experiences involving unstructured play. You should see how happy and successful these little ones are! They thrive on their learning success.
>
> (Carol Turquette)

The following quotes demonstrate the passion for Visible Learning that is now typical of Wolford teachers:

> The learner quality I have focused on the most this year is being self-aware. Students continually evaluate themselves and their peers to determine their strengths as learners and the areas that they want to focus on for improvement. They dialogue with me and with each other about who they are as a learner and where they want to be.
>
> I also try to continually instill a sense of wonder and let students see that trait in me as well. I honestly believe that once you stop wondering and imagining the possibilities, you are no longer a true learner.
>
> (Lara Patterson, fourth-grade teacher)

> We use rubrics to communicate high expectations for learning. Students can see very clearly what the expectations are for an assignment or project before

they even begin. We begin with the end in mind so to speak. This allows students to set goals for themselves, which promotes commitment to the task. I find that giving students these clear and compelling standards is very motivating and fosters engagement with the learning. For the more reluctant learner, it removes the 'I didn't know we were supposed to do that' excuse.

(Cindy Megelich, fifth-grade teacher)

As much as inspiring and passionate teachers understand there needs to be a warm and caring classroom climate where errors are welcome, inspiring and passionate school leaders understand that as well. Visible Learning requires deep learning and change for teachers that can be particularly challenging for experienced teachers who have long-established philosophies of teaching that are not always grounded in research. A few staff members at Wolford needed extra support to be encouraged and made to feel safe to try and evolve their practice. However, as they saw increasing examples of student success, most willingly jumped aboard.

Carol is delighted by the changes she sees:

Over 30 years in the field of education have proven to me that teaching programs are seldom as effective as we may be led to believe or as effective as we need them to be. I have seen many such become the flavor of the day and come and go. It is imperative that our teachers have the skills necessary to be effective in enabling children to become successful learners. This is why I have embraced Visible Learning.

Carol says she does not want even one student to fail. With inspired and passionate teachers like the ones at Wolford Elementary, she just might meet her goal.

Continuing the cycle

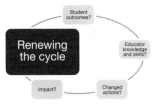

It is clear that Visible Learning has helped Wolford teachers to become inspired and passionate, which undoubtedly has a positive effect on students. However, they all know there is still more work to do, and that Visible Learning is a never-ending quest. Wolford Elementary School has lofty goals, which is another testament to how inspired and passionate teachers are about Visible Learning. They want to:

- get better at displaying and using well-developed learning intentions;
- continue to focus on refining teacher use of specific, focused, and effective feedback to students, as well as their ability to garner feedback from students in a manner that will facilitate deeper learning;
- continue to develop and use annotated exemplars across the curriculum;

- consistently support students to understand what it means to be a learner, talk about their own learning, and use metacognitive strategies to facilitate learning (for example, involving students in becoming their own record-keepers, being self-assessors, and designing assessments);
- continue to infuse the learner qualities throughout the campus (for example through the video club's production and broadcast of a video demonstrating the gestures associated with the learner qualities);
- implement the use of effect sizes to evaluate impact; and
- use the Visible Learning template "Teacher Action Plan for Assessment-Capable Learners" to help planning for the establishment of professional learning communities that are designed to support and encourage deeper teacher collaboration, professional learning, and student learning.

The professional learning communities will be a significant investment for the school. Teachers will be able to select from four such communities, which will be developed and managed by the teachers, but with administrative oversight. Three communities will have a specific focus, with one on feedback, one on collaboration, and one on students as their own data-keepers (or evaluators) of learning. The fourth will provide teachers with the opportunity to conduct evidence-based inquiry into an area of deep personal interest. Each will run for a year and will include timetabled opportunities for collaborative inquiry into impact.

Notes

1 MAP refers to Measures of Academic Progress. It is a norm-referenced, standardized, computer-based assessment designed to show student growth. It is not aligned to the school's curriculum.

2 This adds up to be more than 100%, but "Hispanic" is considered an ethnicity and reports in more than one category, the second being race. So, most Hispanics will report as Hispanic/White, and a few as Hispanic/Black or even as Hispanic/American Indian.

3 Texas Essential Knowledge and Skills – the state standards for what students should know and be able to do.

4 This is the idea that improvement comes from conscious and intentional evolution.

5 James Nottingham introduced the metaphor of "the pit" to communicate to students the concept of the zone of proximal development: the place where they feel stuck and need to consciously reflect on the learning process and the necessary relevant qualities to get out again.

6 Downloaded from http://visiblelearningatwolford.weebly.com

Part IV
Appendix 1

Active reading guide

Now that you have read Part IV, you may like to use the following template to record what you noticed about how the characteristics of Inspired and Passionate Teachers are made manifest in the staff at Clevedon School, Moberly School District, and Wolford Elementary School, and what it was that the school leaders did to foster these behaviors. The prompts are from a Personal "Health" Check for Visible Learning developed by the Visible Learning[plus] consultants for personal reflection and follow-up dialogue with trusted colleagues and coaches.

	Examples observed in the learning story	Inferences about how this was achieved
I am actively engaged in and passionate about teaching and learning.		
I provide students with multiple opportunities for learning based on surface and deep thinking.		
I know the learning intentions and success criteria of my lessons, and I share these with students.		
I am open to learning and actively learn myself.		
I have a warm and caring classroom climate where errors are welcome.		
I seek regular feedback from my students.		
My students are actively involved in knowing about their learning (that is, they are assessment-capable).		
I can identify progression in learning across multiple curriculum levels in my student work and activities.		
I have a range of teaching strategies in my day-to-day teaching repertoire.		
I use evidence of learning to plan next learning steps with students.		

Part IV
Appendix 2

Theory to practice

The chapter stories have provided you with examples of what John Hattie means by the concept of Inspired and Passionate Teaching, the impact of such teaching on students, and the approaches three schools took to get there. The active reading guide invited you to reflect on these schools' stories in relation to a Personal Health Check developed by the Visible Learning[plus] consultants. Now, you might like to use that same checklist to reflect on your own practice alongside colleagues and coaches you trust.

Inspired and Passionate Teaching: thinking prompts	How am I doing? Why do I think this?	What would I like to get better at? What can I do to improve in this area?
I am actively engaged in, and passionate about teaching and learning.		
I provide students with multiple opportunities for learning based on surface and deep thinking.		
I know the learning intentions and success criteria of my lessons, and I share these with students.		
I am open to learning and actively learn myself.		
I have a warm and caring classroom climate where errors are welcome.		
I seek regular feedback from my students.		
My students are actively involved in knowing about their learning (that is, they are assessment-capable).		
I can identify progression in learning across multiple curriculum levels in my student work and activities.		
I have a range of teaching strategies in my day-to-day teaching repertoire.		
I use evidence of learning to plan next learning steps with students.		

The Visible Learning School

13

Oxley College

Australia

At Oxley, we learn how we should learn, then we love how we learn, then we love what we learn.

Cordelia, year 2

At seven years of age, Cordelia already exhibits the characteristics of a visible learner. In this story, you will read about how Oxley College has used the Visible Learning framework to make learning visible for students like Cordelia, for their teachers, and for the whole school community.

Context

Oxley College is a co-educational, non-denominational, non-selective independent school located in the Southern Highlands of New South Wales, Australia. It is situated in an idyllic rural setting, approximately an hour and a half's drive south west of Sydney.

The college opened its doors in 1983 as a year 7–12 secondary school with 23 students. In 2012, it expanded to become a seamless kindergarten to year 12 (K–12) school with 525 students. Many are from local farming families, while others are the children of professionals who have relocated from the city to the Southern Highlands for lifestyle reasons. The secondary school draws from over 20 local primary schools, including its own.

Overview

Oxley College has always espoused a commitment to excellence in student learning. The extension to a full K–12 school provided a unique opportunity for its community to reflect on the school's purpose and how that might continue to be achieved. Like people all around the world, the school understood the critical role of a sound education in ensuring young people thrive in a time of rapid global change. Oxley College wanted to be sure that it was providing its students with an education that inspired them to be thinkers and passionate lifelong learners, preparing them for their futures in the 21st century.

Prior to its involvement in Visible Learning, the school had engaged in a range of staff professional learning and other initiatives intended to achieve their vision. Many of the activities were related to strategies that make a difference in student learning, but there was little hard evidence to suggest that they had been successful. A search through the research on effective schools led to the discovery of a set of criteria that resonated with the school: consistency, innovation, and capacity (Zbar, 2009). When deputy head Kathryn Cunich attended a presentation on Visible Learning in September 2012, she recognized an opportunity to engage in whole-school improvement that met those criteria.

A guiding coalition was established, consisting of the then head of college, Grant Williamson, and the executive team of Stuart Bollom, Emma Calver, Kathryn Cunich, and Beverly Harris. Kathryn led the delivery team, which consisted of Steven Armstrong, Sarah Offner, Jacqui Pugh, Callum Ross, and David Whetton as the inaugural Visible Learning team leaders, each working with eight or nine teachers. In 2014, Michael Parker joined the college as the new head of college, taking his place in the coalition.

As the school implemented the Visible Learning framework, refocusing from curriculum to learning and from assumptions to evidence, the characteristics of visible learners have become manifest, not just in students but also in teachers and school leaders. The journey has not been the same for everyone, and the change has not been an easy one. This story gives you a glimpse into the successes and challenges that have been part of Oxley College's ongoing transformation into a Visible Learning school.

Featured teachers

This story features three teachers in particular:

David Whetton is a year 2 teacher and a Visible Learning team leader. He is connecting his practical experience of Visible Learning to the research he is undertaking as he works towards a Masters of Education (leadership). David has been challenged to "Know Thy Impact" and reflects constantly on whether his practice as a teacher is facilitating the most effective learning for his students.

Ben Hicks is an early career mathematics teacher who has taught in Australia, Turkey, and the United Kingdom. He has a passion for instilling a sense of exploration and wonder in his students, whilst ensuring they are progressing and assessment-capable. Ben is currently focusing on quantitative feedback through the Visible Learning framework.

Victoria Rintoul teaches English to students in years 7–12. Victoria believes that Visible Learning has brought home some powerful truths for her as a practitioner, illustrating how a teacher can be judicious in selecting pedagogical approaches when the aim is to have a positive impact on student learning in every lesson. She sees great benefit in Hattie's focus on seeing evidence of learning – not evidence of being busy or that students can restate what has already been understood, but evidence of fresh connections and new skills.

Oxley College's Visible Learning story

What were the desired student outcomes?

Oxley College's extension from a secondary school to a full K–12 school provided a unique opportunity for its community to reflect on the school's purpose and how that might be achieved. A statement by leadership expert Viviane Robinson captured the attention of the leadership team:

> The most powerful predictor of a student's performance in a subject in any given year is what he or she learnt in previous years. Because what any one teacher achieves, therefore, is critically dependent on the teaching quality of his or her colleagues, it makes sense that teachers take collective responsibility for their students, including helping each other learn how to reach shared goals.
>
> (Robinson, 2011, p. 106)

The school wanted to offer its students a seamless learning journey supported by teachers who shared a common understanding of progression and a shared pedagogy. However, it was faced by the challenge of integrating primary-level teaching into a long-established secondary school, and with the different pedagogies that tend to be associated with those different levels of learning. To this complex picture was added the uncertainty caused by a lack of data. As in many other schools, the collection and analysis of data was not part of the Oxley culture. The only sound source of external achievement data was the Higher School Certificate (HSC)[1] data collected in students' final year of school, but this was analyzed by external consultants and heads of department and played little or no role in informing daily teaching and learning. This meant that the school's first step had to be to gather baseline evidence in order to unpack how students were learning at Oxley.

This first step was facilitated by the school's participation in a Visible Learning[plus] Evidence into Action Day led by Kate Birch and Helen Butler (Visible Learning[plus] consultants from New Zealand and Australia respectively) in March 2013. The opportunity to unpack the five Visible Learning strands and start building a plan for collecting school-wide evidence in relation to each of those strands was a turning point for the school's newly-appointed Visible Learning team. As Jacqui recalls, "We were so inspired that despite a 4 am start, we were all still discussing, planning, and working together at 7 pm on the bus ride home!" On return to the school, the Visible Learning team ran a staff meeting at which each teacher completed the Visible Learning^{plus} Matrix. The team also launched into collecting data with regard to each of the strands, using the tools set out in Figure 13.1.

Analysis of the data made it clear that:

- students at Oxley were not visible learners;
- students' understandings about good learner attributes were mostly about organization and behavior;
- students spoke mostly about what they were doing in class, rather than what they were learning; and
- students were not in the habit of providing feedback to their teachers.

The secondary school's whole-school achievement data showed an average annual effect size of less than 0.4 in spelling, grammar, and punctuation.

Strand	Focus	Tool	Tool	Tool	Tool
The Visible Learner	Students	Student focus groups	Classroom interview	Walkthroughs	Audio and Video diary
Know Thy Impact	Data	NAPLAN (years 3, 5, 7, 9)	Three classes: Effect sizes for each class Effect sizes for individual	Grid, page 50	Visible Learning School Matrix
Inspired and Passionate Teachers	Teachers	Student focus group	Teacher feedback survey	Walkthroughs	
Effective Feedback	Feedback	Measuring relational trust	Feedback observation	Interviews on feedback	Student feedback survey

Figure 13.1 Data collection tools

The guiding coalition agreed on the following aspirations for students:

> We want our students to be active and engaged in their learning, exhibiting a growth mindset as they develop the attributes of a lifelong learner: striving, thinking, and curious.

> We want to show that students at Oxley College achieve a 0.4 or greater effect size in core learning areas (literacy and numeracy).

> Most importantly, we want all our students, from Kindergarten to year 12, to understand what they are learning, how they are going, and where they will go next … that is, to understand how they learn.

What knowledge and skills did the teachers and school leaders need to support these outcomes?

To deepen their understanding of the current teacher practice and its impact on students, the guiding coalition used the data collection tools shown in Figure 13.1 to create a strengths and needs analysis. "We [the guiding coalition] were confident that we were all passionate, inspired, and effective but without observing student learning, we did not have the data to evidence this."

Their analysis of the issues affirmed the perception that teachers were dedicated and committed to their students but also revealed that:

- there was little use of learning intentions and success criteria, which in turn, limited the value of feedback;
- students and teachers did not share a common language of learning;
- students perceived inconsistencies in the way they were taught by different teachers and across different curriculum areas and year groups;
- feedback, particularly from students to teachers, was not an embedded or consistent practice, despite having been a focus of previous professional learning;
- there was limited evidence of collaborative planning;
- the timetabling process was not providing groups of teachers time to meet; and
- the school did not routinely collect evidence to analyze teacher impact and support teaching and learning.

The Visible Learning team shared the collated evidence with the College Executive, the Board of Governors, and the staff as a whole. In their discussions, they drew out the specific knowledge, skills, and understandings they and their colleagues needed to develop to support the outcomes the school wanted for students. On this basis, they decided that the initial priorities for teacher and school leader professional learning would be to:

- develop a shared definition of an effective learner;
- develop a shared language of learning across the school and across all stakeholders;
- use learning intentions and success criteria and make them the focus for feedback;
- develop a shared understanding of learning progressions;
- use the SOLO (Structure of the Observed Learning Outcome) taxonomy to show progression and promote student ownership of learning;
- encourage more dialogue in classrooms;
- encourage teachers to seek feedback from their students;
- foster an "open to learning" mentality that would include engagement with research and the use of evidence to measure impact;
- adapt the school's professional development systems to align with the Visible Learning approach;
- introduce walkthroughs and observations focused on student learning;
- implement the calculation of effect sizes to measure progress;
- provide feedback to teachers that focuses on the impact of teaching on student learning;
- encourage teachers to plan lessons collaboratively by developing a lesson planning process for K–12; and
- embed Visible Learning in strategic planning.

Following their attendance at the Evidence into Action Day Two seminar, the guiding coalition worked through the Visible Learning Plan and set initial targets. These were shared at staff meetings and in Visible Learning team meetings:

2013 Visible Learning Target 1: By September 2013, during walkthroughs, it will be evident that our students and teachers are routinely using learning intentions and success criteria, that students fully understand what these mean, and feedback to students will be based around these.

2013 Visible Learning Target 2: By November 2013, students asked during class walkthroughs will be able to talk about the assessments they take, where they are at, and their next learning steps.

2013 Visible Learning Target 3: By April 2014, all students at Oxley College will show a 0.4 or greater effect size in the core learning areas (literacy and numeracy).

What new actions did the teachers and school leaders try?

The school's work began in earnest in December 2012. This section outlines some of the most significant aspects of implementation at Oxley College.

Restructuring school leadership

The focus on providing observations and feedback to teachers based on student learning was a cultural shift for the school that meant that teachers had to open their classrooms and their practice to critique. The guiding coalition knew that it was vital to support teachers through the change. Kathryn explains:

> We needed a means by which to encourage and mentor sensitive staff through the implementation stage and we thought a cross-curricular, mentor model may be more effective than a traditional hierarchical structure.

Early in 2013, staff were invited to apply for a newly-created middle management position, that of a Visible Learning leader. Six leaders were appointed on the basis of the evidence they could produce of their own implementation of Visible Learning in their classrooms. Their purpose was to "facilitate the implementation and monitoring of the Visible Learning framework, K–12 in order to ensure that students achieve the best possible learning outcomes." Each new leader is responsible for a K–12, cross-curricular team of eight or nine teachers, consisting of a deliberate combination of primary and secondary teachers and of beginning, mid-career, and experienced teachers. The leaders meet weekly as a leadership team, fortnightly for one-to-one mentoring sessions with individual teachers, and monthly as a cross-curricular team of teachers.

The mindframes

The leaders in the guiding coalition introduced the eight mindframes of Visible Learning at the very beginning of the school journey. They and the Visible Learning team have continued in their quest to inspire, encourage, and unite staff in their commitment to maximizing their impact on student learning. They deliberately use the language of Visible Learning to shift the focus from teaching to learning and from a fixed mindset to a growth mindset:

> The best thing for me is the dialogue, ongoing dialogue with teachers and that you've got a framework where you are going to talk about learning … and the focus is on "What are you trying?" Did it work? Did it not work? And experimenting, failing, succeeding, and sharing that with the students, as they are part of the journey.

> (Ben Hicks)

Classroom learning visits

The fortnightly individual mentoring sessions are linked to classroom "learning visits." During these visits, the Visible Learning leader completes an observation template that is linked to the Visible Learning framework.

> Such observation adds another pair of eyes to help the teacher to see the effect of his or her teaching, and moves the discussion away from the teaching towards the effect of the teaching.
>
> (Hattie, 2009, p. 13)

Often, the teacher and leader use their mentoring sessions to collaborate on the observation focus, ensuring that this is aligned with the goals for both teacher and student learning. Following each visit, the leaders provide feedback to the teacher and make suggestions on the "where to next."

Initially, these meetings and the visits provoked anxiety amongst teachers. This was exacerbated by some inconsistency in the way feedback was provided. The Visible Learning team has reviewed the processes for feedback and reflection and worked through several versions of the template (Figure 13.2) as it has sought to alleviate those fears. Many teachers now welcome the one-on-one support they gain through the mentoring sessions and visits.

Walkthroughs

The introduction of whole-school walkthroughs was another vital part of Oxley's strategy. The Visible Learning leaders understood it was imperative to focus observation on student learning. As John Hattie advises:

> I allow teachers only to observe students – the reactions that students have to incidents, to teaching, to peers, to the activity. Then, they interview and listen to the student about what the student was doing, thinking, and not understanding.
>
> (Hattie, 2009, p. 138)

With this in mind, the school developed a methodology for walkthroughs that enables it to track the implementation of the strategies that make the biggest difference to student learning, as identified in Hattie's research:

> On an agreed day, the walkthrough team, usually a combination of executive, Visible Learning leaders, curriculum leaders, and teachers gather at an agreed meeting point. The K–12 timetable is on the board and we plan a series of routes that will take us through every classroom in the course of the walkthrough. In a 50-minute period, we usually visit four or five classrooms.
>
> We work in pairs, with each teacher taking a different role. One records the number of students in the class, the amount of questioning, and the

Learning that is Visible – Learning Visit template

Date	Term	Week/ Period	Curriculum	Year Group	Teacher	Time in lesson		
						Beginning	Middle	End

Content/Context/Activity Underway: _____

	Tick	
Learning intention displayed		
Learning intention communicated		
Learning intention understood by students		

Success criteria displayed		
Success criteria identified		
Success criteria understood by students		

Hook to build commitment and engagement		
Teacher input		
Teacher modelling		
Teacher checking for understanding		
Guided practice		
Independent practice		
Classroom discussion encouraged		
Closure		

Student questions encouraged		
Mastery practice evident		
Feedback given to students		
Shoulder-to-shoulder learning		

Differentiated task/activity		
Visual auditory read/write kinesthetic		
Percentage of teacher talk		

Teacher/Leader Reflection: _____

Strengths:

-
-
-

VL Team Leader/Curriculum Leader: _____ **Teacher:** _____

Figure 13.2 "Learning that is Visible" observation template

activities underway. The other sits with at least two students and asks about their learning. ("What are you learning today?" "How are you going?" "Where to next?")

The observations of student learning are recorded on a template that identifies the year group and curriculum areas, but not the teachers' names. The data collected reflects the strategies that will make the most difference to student achievement, as identified by Hattie's research into effect sizes: understanding of assessment, active learning, student questioning, dialogue, and so on. The template has gone through several edits as we find we can observe more.

The data is collated and published to the staff as soon as possible so that everyone can get a sense of how we are progressing – what is going well, what may have slipped, and where we need to focus our next targets.

(Peter Crawford, Visible Learning leader and walkthrough coordinator)

To illustrate this process, Figure 13.3 shows you the template that was in place in March 2014.

Creating a shared Visible Learning pedagogy

The shift towards a shared pedagogy was supported by the development of a lesson plan template based around Visible Learning concepts. The template was developed by the heads of department and Visible Learning leaders prior to a two-day whole-school Visible Learning seminar. There it was implemented in a jigsaw approach that saw it trialed first by the cross-curriculum Visible Learning teams and then within curriculum and year level teams. It serves as a prompt for teachers to include challenging goals, hooks to improve engagement, and guided and independent practice toward mastery of the learning intentions.

Figure 13.4 is an image of the refined template that eventuated.

Collecting evidence of impact

The theme for 2014 was "evidence, impact, action." Every four weeks, each teacher was required to provide physical evidence of student learning to their curriculum leader. This did not have to be summative data and teachers were encouraged to explore the type of evidence that would show progress in their area. Initially, this new expectation was also met with some apprehension; however, it has turned out to provide a rich opportunity for teachers to talk, share, and inspire each other.

The result was a celebration of things that were wonderful about teaching and learning! We're learning from each other and discovering the progress that can be made in just a few days, let alone a few weeks.

(Curriculum leaders)

These are some of the responses when teachers were asked what they had learnt from collecting the first round of evidence of learning:

Visible Learning Walkthrough

Date	Friday 14 March
Time	Period 1–4
Team members	EC, JP, PCu, PCr, DW, VF, BHi

	Oct 2013	today
Number of classes visited	45	33
Number of students observed	762	576

What time in the lesson?

		today
Beginning of lesson	12	8
Middle of lesson	19	17
End of lesson	14	7

Are the Learning Intentions and Success Criteria of the lesson known by the students?

		today
Learning Intentions displayed	56%	88%
Success criteria displayed	51%	76%

		today
Learning Intentions known by the students	69% (previously 80%)	76%
Success criteria known by students	67% (68%)	55%

What are the students doing?

		today
Listening to teacher	46% (previously 35%)	39%
Reading	22% (previously 11%)	15%
Active	60%	76%
Working independently	38%	67%
Working in groups	38%	42%
Asking questions	38%	33%
Receiving teacher feedback	73%	67%
Receiving peer feedback	36%	42%

	Oct 2013	today
Do the students understand their assessment task?	Insufficient data	70%

Figure 13.3 Visible Learning walkthrough template

Learning that is Visible Lesson Plan

Teacher	
Subject	
Year group	
Topic/unit	
Lesson number	
Date	

Visible Learning Checklist	Time	
Learning intention (Challenging Goal)		
Success criteria		
Hook (to build commitment and engagement in the learning task)		

Presentation:
   • Input
   • Modelling
   • Checking for understanding		

Guided practice (toward conceptual understanding)		
Closure		
Independent practice		

The format of the PL day ran in a tapestry of cross-curricular teams interspersed with curriculum teams (see format below):

- VL leaders taught a lesson using the LTIV template
- Planning lessons using LTIV template
- Planning a set of lessons collaboratively, with a "product of learning" as the results

Figure 13.4 "Learning that is Visible" lesson plan

"I realized the year 9 boys need as much hands-on activity as possible."

"I need to chunk tests into more manageable pieces of evidence."

"Four students needed extra support in inverse operations."

"Some year 8s knew more than I realized."

"Two students required extra support for recount structure and all students needed greater editing skills."

"The vocabulary test informed me that year 8 had prior knowledge of the food web from science."

"In half an hour, my year 7 students improved their drawing three-fold."

Teachers were trained in how to use effect size calculations to support their evidence of learning. The data was accompanied by a discussion with colleagues, Visible Learning Leaders, and Curriculum Leaders about the interpretation of the data, looking at critical questions such as:

Who can be challenged more?

Who needs intervention?

What worked and what didn't?

Where are the gaps and where are the strengths?

What was achieved and what still has to be achieved?

Restructuring professional meeting times

The jigsaw approach taken at the Visible Learning seminar proved effective. It has now become embedded practice, with staff regularly gathering on Monday afternoons, first in their Visible Learning teams and then in their curriculum and year level teams. In both meetings, the focus is on using evidence of impact to guide planning for student and professional learning.

> This is proving to be a highly successful combination, simultaneously empowering teacher voice in two teams within the one timeframe. The result is the richest and most affirming combination of teacher collaboration in our school to date.
>
> (Delivery team)

During this time, teachers have the opportunity to share their students' evidence of learning and effect size calculations. They then gain feedback from their colleagues about what to do next – the vital component of moving learning forward. This change in structure provides the time teachers need to gather and work together in teacher groups to interpret the evidence about their impact.

Student to teacher feedback

The school uses a variety of methods to ensure student voice informs teacher learning and change, including student interviews and focus groups. Recently, it has adopted the Irving Student Evaluation of Accomplished Teaching Scale (Irving, 2005), a Visible Learning tool that enables the consistent collection of data that can be used to identify "where are we, how are we going, and where to next for teachers" (Figure 13.5). Again, implementation of this tool caused some initial anxiety but in fact much of the feedback is affirming and all of it has promoted healthy discussion.

Students complete the survey online at regular times in the term or semester and the results are collated and graphed. This gives teachers the opportunity to track their own progress with each class and set targets for improvement. Teachers and curriculum leaders also discuss and analyze the data, building rapport and relational trust as they work together to improve student outcomes.

Implementing the SOLO taxonomy

One of the key aspects of the new pedagogy was the implementation of the SOLO taxonomy to assess student learning and design curriculum. John Biggs,[2] one of the taxonomy's developers, explains that:

> SOLO is a means of classifying learning outcomes in terms of their complexity, enabling us to assess students' work in terms of its quality, not of how many bits of this and of that they got right. At first we pick up only one or few aspects of the task (unistructural), then several aspects but they are unrelated (multistructural), then we learn how to integrate them into a whole (relational), and finally, we are able to generalize that whole to as yet untaught applications (extended abstract).

Figure 13.6 shows its application in Victoria Rintoul's classroom. Victoria gets her students to reflect on their progress using the SOLO Matrix once or twice every week. They move a sticky tab to indicate where they believe they are up to and read what they need to do next in order to make progress. Victoria says she finds that the taxonomy helps her better differentiate to individual needs and strengths. She has asked her students about their perceptions and they tell her that they like being able to clearly see where they are aiming and what they need to do to get there.

Sharing the language of learning

The shift to a focus on learning and thinking was supported by the introduction of visible cues throughout the school. SOLO taxonomy posters are displayed in every classroom and serve as a visual prompt and a colorful reminder of the verbs required to stimulate the move from surface to deep learning. Classroom walls are covered with drafts of student work with annotations that provide feed forward about the "next steps." Students enter classrooms where physical reminders of learning intentions and success criteria are displayed, whether on an interactive whiteboard or electronically. Teachers are learning to refer to these regularly throughout the lesson, prompting students to notice their progression, revisit, and refocus on the way to success.

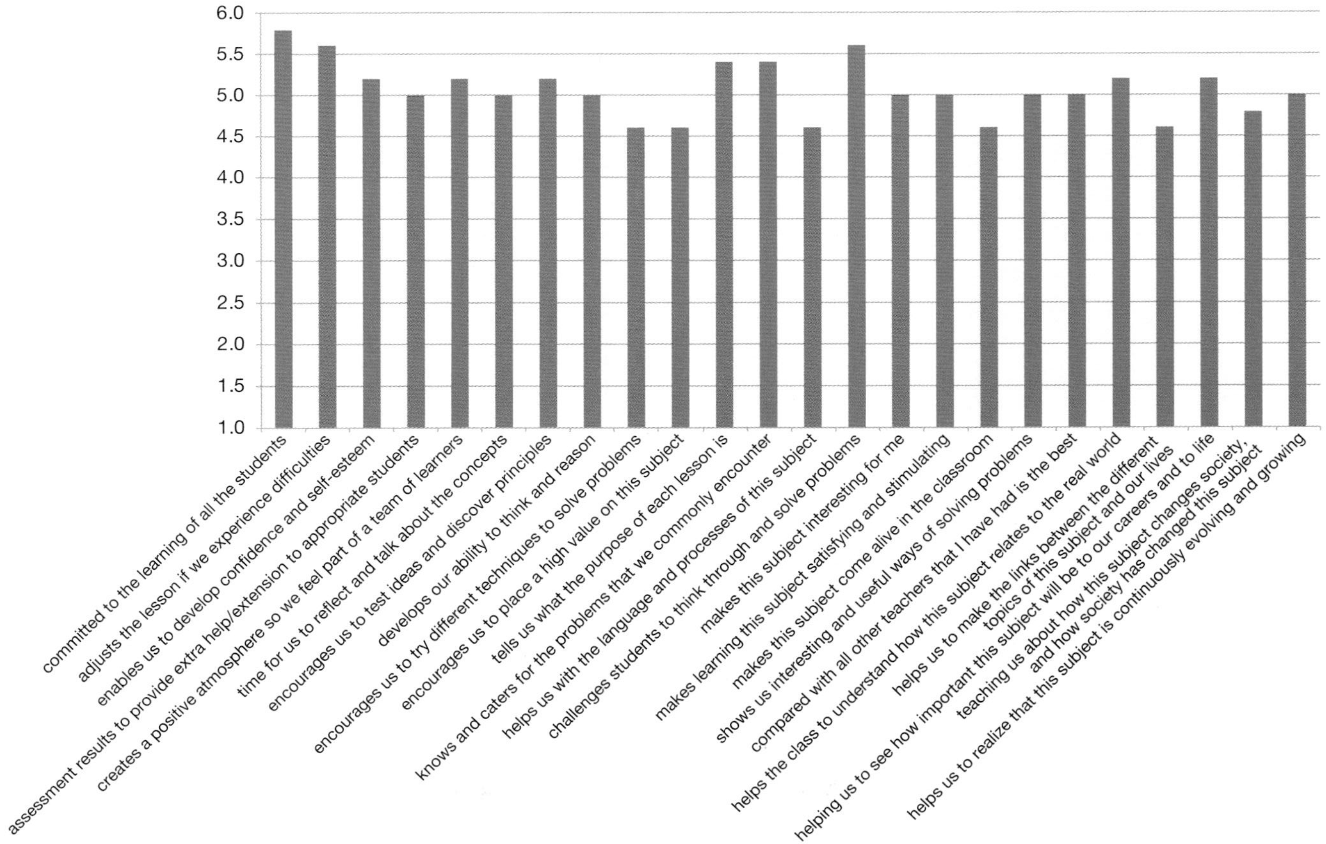

Figure 13.5 The Irving Scale

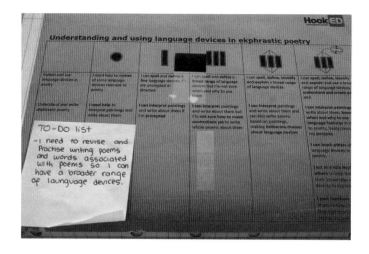

Figure 13.6 Using the SOLO Matrix to monitor progress

Study tour

In December 2013, the Visible Learning team participated in a study tour to Auckland, New Zealand where they saw Visible Learning enacted in several successful schools. The tour culminated in the development of a new action plan for 2014. In their personal reflections, team members expressed delight in the sense of professional camaraderie that was developing and their optimism that despite setbacks, Visible Learning was becoming part of the school's language and culture. Critically, team members were starting to see themselves as professional leaders of learning. David Whetton said:

> I found the honesty and common-voice mentality of our group brainstorm and reflection sessions to be energizing. I felt that we had moved beyond the guidance of Tuesday morning term-time meetings and were encouraged to contribute deeper comments as well as providing evidence or a rationale for our contributions. I felt that we achieved a high level of professional and personal trust.

What was the impact of the changed actions on the desired student outcomes?

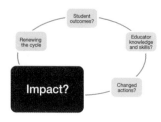

Oxley College has a wealth of evidence to monitor progress with regard to its three Visible Learning targets (see page 242). Leaders also know enough about the dynamics of whole-school change to recognize when those targets need to be revised. For this reason, Target 3: "By April 2014, all students at Oxley College will show a 0.4 or greater effect size in the core learning areas (literacy and numeracy)" was revised to "By April 2014, all students at Oxley College will show progression of learning through collected evidence in all curriculum areas."

School leaders and teachers now routinely use effect size data as the stimulus for conversations about learning and teaching. Effect size data is calculated on NAPLAN data and the conditional formatting used by teachers to ask questions about their impact on student achievement. This group of students achieved an average effect size of 0.8 in numeracy, but the data raised the questions "What caused those in green to flourish while others did not?" and "What could be put in place to assist those who did not progress?"

Ben Hicks, a secondary mathematics teacher, had previously regularly used qualitative feedback from students, but recognized the value of the effect-size model in supporting him to know his impact on students. Ben likes the way the discussion has now moved from a focus on achievement to an equal focus on progression. He comments:

> Questions such as "Are high-achieving students still progressing?" emerge now, questions that were not present in the dialogue before because they were unanswerable.

It excites Ben and his colleagues that this approach also enables them to compare the impact of different approaches to learning. They can try out an interesting new idea for engaging students in mathematics, measure its effectiveness, and discuss whether it really works. Figure 13.7 is an example of the use of effect size to monitor progress and achievement in year 7 mathematics.

The school is using this approach to track whole-school progress in each of the core areas of reading, writing, spelling, grammar and punctuation, and numeracy. Patterns and trends are being used to establish baseline evidence that can be used to decide on specific actions.

The school is already seeing improvements in its whole-school achievement data. Figure 13.8 provides an example of how spelling has now achieved above 0.8 average effect size as a result of a new intervention.

In addition to quantitative data, regular student focus groups, walkthroughs, and video diaries indicate that students at Oxley are growing in their identity as learners. Students use the language of learning to express their progress and how they are going. They speak confidently about their learning and know that they need to "strive, stretch, and stick" in order to achieve success – exhibiting the qualities of a growth mindset.

> When I started at this school in year 2, I didn't know what a success criteria and learning intention was, but now when I don't know what to do in English, and it was up on the board and my teacher said, "Look up to the success criteria," and I did, and I found my way out.
>
> (Year 2 student)

Y7 Geometry: progress vs achievement

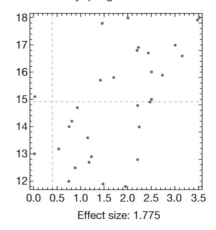

Effect size: 1.775

Figure 13.7 Using effect size to monitor progress and achievement in year 7 mathematics

Year 7: Spelling progress vs achievement

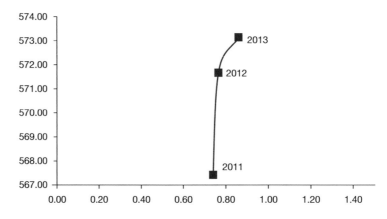

Figure 13.8 Using effect size to monitor improvement

Data from K–12 walkthroughs provides evidence that students are increasingly aware of where they are going, how they are going, and the "where to next" in their learning. In secondary classrooms in particular, there has been a shift from classrooms dominated by teacher talk to where students are more actively engaged in their learning. Students themselves notice the differences:

> I think in science now, we do a lot of group work and it's really great when we get to collaborate with other students and you get to learn a lot from them. And we do a lot of moving around so you get to talk to different types of people and listen to their ideas.
>
> (Year 9 student)

I've progressed most because I can teach other people the topics that we are learning about. Before I would have to ask my peers or my teacher what was going on, whereas now I can actually teach other people who are unsure what's happening. I think I also learn a lot better when I understand what I'm talking about so then I can teach other people and I understand it better in my own words.

(Year 8 student)

Group work in particular has increased as a way of promoting class discussion (0.8 effect size) and there is more dialogue in classrooms than previously observed. Walkthroughs are now unannounced and provide a clearer picture of increased consistency across the campus.

As students are growing in their identity as visible learners, a change is also being mirrored in their teachers.

This year the teachers are really clear ... and the success criteria really helps a lot so that I can figure out whether I'm actually knowing and understanding what I'm meant to.

(Year 8 student)

This beginning secondary teacher says the use of visual cues has been a valuable prompt in her own practice:

It has helped me to clarify what I'm doing in the classroom, the big ideas ... and has helped the students to know what we are doing and what success will look like. And to check in throughout the lesson, looking on the board .... Okay, what are we doing, re-focus ... it's good to see at the end of a lesson or the end of the week, whether we have succeeded and, if not, to think about what do we need to change to make success happen.

Some senior students have struggled with the change to the Visible Learning framework, having done all their prior learning in traditional classrooms. However, others have appreciated the changes, especially the implementation of learning intentions and success criteria and the much more targeted feedback that has accompanied these changes.

Across the board this year, all the teachers have given individual feedback, which has been really effective, teaching what each person needs to work on.

(Year 10 student)

This story has focused on whole-school learning and improvement. It is important to understand that the whole is the sum of the parts – that each teacher has embarked on an individual journey where they have inquired into specific aspects of their own practice and its relationship to where the school wanted to be in

Are the Learning Intentions and Success Criteria of the lesson known by the students?

	Oct 2013	March 2014	May 2014
Learning Intentions displayed	56%	88%	95%
Success criteria displayed	51%	76%	80%
Learning Intentions known and understood by students	69%	76%	75%
Success criteria known and understood by students	67%	55%	68%

What are the students doing?

	Sept	Oct	March	May
Active	53%	60%	76%	78%
Working in groups (from Oct)		38%	42%	39%
Receiving peer feedback (from Oct)		36%	42%	44%

Figure 13.9 Monitoring classroom practice

terms of Visible Learning. For example, teacher and Visible Learning leader David Whetton is excited by the impact of learning intentions and success criteria on his year 2 students, who now speak in the language of learning, as exemplified by Cordelia, who we met on page 237.

One of Cordelia's friends says:

> You know you're learning it if you have learning intentions and success criteria and if you didn't have these on the whiteboard, your mind would just go "wild," but instead, we just stay focused in our class.

David describes it this way:

> When I use Visible Learning strategies with my year 2 children who are 7 and 8 years old, they see why we are doing something, the steps as to how we are going to do it and, at the end, or even through the process, they understand where they sit in the progression of learning. For me, Visible Learning helps my students to understand that learning truly is a progression or a journey and that it's not measured between two points – beginning and end. They understand that the skills they build are skills they can use in the

wider world and beyond the context of learning for whatever we are studying at the time.

An example might be in a maths unit on measurement. I might go back and say to myself, "Did I use the strategies of Visible Learning to the best effect?" I'll know that from my students' feedback to me, my feedback to my own students and also hard test scores, data, summative and formative evaluations. All those pieces of information make me consider my own teaching and learning programs and whether I can make amendments, edit it, or change it – can it be better?

At times, there have been real challenges as teachers, students, and parents have resisted the shift from traditional teaching approaches to something that seems new and unfamiliar. By being sensitive to these genuinely held fears, the leadership team has made significant progress, to the point where Visible Learning is owned and understood by most. This has required the willingness to adjust and change where necessary and to communicate openly, honestly, and frequently. Perhaps most importantly, the school has found that the very process of monitoring progress builds commitment – even small successes reward effort and create a sense of ownership.

When asked for some key messages for other schools, the Visible Learning team and guiding coalition at Oxley College would advise:

Start first with the mindframes, placing students and learning at the center of everything you do.

Visible Learning for a school and teachers mirrors Visible Learning for students: we need to know where we are going, how we are going, and the where to next.

Like our students, we as teachers have differing prior knowledge and in a way, start our journey at different places on the progression of learning. We all learn at different paces and some things work better than other … but keep striving – stretch and stick at it!

Continuing the cycle

The appointment of a new head of college in 2014 might have shifted Oxley College from its path, but Grant and Michael are both skilled educational leaders who understand the importance of maintaining coherence and a clear sense of direction, provided the evidence indicates that this is justified. Consequently, the school has committed further to instilling a growth mindset, to mastery, and to evidence-based learning and teaching. The Visible Learning plan will continue to be monitored, with the future focus on:

- curriculum design that explicitly includes learning intentions, success criteria, evidence of learning, student to teacher feedback, and effect size data;
- developing an understanding of what progress looks like across the curriculum for Visible Learning;
- developing teachers as expert teachers; and
- extending and empowering leaders as evaluators.

Head of college Michael Parker says:

> The most curious citizens are the ones that are most likely to give back to society as well. Having such students go into the world does not just benefit the students themselves, but helps in the creation of a vibrant, forward-looking society and civilization. As a result, our school will continue to transform into a 21st century learning environment that embraces ethics as a cornerstone, alongside a curriculum that embeds thinking skills, curiosity, and the "big ideas" in its learners.

Notes

1   This is the credential awarded to students who successfully complete senior high school-level studies (years 11 and 12 or equivalent) in New South Wales.
2   From John Biggs' website at www.johnbiggs.com.au/academic/solo-taxonomy/

14

Wodonga Primary School

Australia

Context

Wodonga Primary School is a large, state-run primary school situated on the Murray River in rural north east Victoria in Australia. It has a long history, having been established in 1857. Today, the school caters for around 760 students, ranging from the foundation level (five years old) to year 6 (11–12 years old).

Despite being located on the Wiradjuri tribal lands, only 6.5% of the student population are Indigenous Australians. The school is becoming increasingly diverse, as reflected in the fact that in 2014, 7.6% of the students were learning English as a second or additional language. Challenges arise from the facts that one third of students are classified as coming from a low socio-economic background, and there is an unusual degree of transience associated with the growing percentage of students whose parents are employed at the local Defence Force base.

The leadership team consists of principal Pam Thibou-Martin and assistant principals Roger Fiedler and Damian Duncan. Other teachers take on specific leadership roles, with Leanne Bishop designated as the school's Visible Learning coordinator. The leaders have served in their positions for periods ranging from eight to 13 years. The teaching staff is also quite stable, though highly diverse in terms of experience, training, and educational approach.

Overview

The process of change described in this story was prompted by the leadership team's recognition that while student outcomes were "adequate," as indicated by the school's five-year standardized external trend data, they were not what they could be. The school's achievement outcomes had plateaued – the leadership team wanted to see an upwards trajectory and believed that the solution lay in teacher professional learning.

Prior to this program, the school's professional learning focus had tended to be directed by the Hume Regional Office on the basis of its examination of the school's data. While much of the learning had been valued and is still integrated into the school's culture, it was not making the kinds of difference the school sought for its students.

This learning story describes some of what the school has done to create a Visible Learning school. In that environment, school leaders are "instructional leaders" who make time for collaboration, have regular walkthroughs, and engage in evidence-based discussions with teachers about the relationship between practice and its impact on student outcomes. Leaders, teachers, and students open their learning to themselves and to each other, taking control of their own destiny and driving towards a shared vision of a school where the focus is always on learning.

Featured teachers

Pam Thibou-Martin has been an educator for 29 years. She has been Wodonga's principal for the past 11 years.

Roger Fiedler has been assistant principal for 10 years and an educator for 24 years.

Damian Duncan has been assistant principal for eight years, as part of a 24-year career as an educator in Australia and the United States.

Leanne Bishop has taught for 29 years. She has had the additional role of a leading teacher for the past 13 years and is now the school's Visible Learning coordinator.

Emma Walker is a year 6 teacher who has taught at Wodonga Primary School for three years.

James Harris currently teaches students in year 2. He helps lead the school's work on well-being.

Wodonga Primary School's Visible Learning story

What were the desired outcomes?

Traditionally, Wodonga Primary School has collected student outcome data in relation to a variety of foci. These include:

- the literacy and numeracy data collected through participation in Australia's National Assessment Program – Literacy and Numeracy (NAPLAN);

- data on student attitudes to school and well-being;
- student attendance data; and
- analysis of the trends revealed in data collected over time from school-based assessments.

On the basis of this data, the school has worked hard to engage its students in learning through focusing on well-being and community. In particular, the school has sought to align the values of the local community with the learning it offers students across the curriculum.

The school's internal review suggested that the interventions were being implemented faithfully and there had been improvements in students' behavior and well-being. For example, the 2009–10 data from the years 5–6 Student Attitudes to School Survey showed a positive trend in "school connectedness" and "connectedness to peers." The school's success in growing its own sense of community and its connection with the wider community was recognized by a number of awards. However, these outcomes, while positive, were not being translated into improved outcomes in other areas, and particularly not into achieving the level of academic success that the school community sought. In particular, the leadership team had a sense that high-achieving students had been neglected in favour of a focus on improvement for students who were not achieving well.

> There was an underlying leadership concern that something was still missing and that we lacked the complete package to make our school a high-performing school with highly effective teaching and learning and enhanced student outcomes.
>
> (Pam Thibou-Martin)

The leadership team acted on their hunch, looking further into their data to find out what was going on. It helped that the school already had robust data-collection processes that enabled staff to reflect on student learning outcomes in multiple ways: individually; at the class, year, and whole-school level; and longitudinally.

> A school-based approach to reform a whole school on its purpose of education was evident as we dug into the data on an individual and whole-school basis. Through rigorous analysis, we were able to clarify our understanding of the core issue of student learning outcomes and the need to systemically alter the course of the school's learning journey.
>
> (Damian Duncan)

Despite all the hard work, students were not improving against nationally benchmarked standards. In particular, while the school had experienced some success in improving outcomes for students who began at the lower end of the achievement scale, the more able students were making limited progress. You can see this in Figure 14.1, which shows shifts in year 3 writing from 2009 to 2013.

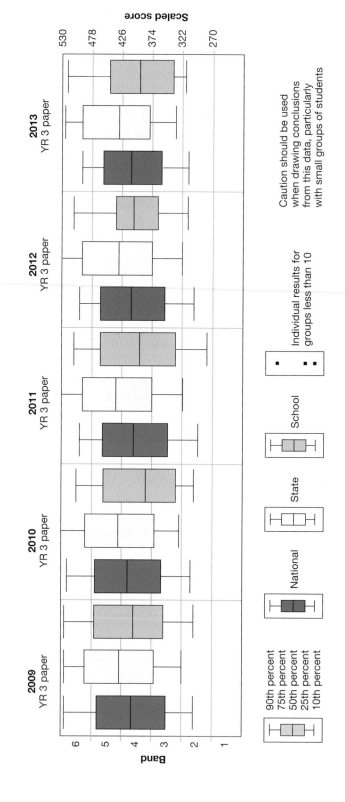

Figure 14.1 Box and whiskers graph from NAPLAN

The data analysis led to the school asking itself some tough questions:

> Why were we not making year-over-year progress when we were working so hard and focusing on applying what we interpret from our data to classroom practice? Our own diagnostic data trends were supported by our standardized test results where the mean of our cohorts were not progressing as our "like schools" were. The school leadership team was perplexed by the conundrum that our "effort in" did not equal better outcomes for students. Plateaued data was frustrating for all.
>
> (Pam Thibou-Martin)

If what they were doing was not getting the results they wanted, then they needed to do something different. The inquiry became a catalyst for change.

> An emerging picture of our school performance was that we were not extending our more successful students. The evidence that we were somehow holding back students who were high-achieving made our collective staff understand a great need for change.
>
> (Roger Fiedler)

It is important to understand that the culture of community and inclusion that the school had developed over time was not abandoned, with this refocusing from well-being outcomes to academic outcomes and from low-achieving students to students at higher levels of achievement. Instead, those aspirations informed a drive to ensure that any new program would benefit all students and take along the whole community.

> We wanted the home–school connection to go beyond the traditional, amicable relationship between school and home to the creation of a real educational partnership with shared knowledge and understandings about learning, along with a shared language and set of values.
>
> (Guiding coalition)

What knowledge and skills did the teachers and school leaders need to support these outcomes?

Fortunately, as the leadership team began its in-depth inquiry into the school's long-term data, an opportunity arose to attend a Visible Learning[plus] workshop led by Deb Masters. The concept of a Visible Learning school resonated with the leadership team, who could see that it provided a means through which they could achieve their aspirations for students.

> We wanted a school where students perceive themselves as learners and understand the process of learning. ... We needed to develop a whole-school Visible Learning language and learning pathways to support this outcome. All stakeholders knowing where students have been, where they are, and where they are going with their learning.
>
> (Leanne Bishop)

The team recognized that achieving this shift would entail redefining the school's vision, purpose, and pedagogy. This was a significant undertaking in a school with many experienced teachers who had developed personal philosophies of teaching that had not been subjected to a great deal of challenge. Teachers could see that there was an issue with student achievement. However, they did not have a shared understanding of how their current educational beliefs and practices impacted on student outcomes or about the kinds of changes needed for improvement. Consequently, the search was on for professional learning that would:

> put student learning at the centre of our work and enable us to develop a whole-school approach to support teachers to reflect on all elements of their core business and to build rigorous professional dialogue.
>
> (Pam Thibou-Martin)

The school contracted Visible Learning^plus consultant Jayne-Ann Young to be its critical friend on this new journey. Jayne-Ann supported the leadership team through the intensive data analysis described in the previous section, providing an external lens that helped the team to dig deeper and understand the lessons that had been missed. As well as helping the team to recognize that the school was not extending its high-achieving students, she also helped in the recognition that the school had promoted a culture of student compliance rather than student learning.

> This outside lens alarmed our leadership and our staff, denting our professional pride in an engaging and thought-provoking manner. It really emphasized to all the need for change and for establishing a commitment to the change vehicle, Visible Learning.
>
> (Damian Duncan)

Applying the Visible Learning^plus School Matrix

Application of the Visible Learning^plus School Matrix (see page 298) was a critical step in the process of understanding the professional learning needs of teachers in light of the learning needs of students. The Matrix is designed to enable whole-school self-review around the Visible Learning themes: Know Thy Impact, the Visible Learner, Inspired and Passionate Teachers, Effective Feedback, and the Visible Learning School.

The Matrix gave our school a greater understanding of the need for strategic planning on what to focus on in our change process, as opposed to simply choosing a high effect size strategy. The Matrix also opened our eyes to our teachers' perceptions of the quality of feedback in our school. It highlighted the need for a continued focus and deliberate effort in giving, receiving, and monitoring effective feedback.

(Pam Thibou-Martin)

On the basis of this analysis, the school decided that it would focus first on the development of learning intentions and success criteria. The leaders intended this to support the use of explicit feedback, first by teachers and later by students.

The fact that the new targets came from the school's inquiry into its own evidence helped to grow a sense that Visible Learning was not new work on top of what staff were already doing, but that it would build upon current practice and help make it more effective. Alongside this, the learning about effect sizes gave the school a powerful new tool for measuring and monitoring the impact of change.

What new actions did the teachers and school leaders try?

Developing an action plan

The first step in the change process was for the school to develop a 100-Day Plan that would support the implementation of Visible Learning in 2012. There were two key aspects to this plan:

1   establishing shared pedagogies; and
2   establishing structural supports.

The 100-Day Plan: Establishing shared pedagogies to support implementation

While the leadership team led the plan's development, all teachers had the opportunity to engage in the change process through conversations that focused on their pedagogy, practices, and purpose as educators. The experience helped create a sense of urgency and commitment.

In these workshop-based professional learning team meetings, our teachers confronted the question "Why do you do what you do?" The conversations focused on the impact of their instruction and their understandings of successful practice in light of the kinds and levels of impact highlighted in Hattie's research. We were not imposing something new on staff; instead, we pressed teachers to express their core beliefs and form a consensus about the school's purpose, vision, and the qualities we want to grow in our learners. We did so by using these questions as prompts:

- Why?
- How do you know?
- Is it really working?

(Guiding coalition)

Figure 14.2 provides an example of the output from one of these workshops. It shows how the year-level teams developed common understandings and expectations about writing:

- The inner circle sets out the school's writing beliefs.
- The middle circle sets out individual teachers' writing beliefs.
- The outer circle sets out the year level team's understanding of writing.
- The term goals are set out on the pencils.

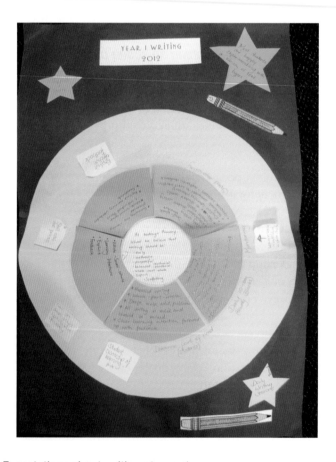

Figure 14.2 Expectations about writing at year 1

Visible Learning schools typically go through a process of determining the particular set of learner qualities that are most valued at their school. Wodonga School began this process by brainstorming an extensive list of suggestions. The teachers then worked in groups to create a final list of five, a process that prompted passionate conversations about what was most important.

The final output from this work is the Visible Learning Framework set out in Figure 14.3.

The 100-Day Plan: Establishing structures to support implementation
Concurrent with the establishment of a shared pedagogy was the establishment of structures to support implementation. The school formed a delivery team consisting of a guiding coalition (Pam Thibou-Martin, Roger Fielder, Damian Duncan, and Leanne Bishop) and the wider leadership team. Every leader was expected to take a Visible Learning lens to their role, ensuring that Visible Learning was a focus across the curriculum.

Leanne took on the specially-created part-time (0.5 FTE) role of Visible Learning coordinator. Creating a job share situation and ensuring the funding was available to provide this opportunity was a significant commitment for the school. In this role, Leanne became an internal critical friend, attending staff meetings

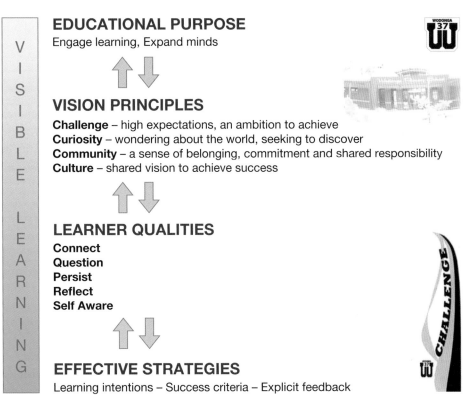

Figure 14.3 The Visible Learning Framework

and providing individual mentoring. She had to balance challenge with support, asking provocative questions while also offering advice and encouragement, materials, and feedback. She was also expected to play an integral part in the school's strategic development of Visible Learning, attending weekly meetings with the guiding coalition, assisting with planning, and helping to monitor the reform's impact.

> Having the opportunity to take a lead role in the implementation of Visible Learning in a whole-school context required an inclusive, collaborative approach where each teacher was valued and their contribution to the development of Visible Learning was shared across the school. Being in the classroom and in the leadership role provided me with a chance to practice Visible Learning in the classroom, as well as have a leadership lens when working with other staff. It was a unique opportunity to be able to trial, share, and lead the strategic work with leaders, teachers, and students.
>
> (Leanne Bishop)

While the purpose of the reform was to improve student learning, the means for achieving this was through learning for adults. Because of this, appraisal and meeting times were reoriented to prioritize learning about and implementing the principles of Visible Learning in ways that were tailored to the values and ethos of Wodonga Primary School.

The 100-Day Plan included the establishment of professional teams to provide teachers with support and explicit feedback around observations of Visible Learning in each other's classes. Called "triads," these groups are comprised of three teachers of varied year levels, years of experience, and roles within the school. Every teacher belongs to a triad. As well as the observations and feedback focused on key areas of focus, the triads read and discuss professional literature. While these include a variety of readings, the core text is John Hattie's (2009) *Visible Learning for Teachers*.

The triads provided the primary context in which teachers could develop an understanding of the practices and routines of what the school calls "curious conversations." The focus of these conversations is on knowing thy impact. Teachers are expected to question aspects of each other's practice in a professional and respectful manner, using evidence to frame their inquiry (for example, "I was wondering why the students were grouped that way, given that the task was centered around a like need?") This use of evidence is intended to make it safe for teachers to give and receive critical feedback without feeling personally judged.

As Figure 14.4 demonstrates, the triads were a significant commitment in terms of timetabling and resourcing.

The leadership team also reviewed the school's professional review process (that is, the appraisal process) to include a focus on Visible Learning professional understandings and growth. This means that professional learning and appraisal are in alignment with each other, with the evidence about the areas of greatest need, and with the school's Visible Learning Framework.

2013 Wodonga Primary School Performance and Development Plan

"What does matter is teachers having a mind frame in which they see it as their role to evaluate their effect on learning."

John Hattie

Professional Learning Triad

2013 sees the continuation of Triad groups. By focusing on what we can learn from our colleagues we are able to develop our capacity as teachers of focused instruction on a non stand-alone Professional Learning Model.

You have been placed in a Professional Learning Triad that creates opportunities to learn and grow in your practice by observing, talking and reflecting with colleagues of varying experience and background knowledge. As with all Professional Learning opportunities, you only get out of the experience, what you put into it!

The school will support the professional growth of teachers through the coaching support schedule developed by the leadership teams as well as any external professional growth opportunities that you nominate.

Throughout the year, you and your Professional Learning Triad members will be getting together to discuss your professional learning intentions, watch each other teach and provide each other with constructive feedback. The Principals will aid the coordination of your visits to each other's classroom when you are ready to proceed.

Page 3 of this Performance and Development Plan is where you annotate your Triad's experience, discussions and Professional Learning.

Figure 14.4 Performance and development plan (excerpt)

Implementing the plan

In 2013, Wodonga Primary School moved into its implementation phase. Some of the new actions that this involved are listed below. For the sake of clarity, they are roughly split according to the elements that were most pressing for leaders, teachers, students, and the wider school community. While this is a rather artificial split, its purpose is to communicate the fact that this was, indeed, a whole-school reform that impacted on all parts of the community. Changes in "how we do things here" were felt across the school community, as the learning was made visible to all.

New actions for school leaders

The guiding coalition realized that it needed more time to explore its beliefs and understandings about Visible Learning and to set a clear direction for implementing Visible Learning at Wodonga Primary School. To support this, it held a leadership summit during the 2012–13 summer break. The "curious questions" the leaders posed themselves included "What do you believe Visible Learning is?" and "What confusions do you have about Visible Learning?"

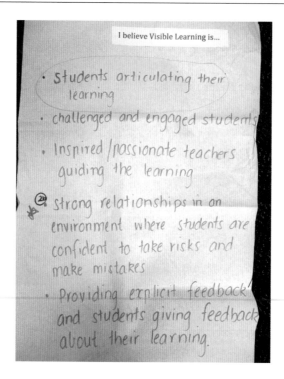

Figure 14.5 Leaders' thinking about Visible Learning (a)

Figure 14.6 Leaders' thinking about Visible Learning (b)

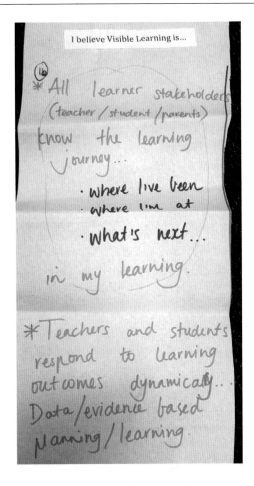

Figure 14.7 Leaders' thinking about Visible Learning (c)

Following the summit, the guiding coalition initiated the following actions:

- The guiding coalition developed resources that would expose the whole school to the language of Visible Learning. For example, flags representing the four vision principles now line the main entrance to the school.
- They developed a homework activity where students created "chatterbox" toys to support their reflection on the qualities of an effective learner.
- In her role as Visible Learning coordinator, Leanne took the lead in gathering and monitoring evidence in relation to the implementation of Visible Learning at the school level. This was used on an active, ongoing basis to monitor growth, reflect on success and challenges, and maintain awareness of progress.
- The team established Know Thy Impact meetings (staff professional learning meetings where the Know Thy Impact quadrant data is analyzed) that are held mid-year and at the end of the school year.

- The leaders changed the meeting timetable to enable weekly collaborative planning meetings for teachers at each year level, supported by the attendance of a leading teacher.
- The Junior School Leadership team developed social story books focused on the learner qualities.
- The literacy, numeracy, and well-being group leaders developed comprehensive learning pathways for reading, writing, and numeracy that connected the school's Visible Learning overview to the Australian Curriculum.
- The leaders embedded the language of Visible Learning in all communications.
- The leaders modeled the practice of putting students at the forefront of professional dialogue and of weaving through the use of a range of evidence, including student achievement data and student voice. As they did so, they promoted the concept of "curious conversations."
- The leaders fostered the creation of data wall charts as a means of supporting planning by making student learning progress visible.
- Student voice was captured on video, as well as in print.

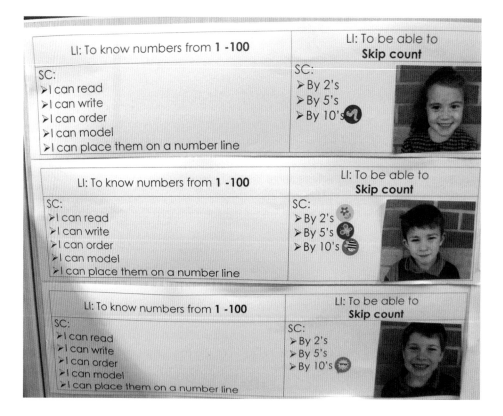

Figure 14.8 Establishing learning pathways

Figures 14.9 Data-tracking wall (a)

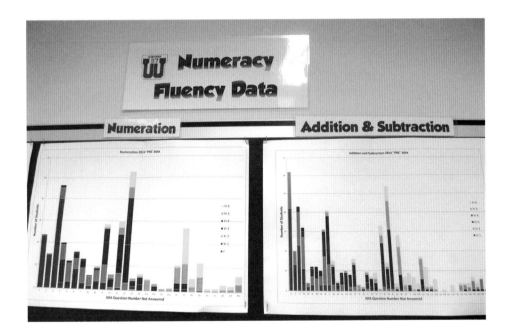

14.10 Data-tracking wall (b)

- The leaders planned and implemented whole-school units of inquiry based on the school's vision principles of Community, Culture, Curiosity, and Challenge. These units were linked to the learner qualities. For example, the unit on Curiosity was linked to the learner quality of "question" and included a science curiosity night and classroom-versus-classroom volcano experiments.
- The team created the document "The Way We Work" to help to embed and sustain the reform over time, ensuring the school's learning is not lost through attrition or a lack of impetus. "The Way We Work" captures key concepts about Visible Learning and sets out the school's expectations of its staff.

New actions for teachers

Visible changes in teacher practice included:

- incorporating learning intentions, success criteria, and explicit feedback into learning and teaching interactions;
- using the language of learning with all in the community: students, colleagues, parents and leadership;
- implementing the language, behaviors, and reflections associated with the five learner qualities;
- using data to drive planning and teach to student need;
- collecting year-level evidence and using it to monitor their personal Visible Learning journeys; and
- applying their learning to ensure explicit, goal-directed and student-centered instruction.

New actions for students

- Students were taught about the qualities of a successful learner and the difference between a growth and a fixed mindset. They learnt about James Nottingham's concept of "the pit" (see page 133) and the strategies required to climb out of it. They were taught about the different approaches to use when in the "learning zone" as opposed to the "practice zone."
- Students were encouraged to be self-aware and recognize the language of learning. The teachers used the new learning pathway resources to encourage their students to articulate their learning goals, identify their progress, and set new challenges.
- The school established student forums and a junior school council and these included opportunities for students to participate in decision-making about how the school enacts Visible Learning.
- Student leaders developed library books relating to each learner quality, and these can be borrowed by families and students.

New actions for the wider school community

- The school council (the school's governance group) includes Visible Learning as a regular agenda item.
- The school created the document "How We Learn at Wodonga Primary School" (Figure 14.11) as a means of communicating the language of learning with parents. That language is now used consistently in all communications to families, including the newsletter and school website.
- The traditional parent–teacher interview process was replaced by student-led conferences. This was a clear signal that it is students who are at the center of learning, and demonstrated that at Wodonga Primary School, students are empowered with the language of learning.
- The school joined the Wodonga Cluster learning community, which gives pre-school, primary school, and secondary school representatives the opportunity to meet every term to share their Visible Learning journey.

At Home ~

We encourage you to support your child's learning
by reinforcing the Learner Qualities at home.

I tried a different idea by . . .

I wondered about ...

When I don't know how to ... I ...

Something tricky for me was... but I

A great strategy I used was...

Figure 14.11 "How We Learn at Wodonga Primary School"

What was the impact of the changed actions on the desired student outcomes?

When thinking about the impact of the changes on students at Wodonga School, we need to think about two questions:

First, to what extent have the changes so far led to Wodonga Primary School becoming a Visible Learning school?

Second, assuming that there has been a significant shift towards becoming a Visible Learning school, what impact has this change had in terms of its fundamental purpose of improved outcomes for students?

To what extent has Wodonga Primary School become a Visible Learning school?

The guiding coalition reports that the concept of Visible Learning now permeates all aspects of the school:

> A whole-school approach across all areas of leadership brings a consistent message and builds a culture of understanding and commitment. We have passionate, committed teachers who want to make a difference and are prepared to change their practice to ensure this occurs. Partly this has been achieved through the culture of our school. Our leadership team is supportive, open, accessible, and dedicated to challenging our teachers to model what they teach – "A love of learning, with a growth mindset." At every level, we practise what we talk about. Integration aides, specialist teachers, principals, and classroom teachers all use the language of Visible Learning in every element of our school. Being collaborative through the process of change has ensured teachers feel ownership of the Visible Learning initiative in our school.
>
> (Guiding coalition)

Teachers are using student data to establish learning intentions that set ambitious but achievable targets. They are able to separate the learning intention from the learning task and then collaborate with their students to design success criteria that enable both teacher and students to monitor progress. The leaders have observed that this greater clarity has made teaching more explicit and means that teacher feedback is better directed to the learning purpose.

Teachers and school leaders have learnt to link evidence of student achievement and progress to their own practice as educators. They habitually use effect sizes to identify the impact of teaching sequences on students in their classrooms and across the year group. The data is interpreted in collaborative professional conversations where teachers unpack the reasons for different rates of progress and use what they learn to set new goals for both student and teacher learning

Teacher and school leader James Harris is excited about the changes he sees:

> The timing of our implementation of Visible Learning was great for me as an educator. I was still figuring out my beliefs in terms of pedagogy and teaching approaches. From the moment I started using learning intentions, success criteria, appropriate feedback, and our school's own Visible Learning language, teaching made more sense to me. I feel I have significantly developed as a professional and I'm very excited to be part of our school's Visible Learning journey. In the short time that has passed, there has been an amazing change across the school in teaching approaches and student progress. The sky is the limit as to what the school can achieve in terms of student outcomes and I'm looking forward to being a driving force in this area.

The concept of a Visible Learning school took some time to understand:

> Creating an understanding in our teachers around the concept of "Seeing learning through the eyes of the student" (Hattie) and shifting teachers' perspectives from what they were teaching, to what students were learning was a challenge, and one that we are still working on.
>
> (Guiding coalition)

In the following transcript from a videotaped reflection recorded one year after the program began, teacher Emma Walker describes the shifts in her understanding:

> When I first heard about Visible Learning in one of our meetings, I thought, "Ooh, I'd better go back to my class and put up lots of posters and examples of the kids' learning so that it's visible." But through this journey, I've come to realize that Visible Learning isn't about making your class look pretty: it's about having the resources in your class so that students know how to be successful in the learning process. It's not the teacher's secret any more, it's more transparent. Giving the students the knowledge of the learning intentions and of how they can be successful has completely changed my way of thinking, as the students are now more responsible for their learning, and I'm not the only one responsible for their learning.

Despite these caveats, the leadership team has been impressed by how quickly teachers have understood and taken ownership of the new concepts. The team believes that this is because Visible Learning is not about compliance with a particular set of content, processes, or practices, but about coming to understand a set of principles. Throughout, teachers have been given time to explore these principles, to think about how they could be integrated into their practice, and to look at the evidence of impact. Because of this evidence, teachers know they are doing the "right" work and have a growing trust in their ability to make a real and positive difference for all students. They are having "curious conversations" and their triad reflections (Figure 14.12) attest to the impact of these upon their own learning.

As this parent attests, the changes have extended, as intended, into the wider school community:

> The learner quality books at WPS bring into our family a new language that sees our children at the center of their own learning, with both the family and school as active participants. This language allows our children to share and continue their learning at home and allows parents to acknowledge and encourage learning. By sharing these books, our family gets to practise this new way of talking about learning and we are rewarded when we hear our children encourage each other to persist with a tricky Lego design or comment that they are curious about a new species of bird in our yard.

How has Wodonga Primary School's shift to becoming a Visible Learning school impacted on the school's desired student outcomes?

The desired outcomes for students were that they would grow as visible learners and that through this, they would achieve measurable improvements in academic outcomes.

2014 TRIADS

Where have we come from?	Where are we?	Where are we going?
No TRIADs. Limited across year level dialogue. Probably no observations of other classrooms. Inability to provide feedback to colleagues comfortably	Focused observations looking for specific evidence. Confidence in providing warm feedback. Organised visits, readings, prof. dialogue	Ability to work together in the TRIAD to move forward professionally through: - explicit feedback - shared experience - ideas for feeding up.

Where have we come from?	Where are we?	Where are we going?
- Giving warm feedback only - Viewing it as an isolated exercise	- More consistent expectations for success - More grounded in understanding of the value of the TRIAD process. - Growth mindset from most staff around the process and its value	- More value of collaboration as a tool for professional growth - Links to V.L. strengthened.

Figure 14.12 Staff triad reflections

Students as visible learners

Within the first term of implementation, teachers noticed a significant increase in student talk about their learning, matched by a decrease in their talk about behavior. It has become a habit for students to use the language of Visible Learning to reflect on their learning and talk about it with others.

> As a student I find that I can concentrate on my work for long periods of time. I will often have a growth mindset but I can sometimes have a slightly fixed mindset when there's a challenge. I work best independently because it is much easier to not get distracted. I will usually persist in challenges. When I must multiply decimals I will constantly switch between a fixed and growth mindset. I believe that I have improved in my letter writing, both formal and informal and I know what to include. I find that the learning zone, the pit and the fixed mindset are similar because they mean that I am learning something new and taking a challenge which is important to me. I feel that I have progressed in my spelling and my reading. I have enjoyed being in year 5.

Students at all levels of the school are growing in their understanding of their personal needs and strengths. There is an emerging understanding that the trajectory of progress is more important than current levels of achievement. The students are getting more precise in identifying where they are in their learning pathway and what they need to do to get to the next step. They challenge themselves to achieve and to identify and overcome difficulties along the way. The students come to see themselves as part of a community of learners who support each other.

This sense of community extends beyond the classroom to students' participation in decision-making in the student forums and the junior school council. It was the forums that led to the events focused on curiosity and to the creation of a set of soft toys that represent the learner qualities.

Learning is articulated and shared at year level assemblies, whole-school assemblies, and a range of special events. It is also having an impact beyond the school gates. One six-year-old boy was so inspired by the unit of inquiry on curiosity that he chose to have a curiosity-themed birthday party!

Student achievement outcomes

The leadership team has developed a "quadrant data exercise" that enables staff to compare student achievement to student progress. An example is presented in Figure 14.13. As you can see, one of the benefits of this approach is that it enables the identification of those high-achieving students who are not progressing as they should be. In this particular instance, the effect size for the class as a whole is an impressive 0.73, but there is a group of students whose progress has plateaued.

The quadrant data exercise outcome is a June quadrant for Reading 2013.

5CK PROBE - June 2013

Student name	Time 1	Time 2	Effect size
Jordan	8	11	0.88
Serena	17	18	0.29
Jake	8	11	0.88
Daisy	11	12	0.29
Katelynn	11	13	0.59
Jaydon	4	9	1.47
Brihanna	10	12	0.59
Benjamin	8	11	0.88
Caitlin	12	14	0.59
Adina-Tallara	7	11	1.18
Benjamin	9	11	0.59
Callum	17	20	0.88
Akira	17	18	0.29
Isaak	12	16	1.18
Bree	12	13	0.29
Liam	8	11	0.88
Brodie	16	19	0.88
Lainey	14	16	0.59
Jai	11	12	0.29
Ruby	8	11	0.88
Cameron	9	12	0.88

Average	10.90	13.38	
Standard Deviation	3.63	3.15	
Average SD	3.39		
Effect size group	0.73		

	Counts
<0.00	0
0.00-0.39	5
0.4-0.79	5
0.8>	10
total	20

	Percentage
<0.00	0%
0.00-0.39	25%
0.4-0.79	25%
0.8>	50%

Legend:
- <0.00
- 0.00-0.39
- 0.4-0.79
- 0.8>

Bar chart: 25% | 25% | 50%

Barometers of Influence

Mid Year PROBE (11+ High Ach)
Mid Year ES (0.2 + High Progress)

High Achievement Low Progress	High Achievement High Progress
Serena Daisy Akira Bree Jai	Brihanna Callum Caitlin Isaak Brodie Katelynn Lainey Cameron
Low Acheivment Low Progress	Low Achievement High Progress Jordan Jake Jaydon Adina Benjamin Liam Ruby Benjamin

Figure 14.13 Quadrant data exercise[1]

Continuing the cycle

One of the central characteristics of a Visible Learning school is the ongoing self-review that means the journey is never over. At the end of each semester, every year level shares their Visible Learning journey at a professional learning meeting. These opportunities for sharing ensure staff can learn from each other and collaborate in identifying areas for future growth.

When we reflected on our Visible Learning journey at the end of 2013, the staff believed we had a strong foundation established, and that our next steps needed to consolidate and embed what we had already begun. Our focus for 2014 was to deepen our understandings of the framework in place – Educational Purpose, Vision Principles, Learner Qualities, and Using Effective Strategies. With six new teachers commencing in 2014, it was critical to have a successful induction process to support the transition of these teachers into our Visible Learning practice.

(Guiding coalition)

The induction process is supported by the teacher resource, "The Way We Work." Further planned developments include a Matrix setting out progression in relation to the learner qualities. Support for continued professional dialogue includes the introduction of weekly collaborative planning meetings. Another new development is to revisit the school's relationship with the Visible Learning Wodonga Middle Years College. By building cross-sector understandings, the school hopes to smooth its students' transitions into the secondary sector.

Whatever the future holds, the leaders are clear:

We can't deliver change in a "top down" way: any initiative needs to evolve and be developed by all stakeholders if it is to be successful at Wodonga Primary. Visible Learning is a whole-school commitment.

(Guiding coalition)

Notes

1   PROBE stands for Prose, Reading Observation Behavior, and Evaluation, a reading comprehension assessment tool. For more information, see www.education.vic.gov. au/school/teachers/teachingresources/discipline/english/proflearn/pages/velsprobe. aspx

15

Tobermory High School

UK

Initially, some staff were skeptical of Visible Learning and became too hung up on the technicalities of calculating effect sizes rather than how the research could inform decisions that they had to make. I think Visible Learning has helped to clarify clear areas for focus and improvement and has been one of the main drivers behind change within the school.

Richard Gawthrope, Deputy Head Teacher

Visible Learning schools may appear to have been established for many years. Visitors can walk into a school where the Visible Learning philosophy is commonplace and the use of learning intentions and success criteria seems natural to every member of the school community. The truth is that schools that have arrived at this state may have gone through a significant change process to get there. Sometimes the change has been rapid and quite recent. Such is the case at Tobermory High School.

Context

Tobermory High School is located on the Isle of Mull in Scotland. Mull is a semi-rural island but good transport links mean its people are not isolated. The town has 1,000 residents, with the school serving 225 students aged 3–18 years. The pre-5 unit caters to 15 children and there are 66 students in the primary (P1–7) department and 144 in the secondary (S1–6) department. Most come from the town of Tobermory, with others transitioning from the small primary schools in the surrounding villages.

The mission of Tobermory High School is "To work together to create a community with a culture where our young people are included, successful, ambitious, and creative and where they can aspire to be the best they can be." The school's vision is "To create a 3–18 school that is a learning community, respected and active in the wider community, and which prepares all students with the knowledge, skills, and attitudes for learning, life, and work in the modern world." Its core purpose is "Valuing Achievement, Valuing Community" and its central values are respect, resilience, creativity, collaboration, and confidence.

In 2010–11, Scotland adopted a new national curriculum for learners aged 3–18 called Curriculum for Excellence. Its implementation is a priority for Tobermory, as in all Scottish schools.

Overview

Craig Biddick was excited to be appointed the head teacher (leader) of Tobermory High School in May 2012. Having been a facilitator of professional learning, he knew it was important not to make change for change's sake but to get to understand his new school and where he could add value. After taking time to observe what was happening in classrooms, Craig came to the conclusion that while they were generally well ordered, many of the students were not fully engaged in the learning. Despite their teachers' best efforts, students were often passive and tended to leave responsibility for their progress to the teachers. Craig knew how important it was that students were challenged on a daily basis and that it was ultimately his responsibility as school leader to make this happen.

When Craig attended an introductory session on Visible Learning, he knew that this was what he wanted for his school. In collaboration with consultant Craig Parkinson from the Visible Learning[plus] Osiris team based in the United Kingdom, Craig began to introduce staff to the Visible Learning philosophy. He did so with the enthusiastic support of his senior leadership team: Janice Mitchell (deputy head, secondary school), Richard Gawthrope (deputy head, primary school), and Graham Davidson (senior manager and acting principal teacher of mathematics and science). Other staff were also involved as part of the extended Visible Learning lead team: Lynne Horn, John Coyle, and Lilian Mitchell-Stephen. This helped ensure the messages would permeate across all levels and faculties of the school.

Craig knew it would take some work to get teachers on board and that a commitment to Visible Learning was a matter of years, not months. Nevertheless, thanks to his commitment and that of his staff, Tobermory has seen big changes in less than a year.

Featured leaders

The success of the Visible Learning intervention at Tobermory High School rested with the combined efforts of the entire senior leadership team and the extended Visible Learning lead team formed in 2013–14. Two leaders are quoted directly in this story:

Craig Biddick has been an educator for over 26 years. Prior to his appointment as head teacher of Tobermory High School, he was engaged in academic counseling, student guidance, and behavioral interventions, dealing with issues such as student mental health and drug and alcohol misuse. Craig was an in-school facilitator for a major professional learning project from 2004–7. Before becoming a teacher, Craig worked as a university researcher and as a quality control chemist for a pharmaceutical company.

Richard Gawthrope has been deputy head of the primary school since joining the school in 2009, thoroughly enjoying the challenge of leadership. A keen learner himself, he embraces all opportunities to support professional learning for his colleagues.

Tobermory School's Visible Learning story

What were the valued student outcomes?

In 2012, Craig Biddick took up the position of head teacher at Tobermory High School. Craig knew that most students were achieving good exam results but also that there was increasing evidence that students in some classes were not achieving at a level suggested by earlier progress. He undertook an initial audit to find out more. Craig found that most classrooms were well ordered, but there was some drift in the consistency of student management. More importantly, he found that although students were largely motivated to learn, some middle- to low-achieving students were struggling. At the same time, other students were not being challenged to extend themselves. Teachers and leaders at Tobermory had several key questions to ask themselves:

- Why are struggling learners allowed to continue to struggle?
- What teacher actions contribute to that complacency?
- What do we need to change in our students that will help them own their own learning more?

After entry into the Visible Learning intervention, Craig and his leadership team began the systematic data collection process that takes place in the first two phases of the impact cycle. This initial inquiry included classroom observations and student interviews and focus groups. Craig Biddick says:

> In our data collection phase, we found students did not necessarily understand the concept of what a good teacher or student would look like. They had many surface ideas, without a deeper understanding.

As the leaders examined their data, they began to develop a list of "symptoms" that needed to be addressed. The symptoms included:

- disengagement;
- students had poor learning skills;
- students had a fixed mindset in relation to ability;
- students giving up on hard tasks;
- students leaving the leadership of learning to teachers;
- some students manipulating classroom interactions with teachers in order to be spoonfed the information they needed;
- poverty of dialogue; and
- lack of feedback from teachers to students and students to teachers.

Leaders and teachers at Tobermory shared a desire to address and, if possible, cure these symptoms. Having been introduced to the basic tenets of Visible Learning, they agreed on an end goal that all of their students would become assessment-capable. However, they had to lay some groundwork in order to get there. This needed to include:

- ensuring both students and staff thought of themselves as learners;
- coming to a consensus on the attributes of good learning and good learners;
- challenging students to extend themselves;
- increasing the opportunities for classroom dialogue;
- enabling effective feedback;
- fostering the development of students' cognitive and metacognitive skills, including the ability to self-regulate learning; and
- supporting students to understand the expected trajectory of progress and how to assess themselves against such progressions.

This process of learning about student learning needs and prioritizing outcomes for students became the catalyst for improvement. It highlighted the need for both teachers and leaders to identify and work towards a new set of knowledge and skills.

What knowledge and skills did the teachers and school leaders need to support these outcomes?

Craig and his staff now needed to dig into the evidence to understand the teacher practices that had contributed to the current situation for students. While Tobermory had many good teachers, the team found that they often dominated their classes, with students taking a passive role as the recipients of knowledge. Many teachers engaged in monologue rather than leading communities of learners who could co-construct knowledge within cooperative learning conversations.

During the evidence-collection phase, the school also had an inspection by Her Majesty's Inspectorate of Education (HMIe). This was valuable, as HMIe had an intensive focus on teaching and learning:

> This reinforced much of what we found. Teachers needed to be less didactic, differentiate learning by task and not just outcome, and challenge and support all learners, especially those at the middle and upper end of the academic ability spectrum. HMIe also found staff were not constructing their lessons to encourage enough thinking. Many lessons lacked what HMIe termed "creativity," and were therefore missing some of the key constructivist ideas underpinning the Curriculum for Excellence.
>
> (Craig Biddick)

Part of the reason that teachers found it difficult to adapt their teaching to individual student strengths and needs was that they did not have coherent and supportive assessment processes and routines. This also tended to hamper their ability to provide effective feedback or to explore the relationship between their own actions and learning development as educators and the progress of their students. They could not challenge students to make the next steps towards their learning goals because they did not have detailed descriptions of progression setting those steps out. This issue was particularly acute for students from the primary to early secondary levels of schooling. While it appears to have been a wider problem for Scottish educators, Craig and his leadership team felt compelled to develop a solution that would work for their school.

Craig and his colleagues on the newly-formed Visible Learning team considered that teachers' capacity for engaging in schooling improvement was also related to their knowledge and confidence in relation to the new curriculum. For some, the new curriculum posed a challenge to deeply engrained personal theories about knowledge, teaching, and learning. The team recognized that a big part of their work was going to involve reculturing teachers through exposure to new or refined theories about effective teaching and learning and the genesis of the new curriculum. The idea of being involved in a school-wide development process that had agency and authority in a sound research base was a good starting point for asking teachers to think outside their context and think more about these big ideas. At its heart, this is what Visible Learning asks of all teachers. Here was an opportunity to craft a development plan that took these contextual issues into account while enabling the school to realize some of the goals inherent in the new curriculum.

Tobermory did have strengths. HMIe perceived the school as having a positive environment that was friendly and welcoming for both students and parents. This confirmed Craig's own observations that students were largely motivated, polite, and positive, and teachers were well-regarded.

Over the next few months, Tobermory's leadership team created an agenda for change that addressed the challenge of the new curriculum and a government agenda relating to new qualifications for senior students and positive student destinations. They also continued to monitor what was happening in classrooms and, helped by Craig Parkinson, established a plan for using Visible Learning as the school's lever for improved teaching and learning. The agenda was set out in a school three-year improvement plan that included details about the priorities, tasks, strategies, timeline, and personnel, and a process for evaluation. It had two strands: 'Curriculum and Assessment' and 'Learning and Teaching'. In a 30-page booklet for parents, the leaders explained the targets for learning and teaching as shown in Figure 15.1.

What new actions did the teachers and school leaders try?

For staff, the introduction to Visible Learning typically begins with a Foundation Day where they learn about the structure of the Visible Learning intervention, where it originated, and some of John Hattie's key findings. They are introduced to the concept of mindframes and have the opportunity to think about this in relation to their own philosophies and practices. They learn about effect sizes, how to gather and analyze appropriate evidence, and how they will have to put their learning into action.

Richard Gawthorpe responded to a series of questions about the Foundation Day and the early response to Visible Learning at Tobermory.

Strand Two Targets: Learning and Teaching

- Introduce the Visible Learning CPD programme at THS (Primary and Secondary) across key inset days and further professional development activities to embed school-wide practice that involves the use of researched, high effect size strategies relating to teacher–student feedback to improve learning.

- Promote the ethos of best evidence practice teaching across Primary and Secondary as a sustainable model developing from Visible Learning.

- Pupil voice across the school (3–18) – including corporate voice and voice learning.

Figure 15.1 Targets for learning and teaching

Early reflections: Example 1

What were your first impressions?

During the initial day, I was intrigued by the effect sizes and the wealth of information and studies that had been carried out to inform these. It was from this that I began to consider how this could improve not [just] teaching and learning in my class but also the school.

What do you think Visible Learning will do for staff?

Initially, some staff were skeptical of Visible Learning and became too hung up on the technicalities of calculating effect sizes rather than how the research could inform decisions that they had to make. Personally, I think Visible Learning has helped to clarify clear areas for focus and improvement and has been one of the main drivers behind change within the school. Visible Learning has demonstrated to staff the commitment to self-evaluation and has also focused in on key aspects during observations. The conversations involving pupils have also given greater insight into specific areas, giving real focus. Linking aspects of the improvement plan to Visible Learning has helped to identify key areas for improvement that can be measured. This will allow us to feed back on key areas, using data to validate what has been found. Over time, this will hopefully be used to show improvements.

What do you think it will do for students?

Students are becoming increasingly aware of Visible Learning and hopefully, through using aspects such as questionnaires, this will continue, as well as give them greater opportunity to reflect upon and influence their own learning.

What is one interesting thing you found?

I have found the matrices to be useful as tools to assist self-evaluation and also to give prompts for discussions that have then informed the action plan. I particularly like the headings and have found these give clear focus for carrying out rigorous self-evaluation.

Richard's very positive response was informed, in part, by his early commitment to Visible Learning as a part of the leadership team. The response from teachers who had not had this early involvement tended to be more equivocal, as shown in 'Early reflections: Example 2' and 'Early reflections: Example 3'.

Early reflections: Example 2

What were your first impressions?
I wasn't sure at first.

What do you think Visible Learning will do for staff?
It will provide a focus for specific areas to improve.

What do you think it will do for students?
It should allow for better learning environments and improved teaching.

What is one interesting thing you found?
I found the effect size very interesting and would like to investigate it further.

Any negatives?
The initial day – the general feedback was not so good – it turned a lot of people off.

Early reflections: Example 3

What were your first impressions?
Didn't really know what it was about and initial day wasn't that clear to me. I got more into it [with] the Geoff Petty[1] book, which gave a good background. I was interested in the idea of focusing on using things in class that were proven to work.

What do you think Visible Learning will do for staff?
I hope it will make us more reflective to be able to choose from a variety of teaching and learning styles that we know work well and stop doing things that don't work well.

What do you think it will do for students?
I hope they will become more aware of themselves as learners and that as staff continue to improve feedback, pupils will take on the responsibility of responding to that feedback.

What is one interesting thing you found?
I would like to look again at how we do lesson observations in the light of Visible Learning.

Any negatives?
Unclear at times where we are going/what happens next post-Matrix – that uncertainty can put people off. I think also pupils have been over-surveyed. I think pupil voice is important, but in our small school there is no choice but to keep asking the same pupils.

Craig and the leadership team were not surprised that there was some equivocation in the teachers' responses. Teacher reactions typically vary from those who are really excited to those who feel they have had enough of being expected to learn new things. They knew they were going to have to work hard to get some of the staff on board.

> I think the Foundation Day was good but we probably needed a second day for more discussion about what it meant to the teachers, how it might look in our school, and what the impact might be. We ended up using twilight sessions to further our understanding. We had a number of complex things to look at arising from our Scottish context and the new curriculum, as highlighted in the HMIe inspection report.
>
> (Craig Biddick)

At Tobermory, the Visible Learning initiative needed to be integrated with the demands of the new Scottish curriculum. The Curriculum for Excellence sets out less specific content than its predecessor and encourages schools to pay attention to the learning process. It is designed to be holistic, describing literacy, numeracy, and health and well-being outcomes that are to be taught and assessed across all curriculum areas. The curriculum guidance documents also encourage interdisciplinary learning, encouraging schools to select themes or contexts that will support learning opportunities that cross subject areas.

Working in their curriculum teams, the teachers at Tobermory audited their curriculum and created a written database describing what was being taught, what was being assessed, and the depth of content taught. They then started to look at how they could link up learning through interdisciplinary contexts, paying particular attention to how numeracy, literacy, and health and well-being outcomes could be joined up. They have begun to review their unit plans and to think about how they could redesign the plans to develop more holistic learning opportunities that progressively deepen and extend student learning and thinking.

Both strands of Tobermory's improvement plan demanded better understanding and tracking of student progression. The leadership team have started to develop clear literacy and numeracy policies that will be in line with new Education Authority (LEA) Policy guidelines. Craig Biddick responded to urgent need by writing the "Tobermory High Assessment Toolkit." It is an important document that provides assessment rubrics and standardized assessment frameworks that teachers can use to guide learning and set challenging targets. Along with the school's assessment working group, he is continuing to develop the toolkit and support teachers to understand and apply its concepts.

The leadership team has started to ask the curriculum teams to take more responsibility for establishing systems for tracking data in relation to the learning outcomes set out in the Curriculum for Excellence and has implemented interim measures that will be further developed in line with the new assessment tools. The teams are now being asked to establish key targets for progression in literacy and numeracy and other areas of academic skill beyond what they presently do. This is so that teachers and leaders in the school will all have a common view of what progress looks like.

The teams are considering what other standardized data, beyond what is used now, could be used at each year level, as well as what curricular area data and what data from wider aspects of learning in the curriculum would provide good learner information. They introduced more standardized testing at the primary level and are beginning to use effect sizes as a means of getting a true understanding of student progress. The curriculum teams have also developed assessment rubrics that explicitly tell students how to achieve higher levels of a particular outcome.

The school has been looking at how it reports on students and profiles their learning. The Visible Learning team wants to communicate the message that students who are assessment-capable learners can identify the knowledge and skills they need in different subject areas and understand how they are progressing. A group of interested staff have formed a working group to look at how they could support students to create records of personal progress and achievement that document all their learning, both in and out of school.

The new curriculum and assessment systems sit well with Visible Learning's emphasis on the use of explicit learning intentions and success criteria that make teacher expectations clear to students. In addition, teachers at all levels of the school have begun to learn how to provide effective feedback to students that is directly related to the intended learning outcomes and the criteria for success. They use the rubrics for both formative and summative assessment.

The leadership team monitored teachers' early implementation of Visible Learning through a cycle of teacher observations and walkthroughs. In order to get the best out of the observations, the team has set out protocols to ensure that teachers understand that the focus will always be on student learning, and not just on teacher instruction.

Craig and his staff know that it takes the whole community to educate a student. Parents need to feel confident that what Tobermory staff are doing is about improving their children's chance to improve their learning and succeed. The parent booklet sharing the details of the improvement plan was one way of ensuring their inclusion. Another was for Craig to help parents understand John Hattie's work on effect sizes and how it helps us to understand what really works in education.

The leadership team at Tobermory have had to keep the focus on the twin goals of creating assessment-capable learners and a Visible Learning school while being cognisant of the various pressures that can take the school off course:

> Time is the biggest enemy, and workload. Our context involves work on a new curriculum and developing tools for criteria-based assessment, which is not-familiar to many Scottish teachers. Staff have also expressed uncertainty and anxiety as they develop new courses that will lead to national certificated exam courses that are seen as high stakes for senior students. There is also an urgent need for schools to revisit the curriculum at primary and early secondary

school level so it reflects the intentions of the Scottish Government for a more flexible and challenging curriculum that teaches across a range of contexts.

(Craig Biddick)

What was the impact of the changed actions on the desired student outcomes?

The Visible Learning leadership team at Tobermory continues to collect and analyze data from a range of sources to monitor progress towards the goals set out in its improvement plan. As well as exam results, the team collects information from small student focus groups and feedback from teachers and parents. Currently, it is too early to discern a tangible impact on student learning but there are indications of impact on teacher practice and students' positioning of themselves as learners. The leadership team expect that this will naturally accelerate as the intervention creates a new dynamic in the school.

During walkthroughs and observations, the leaders can see that teachers are more focused on common goals that revolve around Visible Learning and students are becoming more aware of the need to be assessment capable. Some teachers are offering more time for students to engage in dialogue with each other as well as with the teacher, but they want this to become commonplace. The quality of that dialogue has improved, with some teachers using questioning and prompts that elicit higher order thinking. The leaders see evidence that a number of teachers are now thinking about how they can stretch the thinking of all their students, from those who have tended to struggle to those who have consistently achieved high test results. Craig makes the point that "Sharing good practice will be vital if this is to be the case in all classrooms."

The initial products of the Tobermory assessment toolkit have already proved valuable in enabling teachers, sometimes with their students' assistance, to design rubrics based on constructs such as the SOLO[2] taxonomy and therefore encourage the right sort of feedback. Teachers are using them to engage in discussion with students about how to achieve higher levels of a particular outcome. The leaders can see that teachers' use of the rubrics is encouraging richer dialogue with students about the skills and knowledge that need more attention and what a more advanced level of work would look like. Away from the classroom, teachers are beginning to understand and discuss the new assessment rubrics in a way that encourages professional discourse and collaboration, empowering staff to develop the idea that John Hattie describes as "seeing learning through students' eyes."

Teachers now use walkthroughs, peer evaluation, and discussion to improve learning strategies in the classroom. They also use student evaluation of teaching in their professional development sessions, and this will continue to be analyzed to look at how students are experiencing learning events in the classroom. Some teachers have proposed the use of video recordings so they can better see for themselves.

Recently, Tobermory surveyed its students to request feedback on how everything is going. While the survey provided useful guidance for further improvement, it also gave cause for celebration. For example, over 84% of students felt that they are always or often clear about what they are learning. While we don't have comparative student survey data as a baseline, the information from the school and HMIe indicate that this would not have been the case in 2012.

The June 2014 inspection by HMIe[3] commented favorably on the learning environment that has been created, noting, for example that:

> Across the nursery, primary, and secondary stages, children and young people are polite, engage effectively in their learning and are keen to do well. They have positive relationships with staff. At all stages, children and young people are becoming independent learners and are beginning to take responsibility for their learning. At all stages, they work confidently with each other in pairs and groups when completing tasks and projects in class and outdoors.

The inspection provides an external view on the school's improvement processes:

> The head teacher has a strong vision for developing and improving the school. He has started to develop the leadership qualities of staff, children, and young people with a particular focus on improving the quality of learning and teaching. He has asked staff, children, young people, and parents for their comments on school matters. He has also used current research to inform and improve classroom practice. Senior managers observe lessons regularly and provide helpful feedback to teachers. Staff are reflective and committed to improving their teaching and are reviewing and updating the curriculum. The school should continue to develop its self-evaluation approaches and ensure they are included in classroom practice and lead clearly to improvements. Staff are members of school working groups and are producing new materials, sharing ideas and good practice. They feel they have a say in contributing to school improvement and report that leadership and responsibility are encouraged. As a result of these and similar activities, the school is able to identify appropriate areas for improvement. The school has well-established and extensive links with organizations in the community and uses these well to extend opportunities for children and young people. The school should involve partners more in shared planning and evaluation. This would help to ensure that partners' contributions enhance further young people's learning and progress.

Tobermory School's story is that of a school that is just beginning its Visible Learning journey, and doing so in the context of a system that is going through change.

One of the prime drivers of our Visible Learning lead team is to know thy impact. I think there are two streams in the work we're doing: the professional development programs that will make teachers look more closely at assessment and developing assessment-capable learners and the parallel work of developing better curriculum, assessment tools, and infrastructure. In some ways, one relies on the other: we need the tools and infrastructure to provide us with the raw data to understand the impact of Visible Learning and our related initiatives. In the meantime, I believe it is likely that relationships and affective domains will play a big part in the success of Visible Learning. The "soft data" we're getting from the student surveys and observations indicate that we are getting good shifts in classroom relationships, teacher positioning, and student self-concepts. Students certainly know something is up!

(Craig Biddick)

Craig says that the leadership team will further develop the monitoring of teachers' implementation of Visible Learning through an ongoing cycle of teacher observations and walkthroughs based on the lessons learnt from the initial evidence collection phase.

The Visible Learning team was stimulated by the task of collecting a rich variety of data and enthusiastic about the insights it gave into learning in the school. The team is confident it will further catch the hearts and minds of other teachers across the school.

(Craig Biddick)

Tobermory's story demonstrates that when a school takes an approach that builds on evidence and is as inclusive as possible, they can make significant steps on their Visible Learning journey in a short period of time. As we will see in the next section, this also means schools can make good plans for future developments.

Continuing the cycle

"Where to next?" is a critical question in a Visible Learning school. For Craig Biddick and the Tobermory team, it guides them as they enter into their second year with the Visible Learning philosophy. At the time of writing, the school was preparing to share the information garnered from their second implementation of the Visible Learning^plus Matrix activity with staff. This will be a planned, two-stage process, beginning with the leadership team sharing the results of a Survey Monkey questionnaire that focuses on inspired and passionate teachers, as well as some information on feedback. The school already knows that it needs to pay attention to the following areas of need:

- achieving a greater match between the challenge of the task and the learner's stage of development through testing students' prior knowledge and using that information to differentiate tasks;
- encouraging independent thinking through the provision of more challenging tasks, higher order questioning, and structured cooperative learning;
- continuing to work towards consistency in classroom practice, paying attention to both curriculum design and instructional strategies;
- helping learners to see themselves as their own teachers, through continuing to develop students' cognitive, metacognitive, and self-assessment skills and their ability to construct knowledge through dialogue;
- working collaboratively to ensure all teachers know what student progress looks like at Tobermory High School and using that knowledge to improve learners' achievement at all levels of ability; and
- using effect sizes and standardized data to understand achievement and progress in individual classes and across the school.

Based on what they already knew, a number of actions were already in train at the time of writing. These include:

- accelerating the review of unit plans and identifying opportunities for more interdisciplinary work;
- designing new units around themes and contexts that they hope will encourage students to think more deeply, creatively, and critically;
- linking the new themes to the newly-designed progressions so that student learning will be deliberately built from year to year;
- including activities in the new unit plans designed to help students develop their ability to discuss their learning and progress in a more sophisticated manner than has been possible in the past;
- continuing to foster and expect professional dialogue around assessment and progressions as part of the whole-school approach to developing assessment-capable learners;
- using the self-evaluation mechanisms developed with Craig Parkinson as part of the Visible Learning "evidence into action process" to help monitor teachers' classroom practice and support the type of active learning and classroom dialogue the school seeks to make habitual;
- using the adoption of effect size calculations at the primary level as a model for their use at the secondary level;
- sharing its ideas about assessment, progression, and the use of effect size with the local education authority, who collect data on areas such as literacy across a large number of schools; and
- planning and developing systems to ensure teachers who are working on peer observations will develop greater confidence in how to provide feedback to the peer that they are observing, particularly in relation to the key development aims arising from the Visible Learning evidence and the HMIe inspection report.

Notes

1   Geoff Petty is a British expert on teaching and learning whose messages are in close alignment with those of his former colleague, John Hattie. For information on his work, see www.geoffpetty.com

2   As noted elsewhere, SOLO stands for Structure of the Observed Learning Outcome.

3   Inspection of Tobermory High School, Argyll and Bute Council – 10/06/14 (Education Scotland, 2014, available from www.educationscotland.gov.uk).

Part V
Appendix 1

Active reading guide

It is likely that you are already familiar with the Visible Learning[plus] Matrix, a learning tool that played a key role in catalyzing and guiding the whole-school inquiries at Hodge Hill Primary School, Oxley College, Tobermory High School, and Wodonga Primary School. In this version of the Matrix, the prompts for inquiry have been removed so that if you wish, you can use it to record some of what you noticed about changes at one or more of these schools.

	School climate	Strategic planning	Position allocation and responsibilities	Assessment and student management systems	Professional development program	Staff and team meeting schedules and agendas	Lesson planning	Timetabling and streaming/ tracking	Walkthroughs and observations	Appraisals
The Visible Learner										
Know Thy Impact										
Inspired and Passionate Teachers										
Effective Feedback										

Part V
Appendix 2
Theory to practice

As you read the stories in Part V, you were invited to record what you noticed about the schools on the Visible Learning^{plus} Matrix. As you did so, it is likely you will have been thinking about your own context and any similarities or differences. Now, you may like to select one specific area of interest and explore it in relation to your school or institution.

In conclusion

At the 2013 Visible Learning Conference in Brisbane, John Hattie stood up in his opening address and said, "I'm looking at you all and thinking 'What if I got this wrong?'" I feel the same way when educators ask to visit and I always end up in the same place – that Keilor Views is a living, breathing example that he didn't.

Charles Branciforte, Principal of Keilor Views School

The story underlying the Visible Learning research aimed to motivate educators around the world, and these fifteen chapters are set out to exemplify the multiple ways in which schools have interpreted these messages to create their own stories of change and impact. The purpose of this book is to inspire you and illustrate how you too may undertake a similar journey of self-review and evidence-gathering to achieve even better outcomes for your students. As said in the introduction, the place to begin is by considering your impact, and if this impact is above what is deemed acceptable, then validate and continue this practice. If not, the aim is to refine, adapt, and change, using the big ideas of the Visible Learning research as your framework. You can see the multiple journeys and decisions made are all based on the same theme of knowing thy impact and being an evaluator, which are the key messages of the Visible Learning research and the work around this.

Cognition Education has designed a professional learning program that provides school leaders and teachers with the knowledge and tools to engage with the research and consider what works best for their students. Its rigor is assured by the close and ongoing collaboration between program director Deb Masters and John Hattie. The program's purpose is to set up a professional learning process that will continue after the providers have disengaged from a particular school, cluster, or system. The focus is on the process of and tools that will enable self-review, which is contextualised and unique for each and every educational setting. The model the Visible Learning[plus] team at Cognition Education has developed is premised on showing and evaluating impact. The full suite of professional learning opportunities is summarized in Figure 16.1 and is explained in more detail in the introduction on pages 7–9.

The reading guides in the appendices of each part, related to the strand, have been designed to help you kick-start your self-review process. They may be the stimulus for a leadership group, or a staff meeting to consider your own evidence of impact; what impact means across teachers in your school, in your context; and to begin your own unique Visible Learning story. Close reading of each school chapter will give ideas and practical examples of what the people in your story may do and say, but we urge you to remember that your story is unique, that your decisions will always be steeped in evidence, and that all decisions are guided by the Visible Learning mantra: "When teachers see learning through the eyes of their students, and students see themselves as their own teachers."

The fifteen schools in this book have begun the change process, and they are celebrating successes and finding ways to work through the challenges. Some of these schools are at the very early stages of becoming Visible Learning schools and others are well on the way, in their second and third years of impact cycles. Each cycle brings a new set of evidence and challenges, yet the processes and tools are a constant framework. These are early days for the measuring of impact, and there is never a foreseeable endpoint. However, as we have already said in the introduction to this book, it is the combined expertise of teachers and school leaders that makes the difference. Developing such expertise, nurturing it, and building a coalition of expertise is among the most expensive but worthwhile investments a system can make to enhance learning.

We wish you well on your own Visible Learning impact cycles.

The Visible Learning Program

Single schools can engage in an Impact Program or many schools and system leaders can engage in a Collaborative Impact Program.

Becoming Visible Learning Aware

- John Hattie research and publication of Visible Learning texts
- Visible Learning Conference or Institute
- Visible Learning website and social media
- Visible Learning news and journal publications

- Ⓛ Learner
- Ⓣ Teacher
- Ⓢ Student

Ⓛ Ⓣ

Year 1 — Impact Cycle One	Year 2 — Impact Cycle Two	Year 3 — Impact Cycle Three
Professional Learning and Development from the Visible Learning Foundation Series	Professional Learning and Development from the Visible Learning Foundation Series	Professional Learning and Development from the Visible Learning Foundation Series
• Foundation Day (whole school)	• Foundation Day (people new to the school or district)	• Foundation Day (people new to the school or district)
• Evidence into Action 1 and 2 for school Leadership Team	• Evidence into Action 1 and 2 for new members of the school Leadership Team	• Evidence into Action 1 and 2 for new members of the school Leadership Team
• Visible Learning into Action for Teachers	• Evidence into Action 3	• Evidence into Action 4
Identification of focus areas	• Visible Learning into Action for new Teachers	• Visible Learning into Action for new Teachers
Targeted workshops from the Visible Learning Inside Series	Review your focus areas and design next steps	Review your focus areas and design next steps
Develop your school baseline data and action plan	Targeted workshops from the Visible Learning Inside Series	Targeted workshops from the Visible Learning Inside Series
Ⓛ Ⓣ Ⓢ	Ⓛ Ⓣ Ⓢ	Ⓛ Ⓣ Ⓢ

Professional Learning and Development in the Visible Learning program and workshops leads to increased capabilities of system and school leaders, teachers and learners and improved learner achievements.

Figure 16.1 The Visible Learning^plus program

References

Barber, M., Kihn, P., & Moffit, A. (2011a). *Deliverology: From idea to implementation.* Washington, DC: McKiney and Co.

Biggs, J. (n.d.). SOLO taxonomy. Available from www.johnbiggs.com.au/academic/solo-taxonomy/

Cognition Education. (2012a). *Visible Learning^plus: Evidence into action: Workbook one.* Auckland: Cognition Education.

Cognition Education. (2012b). *Visible Learning^plus: Foundation Workbook.* Auckland: Cognition Education.

Fullan, M. (2008). *The six secrets of change.* San Francisco: Jossey–Bass.

Hattie, J. (2009). *Visible Learning: A synthesis of over 800 meta-analyses relating to achievement.* London and New York: Routledge.

Hattie, J. (2012a). Know thy impact. *Educational Leadership,* 70(1), 18–23.

Hattie, J. (2012b). *Visible Learning for teachers: Maximizing impact on learning.* London and New York: Routledge.

Hattie, J. (2013). [Interview with]. Know thy impact: teaching, learning and leading: An interview with John Hattie. *In Conversation*, Vol. IV(2). Available from http://www.eosdn.on.ca/docs/In%20Conversation%20With%20John%20Hattie.pdf

Hattie, J., & Timperley, H. (2007). The power of feedback. *Review of Educational Research,* 77(1), 81. Sage Publications. Available from: http://education.qld.gov.au/staff/development/performance/resources/readings/power-feedback.pdf

Irving, E. (2005). *The development and validation of a student evaluation instrument to identify highly accomplished mathematics teachers.* (Unpublished doctoral dissertation). University of Auckland.

Levin, B. (2012). *System-wide improvement in education.* Geneva, Switzerland, International Academy of Education/International Bureau of Education. Available from www.ibe.unesco.org

Ministry of Education. (2009). *Reading and writing standards for years 1–8.* Wellington: Author. Available from http://nzcurriculum.tki.org.nz/National-Standards

Ministry of Education (ongoing). e-*asTTle: Electronic assessment tools for teaching and learning*. Auckland: University of Auckland School of Education. Available from http://e-asttle.tki.org.nz/

Ministry of Education (ongoing). *asTTle: Assessment tools for teaching and learning: He Pūnaha Aromatawai mō te Whakaako me te Ako*. Auckland: University of Auckland School of Education. Available from http://e-asttle.tki.org.nz/

Moss, C., & Brookhart, S. (2012). *Learning targets: Helping students aim for understanding in today's lessons*. Alexandria, VA: ASCD.

Nottingham, J. (n.d.). Challenging students with a learning pit. Available from www.devisa-hb.se/thinkingnetwork/FromJames/ChallengingOurStudentsToLearn.pdf

Nottingham, J. (2010). *Challenging learning*. Cheltenham, Vic.: Hawker Brownlow Education.

NZCER (2001). *STAR: Supplementary tests of achievement in reading: years 4–9*. Wellington: NZCER.

Petty, G. (2006). *Evidence-based teaching*. Cheltenham: Nelson Thornes.

Robinson, V. (2011). *Student-centred leadership*. San Francisco: Jossey-Bass.

Robinson, V., Hohepa, M., & Lloyd, C. (2009). *School leadership and student outcomes: Identifying what works and why. A best evidence synthesis iteration (BES)*. Wellington, New Zealand: Ministry of Education. Available from http://www.educationcounts.govt.nz/publications/series/2515/60169/60170

Rubie-Davies, C. M. (2014). *Becoming a high expectation teacher: Raising the bar*. London: Routledge.

Timperley, H. S. (2009). *Realizing the power of professional learning*. Maidstone, England: Open University Press.

Timperley, H., Wilson, A., Barrar, H., & Fung, I. (2007). *Teacher professional learning and development: Best evidence synthesis iteration*. Wellington: Ministry of Education. Available at http://www.educationcounts.govt.nz/publications/series/2515/15341

Visible Learning[plus:] Foundation workbook. (n.d.). South Yarra, Auckland: MacMillan Professional Learning/Cognition Education.

Zbar, V. (2009). School improvement and reform: the holy trinity of consistency, innovation and capacity. *CSE Occasional Papers. Number 111*. Melbourne: Centre for Strategic Education.

Index

Locators in *italics* refer to figures and tables.